HOLLYWOOD ON LOCATION

HOLLYWOOD ON LOCATION

An Industry History

Edited by
JOSHUA GLEICH AND LAWRENCE WEBB

RUTGERS UNIVERSITY PRESS
NEW BRUNSWICK, CAMDEN, AND NEWARK, NEW JERSEY, AND LONDON

Library of Congress Cataloging-in-Publication Data

Names: Gleich, Joshua, editor. | Webb, Lawrence, editor.
Title: Hollywood on location : an industry history / edited by Joshua Gleich and
Lawrence Webb.
Description: New Brunswick, New Jersey : Rutgers University Press, [2019] |
Includes bibliographical references and index.
Identifiers: LCCN 2018012688 | ISBN 9780813586267 (cloth) | ISBN 9780813586250 (pbk.)
Subjects: LCSH: Motion picture locations. | Motion picture industry—United States—History.
Classification: LCC PN1995.67.A1 G54 2019 | DDC 384/.80973—dc23
LC record available at https://lccn.loc.gov/2018012688

A British Cataloging-in-Publication record for this book is available from the British Library.

∞ The paper used in this publication meets the requirements of the American National
Standard for Information Sciences—Permanence of Paper for Printed Library Materials,
ANSI Z39.48-1992.

www.rutgersuniversitypress.org
Manufactured in the United States of America

CONTENTS

HOLLYWOOD ON LOCATION

INTRODUCTION

Joshua Gleich and Lawrence Webb

Location shooting has overtaken soundstage production as the standard procedure for Hollywood filmmaking, and arguably, it has a longer history than studio-based production as the primary method of filmmaking. Early cinema was largely shot outdoors, where the sun provided the only strong-enough source of light. With the construction of major Hollywood studios in the 1910s, indoor sets and back lot exteriors increasingly took the place of actual locations, but location shooting remained a common supplementary technique. By the mid-1960s, filmmakers increasingly gravitated to international locations, while the physical studios were largely occupied by television productions.[1] In the fifty or so years that have followed Hollywood's classical studio system, this wayward trend has continued. The history of Hollywood's back lot production is overwhelmingly detailed. Yet once we step outside the studio gates, the long history of location shooting as a modus operandi is largely uncharted territory.

Location shooting has been almost exclusively defined in opposition to studio filmmaking. From the Italian neorealists to the French New Wave and the Hollywood movie brats of the 1970s, filmmakers have claimed untold riches in authenticity and creative expression by leaving the confines of studio facilities. Scholars have often taken them at their word, with the phrase "shot on location" decidedly shifting attention toward the real places captured onscreen and away from the production methods that brought them to the screen. What we may romantically picture as a small crew working on location with a handheld camera is, more often than not, a sizeable production team flanked by banks of lights and equipment, working with extras in cordoned-off streets in consultation with off-site production offices and studio executives. Creating the illusion of reality on location is an industrial, technical, and stylistic process, just as it is on the studio lot. Furthermore, by defining location shooting as an alternative practice, we lose sight of the fact that location shooting has always been a component of Hollywood filmmaking, even during the peak of the studio era.

This volume seeks to provide a history of location shooting in its own right, not as part of a style or a movement but rather as an evolving Hollywood industrial practice. Studio filmmakers could not leave the lot without permission, without the technical resources to support location shooting, and without plans in place to address the inherent uncertainties of working outside the controlled environment of studio facilities. While certain filmmakers came up with innovative location techniques, they drew on an industry paradigm for how to most efficiently and effectively capture real environments. Such a practice followed and precipitated shifts in the larger industry, balancing the potential financial and pictorial assets gained outside the lot against the economy and resources found at the studios. Soundstage filmmaking has defined location shooting, but the opposite is true as well. Decisions to pursue and rely on actual locations helped redefine the role of Hollywood's physical plant and its centrality within the production process.

As the first comprehensive summary of Hollywood location shooting from the silent era to the present, this volume seeks to fill several gaps in our understanding of this process. These chapters bring to light exemplary histories of location filmmaking from outside well-documented periods such as early cinema and the Hollywood Renaissance. They connect location shooting across genres, rather than limiting it to its most famous instances, such as westerns and film noir. Finally, they tie together the industrial and aesthetic histories of location shooting, showing how financial incentives and stylistic decisions informed each other. We hope both to reassemble location shooting as a historical practice and to reconnect it to the larger history of Hollywood filmmaking, in which its contributions remain surprisingly underexamined.

LOCATIONS ON THE MARGINS OF FILM HISTORY

Location shooting is often invoked in histories of American cinema, but it is seldom discussed in depth or with precision. While the term "location shooting" appears relatively frequently in existing scholarship, it has rarely been directly examined, and though it appears in the background of many studies of American cinema, its meaning is frequently taken for granted. For example, location shooting is often made synonymous with the techniques of cinematography that are closely associated with it, such as the use of available light or handheld camerawork, or deployed as a shorthand for realism or authenticity, collapsing its significance into the qualities that it seems to produce. Location shooting is also commonly identified with specific genres, whether one thinks of the sweeping vistas of the western or the rain-slicked streets of film noir; this frames it primarily as a generic marker rather than a mode of production. In the now-extensive literature on film, space, and place, an emphasis on the specificity of locations frequently supplants discussion of location shooting as a method: buildings, streets, and landscapes take center stage, while the techniques that placed them in the frame recede into the shadows. While drawing on these multiple perspectives, this book seeks a more precise understanding of location shooting as a practice, focusing on its economics and logistics, its technologies and techniques, its ethics and aesthetics. Our aim is to bring location shooting to the foreground, to illuminate it as an industrial and aesthetic strategy that has largely appeared invisible or transparent, both onscreen and in existing scholarship. As each contributor to this volume demonstrates, location shooting is not just a stylistic flourish but rather a complex, evolving practice that has shaped the history of American cinema.

Presently the history of location shooting is scattered among existing histories of American cinema. Though studies of specific periods, places, and genres occasionally offer more detail, canonical Hollywood histories only marginally address location shooting.[2] In historical surveys of the American film industry, such as the multivolume series *The History of the American Cinema*, location shooting persists in the background but rarely receives direct attention. For example, David Cook's authoritative survey of Hollywood in the 1970s devotes less than a page to explicit discussion of location shooting as a technique, despite its ubiquity during that period.[3] Similarly, David Bordwell, Janet Staiger, and Kristin Thompson's landmark study *The Classical Hollywood Cinema* only occasionally draws a clear distinction between studio and location work as distinctive technical and aesthetic practices.[4] As this suggests, the preeminence of studio filming in the classical era as the dominant mode of production has displaced location shooting as a key variation and potential alternative to that model. But how was location shooting integrated with studio procedures and integrated into the "seamless" classical text? And to what extent did its popularity after World War II challenge, disrupt, and eventually overtake the studio-based mode of production and its narrative and aesthetic patterns?

Some recent scholarship has approached these questions more directly. R. Barton Palmer's *Shot on Location* establishes the importance of what he calls "locative realism" for a strand of films produced in the postwar years, such as *The Big Lift* (George Seaton, 1950), that were driven by contemporary ideals of journalistic authenticity and reportage.[5] Two recent volumes from the Behind the Silver Screen series, *Cinematography* and *Art Direction and Production Design*, discuss aspects of location shooting, especially in the postwar period, though primarily as an ancillary concern to those specific crafts.[6] Recent historical work by Lawrence Webb and Adam O'Brien on the 1960s and 1970s has also emphasized the importance of location shooting to New Hollywood's political and visual economy, viewing it as a catalyst for an urban aesthetic on the one hand and an emerging ecological sensibility on the other.[7] From an industrial and economic perspective, location shooting has also been important to recent media industries scholarship—in particular, production studies—though this work is largely focused on the present and often excludes questions of narrative, style, and filmmaking technique.[8] A spatial turn in film scholarship since the 1990s has likewise focused greater attention on location shooting practices in specific places or in particular genres—for example, Edward Dimendberg's work on film noir and Mark Shiel's and Stanley Corkin's respective studies of Los Angeles and New York.[9] More generally, a series of edited collections on cities and landscapes have focused on location, though these volumes have largely elided the historical development of location shooting, approaching film locations as products of cultural representation and critical theory.[10]

Beyond the North American context, sustained attention has been paid to location shooting as a component of the creative process, especially for postwar "art cinema." In *Making Waves*, Geoffrey Nowell-Smith devotes a chapter to the importance of location shooting for the Italian neorealists and the various New Waves of world cinema in the 1960s. As Nowell-Smith shows, the preference of many filmmakers for working outside the studio was frequently an attitude, a philosophy, or an artistic practice as much as an indicator of limited means. For filmmakers such as Roberto Rossellini and Vittorio De Sica, location shooting became part of a search for cinematic "truth" and a closer engagement with reality and helped establish an aesthetic of imperfection and improvisation, a working method that opened up the filmmaking process to the contingencies of the social and natural environment. For the filmmakers of the French New Wave, leaving the studio behind became a central component of their challenge to the "cinema of quality."[11] Though location shooting in American cinema has its own semiautonomous history, the influence of these global film movements and their approach to location shooting has directly impacted Hollywood's development.

DEFINING LOCATIONS

At the most basic level, "location" serves as an antonym for the "studio." The Oxford *Dictionary of Film Studies*, for example, defines "location" as "any place other than a studio where a film is partly or wholly shot."[12] While adhering to this relatively open and flexible definition, this volume explores the historical complexity of the relationship between "location" and "studio." The distinction between the two has long been meaningful for filmmakers, audiences, and critics, but the dividing line can nevertheless be blurry. At different historical moments, Hollywood studios have encompassed open-air stages, interior shooting space (from the coming of sound, "soundstages"), and extensive back lots and ranches for exterior work, such that the difference between location and studio is not always visible onscreen. And as Jennifer Peterson demonstrates in the first chapter of this volume, the notion of "location shooting" did not arrive fully formed in the early years of cinema; its meaning necessarily emerged as a counterpart to the consolidation of the "studio" as a material and conceptual

reality. Tracing the history of location shooting therefore requires paying attention to shifts in critical and industrial discourse as well as evolving economic and
technological considerations.

In the first instance, then, "location" implies any filming site beyond the
immediate ownership and control of the production company. But locations can
be viewed from multiple perspectives. Filming locations are physical, material
spaces that constitute the basic infrastructure of the filmmaking process outside
the studio. They are also *places* with culturally constructed uses and meanings
that interact with the story material and resonate for the audience in complex
ways. Locations are transformed, through the filmmaking process, into the
manufactured place of mise-en-scène: they become cinematic landscapes. For
filmmakers, cast, and crew, the location can be a catalyst of artistic creativity, col-
laboration, and performance. From a political-economic perspective, the location is also a site of labor and a regulated space subject to legal jurisdiction and
institutional oversight. The question of who can film where and when is subject
to control by state and municipal governments, law enforcement, and local agencies (such as emergency services, parks department, or transit authorities). These
regulations have often provided legal and logistical barriers to location shooting,
though at least since the 1960s, the commercial benefits of a Hollywood shoot
have been widely recognized by city and state governments. Location shooting
also takes place in a cultural territory, in which local communities might provide extras, crew, or simply background texture. As with any other workplace
or social environment, location shoots are stratified by class, race, and gender
relations; unsurprisingly, they have not infrequently been sites of conflict and
struggle. Location shooting can also make a material intervention into a social or
natural environment that leaves an imprint or trace. It might have physical effects
on the place of filming, whether we think of the chipped steps of San Francisco's
Alta Plaza Park left by the car chase in *What's Up, Doc?* (Peter Bogdanovich, 1972)
or the environmental damage to the Thai coastline caused by *The Beach* (Danny
Boyle, 2010). Alternatively, location shooting may also have sociocultural effects
in particular cities and neighborhoods, as recent work on New Orleans and the
HBO series *Treme* has shown.[13]

HOLLYWOOD LOCATION SHOOTING: FOUR CONSTRUCTIVE FACTORS

Location shooting always connotes a fundamental choice to accept the unpredictability of actual places over the hermetic environment of studio production
facilities. The reasons for doing so largely fall into four categories: economics,
technology, aesthetics, and logistics. While these connote different historical
approaches, they have never existed in isolation. Each contributor to this volume
and each era of Hollywood presents a different type of intersection among these
factors and ascribes varying degrees of power to each potential cause for changes

in location shooting practice. For instance, in the decades following World War II, shooting on location became cheaper with the development of more portable equipment—but the motivating factors to invent this equipment were financial incentives to shoot on location abroad, a desire for greater realism, and the logistical challenges that filmmakers encountered in places that were previously inaccessible or unaffordable to photograph. The following sections provide a historical overview of how these each of these categories affected changes in Hollywood's location shooting practice.

Economics

In a commercial industry such as Hollywood, it is a common assumption that whenever productions shot on location, they did so because it was cheaper. Yet if that were the case, why did American film moguls endeavor to build massive production plants? A more nuanced explanation is that under certain circumstances, location shooting either proved less expensive than building a facsimile of the location on the studio lot or offered surplus values that more than offset its added cost. As Jennifer Peterson shows, the concept of location shooting could only emerge for Hollywood once filming at a physical studio in greater Los Angeles became the industry standard. The emergent studio system eventually changed from a centralized, mass-production industry to a distribution empire with production scattered across the globe, and increased location shooting was both a symptom of these changes and a causal factor in Hollywood's transformation.

Changes in Hollywood's mode of production affected the desirability of location shooting. The high volume of pictures produced during the 1920s and 1930s required the efficiency of mass production on a studio lot, whereas in the postclassical period, fewer pictures and higher budgets allowed greater resources to be dedicated to location shooting. As for independent producers, ranging from the studio veterans of the 1950s to the indie filmmakers of the 1990s, they often shot on location out of necessity, unable to cover the expense of set building and studio rentals.[14] In short, the desirability of location shooting was always contingent on the budget of a given film, the resources available to filmmakers, and the flexibility of the production schedule.

Location shooting could offer surplus values to compensate for its relative unpredictability compared to studio work. Direct financial incentives on the international, regional, state, and urban scale helped promote Hollywood location shooting and expand its geographical scope. Certain sites, ranging from expansive landscapes to bustling cities, offered production values that would be either impossible or unaffordable to recreate on the studio back lot. Yet this economic calculus remained speculative. *Trader Horn* (W. S. Van Dyke, 1931) and *Heaven's Gate* (Michael Cimino, 1980) are famous examples of distant location shoots whose potential production values were overwhelmed by the spiraling expense of shooting delays and dangerous working conditions.[15]

As a unionized labor force, Hollywood personnel also shaped the course of location shooting. Armies of set builders fueled the mass production of the early studio era and placed greater production resources at the studio than on location. Studios pursuing financial incentives to shoot abroad had to reckon with labor resistance at home or pay standby workers, reducing the benefit of employing cheaper foreign labor. Foreign workers' relative inexperience with Hollywood working methods, as well as Hollywood professionals' relative inexperience with extensive location work, further raised production costs. Producers had to cover the expense of housing and feeding personnel on location, which escalated with each day a production fell behind schedule.

Technology

Until the early 1970s, lighting technology placed critical limitations on location shooting. For nineteenth-century cinema, the only strong-enough lighting source was the sun, encouraging early filmmakers such as the Lumière brothers to shoot extensively outdoors. With the advent of more powerful incandescent lighting in the early 1900s, studio filmmaking increasingly moved indoors, where the quality and directionality of light could be controlled. Despite Hollywood's seeming ability to represent any site on film, certain regions and times of day remained impossible or impractical to shoot with proper exposure until the early 1970s. While more powerful lights, faster lenses, and faster film stock emerged to reduce lighting requirements, they could be counteracted by other technologies, such as color and widescreen, that greatly increased the necessary illumination levels. For much of Hollywood history, location shooting almost exclusively favored bright daylight locations, such as the sun-drenched landscapes of the western.

The portability of equipment also shaped Hollywood's approach to location shooting. Powerful arc lights could solve lighting issues on location, but they were massive, making them difficult to transport to a location and cumbersome to set up, not to mention the large generators required to run them. With the coming of sound came more bulky equipment designed to function in sound-proofed stages, not everyday settings. Location shooting required both new types of equipment and creative adaptations of existing equipment to expand its range of possibilities. Even a mundane location, such as an apartment, might leave no room for the actors to stand once all of the equipment was placed on-site. Finally, methods for transporting personnel and equipment informed location practices. The expansion of commercial air travel after World War II made it far easier for studio filmmakers to shoot in Europe. In the 1970s, the Cinemobile, a compact production vehicle that could be quickly moved between sites, proved a boon for urban settings where multiple locations could be captured in a single day.[16]

Studio technologies for recreating real places also had a major impact on Hollywood's standard practices for location shooting. A salient example is rear projection, which provided economic efficiency both on and off location. Real backgrounds could be captured by smaller, second unit crews, sparing the expense of sending a full crew to a distant location. Then on the soundstage, actors could perform under perfectly controlled conditions. A similar dynamic has emerged more recently: CGI allows distant backgrounds to be realistically added during postproduction. In short, Hollywood location shooting asks a question of not just where to shoot but whether a location provides something that could not be adequately captured on the back lot.

Aesthetics

Whether reading André Bazin or an interview with a contemporary director, such as Matt Reeves discussing *Dawn of the Planet of the Apes* (2014), there is an overwhelming association between realism and location shooting. It follows that the common assumption in popular and scholarly texts is that the more one shoots on location, the more realistic a film will be. But photorealism is an aesthetic that changes over time; as Julie Turnock has shown, the rear projection of location footage was standard practice in the 1950s but strikes current audiences as highly artificial.[17] While a desire for realism drove many filmmakers to shoot on location, how they chose to frame, light, dress, and otherwise alter an actual place is just as important as their decision to shoot outside the studio. The celebrated realism of *Bonnie and Clyde* (Arthur Penn, 1967) looks much different than the later realism of *Slacker* (Richard Linklater, 1991).[18]

Trends in documentary filmmaking have been a key determinant of Hollywood's location aesthetics. Louis DeRochemont, a newsreel producer, produced the earliest postwar semidocumentaries, such as *The House on 92nd Street* (Henry Hathaway, 1945), which captured real locations with straightforward camera work and flat lighting. Voice-over narration helped cement these locations as markers of the fidelity of the story. Such an attempt to tie real locations to recreations or fictionalizations of real events dates as early as Edison's *Execution of Czolgosz with Panorama of Auburn Prison* (1901). By the late 1960s, direct cinema and cinema verité (as well as television news) created a rather different documentary paradigm for Hollywood to follow. Location realism in the 1970s featured handheld camera work, zoom lenses, imprecise framings, and shooting with available light. Cinematography that would have appeared distracting and unprofessional in the 1940s now connoted the immediacy of real, unpredictable events unfolding on real locations. Films shot in New York and based on true events, such as *The French Connection* (William Friedkin, 1971), *Serpico* (Sidney Lumet, 1973), and *Dog Day Afternoon* (Sidney Lumet, 1975), typified a gritty style of location shooting that became synonymous with realism and continues to influence more contemporary films such as *Training Day* (Antoine Fuqua, 2001) and *The Hurt Locker* (Kathryn Bigelow, 2009). There is a certain irony to this style of realism that draws attention to the presence of the camera, unlike the seamless dramatic realism of classical Hollywood that can now appear staged by comparison.

Hollywood location shooting also has a strong association with spectacle. John Ford's Monument Valley is not an everyday setting but rather an other-worldly landscape that heightens the drama of many of his westerns. New wide-screen technologies such as Cinerama favored exotic and picturesque locations, and the first Cinerama films eschewed narrative for the immersive spectacle of virtual travel. Hitchcock's 1950s thrillers included similar moments of touristic splendor in scenic European and American locations, as does the entire James Bond franchise. More recently, New Zealand's majestic landscapes combined with computer-generated edifices and creatures to build the fantastical realm of Middle Earth. Real locations are not confined to realist dramas and thus can add glamour and production value to Hollywood films while still providing a realistic sense of place.

Logistics

In a hypothetical scene shot on location, the lead character walks across the street. The film crew will need a permit from the local government to shoot on said street, as well as permission to stop traffic at a set time of day. On a busy street, the crew might shoot day for night with powerful lights in order to prevent a traffic jam. If the lead character is a star, additional police officers or security personnel will need to cordon off the set to keep a crowd of onlookers out of the shot. Even just the presence of a camera and a large crew might be enough to draw a crowd. Depending on the shot, the size of the crew, and the budget of the film, all of the pedestrians and cars might be replaced by extras and rentals steered by hired drivers. Alternatively, each person clearly appearing in the shot would need to sign a photographic release form. The crew would likely be a mix of local personnel and Hollywood personnel, determined by prior arrangements with unions and state and local government.

These procedures, now routinized in Hollywood production, were either nonexistent or slowly developing as location shooting became increasingly common. Concerns about film production interfering with local business and traffic emerged early in Los Angeles but were uncommon elsewhere for several decades.[19] Through the 1960s, shooting unsuspecting crowds with a concealed camera rather than hiring extras was an accepted practice. In the 1940s and 1950s, throngs of onlookers might come as a surprise to filmmakers hoping to get a quick shot or unaccustomed to extensive location shooting. The issue of controlling bystanders and disrupting daily lives was most pronounced in urban locations. In rural locations, local cooperation was often a point of civic pride, allowing film-makers to take advantage of relatively free rein shooting in a small town.

In less populous locations, so often associated with westerns, local people were far less of a concern than a lack of critical resources and environmental

control. Beautiful scenery might be inaccessible without building roads or relying on pack animals to move equipment. Just hours away from Los Angeles,
weather could be extremely unpredictable. For *The Adventures of Robin Hood*
(Michael Curtiz / William Keighley, 1938), weather caused major delays on location in Chico, California.[20] During the production of *Ride the High Country*
(Sam Peckinpah, 1962), an unexpected snowstorm transformed the landscape,
while the color of the sky varied in different locations around Mammoth Lake
in California.[21]

The logistical demands of Hollywood location shooting gave rise to new pro-
fessions, such as the location scout and the unit production manager. Specialists
had to figure out not only where to shoot but also how to gain local cooperation
and to respect local regulations throughout the globe. The more Hollywood filmmakers shot on the location, the more complex such agreements could become
as workers, administrators, and citizens in production hubs outside of Los Angeles gained awareness of their rights or grew disenchanted with Hollywood's offscreen or onscreen treatment of their local environment. Similarly, Hollywood
production companies grew more adept at working with outside personnel and
leveraging potential economic contributions toward greater local cooperation.

Chapter Overviews

Jennifer Peterson's chapter details location shooting practices in the silent era.
Although outdoor filming was widespread in the early years of cinema, the concept of "location shooting" did not crystallize until the early 1910s. As Peterson
explains, the meaning of "location" was necessarily intertwined with its opposite,
the "studio." Peterson sets out a four-part taxonomy of location shooting in early
cinema: scenic shooting, outdoor shooting, narrative integration, and substitute
locations. From the place specificity of early travelogues to the often generic
interchangeability of feature film backdrops, location shooting developed in tandem with the transition from the cinema of attractions to the cinema of narrative
integration. As Peterson shows, location shooting and its associated ideas of realism therefore evolved alongside the consolidation of the studio system and what
would become its primary output, the narrative feature film. When the industry
moved west, location shooting and the idea of the "substitute location" flourished, with the varied landscapes of Southern California standing in for a range
of global settings. In particular, Peterson argues, location shooting in the natural
spaces of the American West became central to the development of the western
genre and the imperialist ideology that undergirded it. If location shooting was
a common practice in the silent era, it was not without problems, as Peterson's
account of MGM's disastrous shoot for *Ben-Hur* (Fred Niblo, 1925) makes clear.

Such challenges and constraints provide the overarching theme for Sheri
Chinen Biesen's chapter on the studio system between 1927 and 1945. During that

period, Hollywood location practices were deeply affected by two shocks, the first internal (the coming of sound) and the second external (World War II). The advent of synchronized sound temporarily pushed filmmaking back into the studio and established the soundstage as the primary infrastructure for feature production. But location work remained an important, if subordinate, component of the filmmaking process, and throughout the 1930s, the studios experimented with ambitious location projects. For high-budget, prestige pictures such as *The Big Trail* (Raoul Walsh, 1930), *Trader Horn*, and *Mutiny on the Bounty* (Frank Lloyd, 1935), location shooting generated spectacular and sometimes exotic backdrops, but its logistical, technical, and financial challenges were frequently considered by studio executives to outweigh the benefits. At the same time, more successful forays into location shooting, such as the Warner Bros. hit *The Adventures of Robin Hood*, demonstrated the potential value of working beyond the studio—if the location shoot might be kept carefully under control. However, the Technicolor extravagance of films such as *Robin Hood* and the overseas shooting used in films such as *Trader Horn* were rendered difficult, even impossible, by the outbreak of war. As Biesen shows, wartime restrictions on filming materials, equipment, and transportation created an austere filmmaking environment that militated against extensive location work and curtailed the experiments in color and widescreen undertaken in the interwar years. Nevertheless, World War II also acted as a crucial catalyst for location shooting in other ways, as the technological and logistical requirements for documentary shooting in combat pushed the boundaries of location filming forward.

The stark, unglamorous aesthetics of wartime documentaries and newsreels influenced the style of filmmaking during and after World War II. The emergence of a "semidocumentary" tendency in Hollywood cinema is a key theme of Joshua Gleich's chapter on the postwar period. In the immediate aftermath of World War II, films such as *The House on 92nd Street*, *Dark Passage* (Delmer Daves, 1947), and *The Naked City* (Jules Dassin, 1948) used extensive location work, especially in urban settings, and established a new kind of naturalist approach that contrasted with much of Hollywood's prewar output. This genre was short-lived, and as Gleich demonstrates, the semidocumentary boom highlighted the persistent problems faced by filmmakers on location. In the following years, the technical gap was narrowed by the development of faster film stocks, smaller cameras and lighting units, and more compact sound-recording equipment, all of which made location work increasingly feasible both financially and logistically. Gleich outlines the complex economic, logistical, and stylistic concerns that attended location shooting as it developed throughout the 1950s and early 1960s. The second part of his chapter explores these issues through a case study of Otto Preminger. As Gleich shows, Preminger's location work in films such as *Anatomy of a Murder* (1959) and *Advise and Consent* (1962) helped establish the economic and technical viability of shooting a feature entirely on location.

However, Preminger's careful integration of location material into the studio-based style of the classical cinema was in some ways self-defeating: the more the two became indistinguishable, the less expressive or aesthetic value location shooting held in distinction from the studio or the back lot.

While domestic location shooting was frequently driven by concerns of realism, the spectacular possibilities of location shooting were explored by a series of overseas productions throughout the 1950s and 1960s. Daniel Steinhart's chapter illuminates this trend of postwar "runaway productions" in foreign locales, offering a parallel history to Gleich's overview of postwar location shooting in the United States. Filming in Europe, both on location and in studios such as Cinecittà in Rome, was incentivized by frozen funds, government subsidies, tax incentives, and a strong dollar. But as Steinhart shows, the industry tended to portray runaways as motivated by narrative and aesthetic values. Authenticity and spectacle were real enough attractions for audiences, but they also operated as a fig leaf for the economic priorities of the studios. Drawing on an extended case study of Warner Bros.' production of *The Nun's Story* (Fred Zinnemann, 1959), Steinhart discusses the practical organization of an overseas shoot, from networks of foreign offices to local production managers, as well as key aesthetic considerations of the period, such as widescreen staging. As Steinhart shows, the development of foreign location shooting between the 1940s and 1960s helped establish an internationalized production network that prefigured the "global Hollywood" of the late twentieth century and beyond.

By the mid-1960s, most of the technological and logistical barriers to efficient location work had been overcome, yet for major studio projects, studio shooting remained a default option for many scenes, especially those involving interiors. Yet this was soon to change. Lawrence Webb's chapter shows how location shooting played a central role in the transition toward a "New Hollywood" between the late 1960s and the late 1970s. As Webb argues, the forces that pushed filmmaking away from the studio in this period were both economic and aesthetic. From an industrial perspective, the industry's financial crisis of 1969–71 acted as a catalyst for organizational change. The accelerated turn to package deals, independent production, and outsourcing favored location work, which also enabled the studios to pursue a new kind of flexible business logic. In turn, a new set of institutions developed at city and state level to encourage Hollywood location shooting. The business remained centered in Southern California, but its production geography became increasingly mobile and decentralized. This emphasis on location work was also underpinned by cultural and political change. Location shooting became inextricably bound up in the shift from the "old" to the "new" Hollywood, with the supposed authenticity and realism of the location staked against the artificiality and illusionism of the studio. As Webb shows, location shooting helped develop new working practices, broke down hierarchies, established new aesthetic conventions and ideas about realism, and became a crucial marker of auteurism. In films such as *The French Connection* and *The Sugarland Express* (Steven Spielberg, 1974), location shooting also enabled a new kind of mobility, whether through the crisis-ridden city streets of New York or across the rural landscapes of Texas. This sense of heightened mobility and flexibility was enabled during the 1970s by technological advances such as the Panaflex camera, the Steadicam camera mount, and the Cinemobile, a portable equipment vehicle that helped standardize the mobile location shoot. However, as the 1970s drew to a close, high-profile location shooting disasters and the renaissance of the spectacular, visual-effects-driven blockbuster helped tip the balance back toward the studio again, with films such as *Close Encounters of the Third Kind* (Steven Spielberg, 1977) employing a layered composition of locations, sets, models, and visual effects.

During the 1980s, American cinema became more clearly bifurcated between the mainstream studios—now fully incorporated into corporate conglomerates— and a flourishing independent sector. Noelle Griffis discusses how the film office or film bureau became a permanent fixture for both strands of production in the 1980s and 1990s, as state and municipal governments across the United States and Canada worked to draw in Hollywood location shoots and to foster sustainable, local production cultures. As Griffis shows, these two aspirations were frequently contradictory. The hypermobility of Hollywood location shooting opened up an intense competition to attract location shooting. In the 1980s, states such as Georgia, Texas, and Florida were at the forefront of developing production incentives and industry liaison; in the 1990s, Vancouver and Toronto were among the most competitive production centers beyond the industry's twin hubs of Los Angeles and New York. In contrast to the place specificity and discourses of authenticity that were dominant in the 1970s, these regional production centers capitalized precisely on their ability to double for other places, emphasizing generic space over specific place. Conversely, as Griffis shows, independent auteurs such as Hal Hartley, Abel Ferrara, and Richard Linklater developed strong associations with specific locales that recurred in their work. In the case of Linklater, his close association with Austin, Texas, has contributed to the city's development as a regional production hub.

Julian Stringer's final chapter looks at *Dawn of the Planet of the Apes* as a paradigmatic example of Hollywood's current integration of digital effects and location shooting into its primary form of output, the franchise blockbuster. Using digital technology to approximate reality and capturing real locations may seem like contradictory impulses, but Stringer shows how they reinforce each other. Financial incentives still favor location production, and iconic cities such as San Francisco still add production value to blockbuster films. The digital era favors locations that are immediately recognizable and eminently destructible, such as the Golden Gate Bridge. Meanwhile, digital technology can create physically impossible or prohibitively expensive characters and events while reducing labor costs on set. Advances in motion-capture technology allowed CGI apes to be seamlessly incorporated into scenes shot on location. Here the reality of place buttresses the realistic illusion of an army of genetically enhanced apes. Through a detailed production history of the film, Stringer analyzes how contemporary filmmakers decide to incorporate new technologies and location shooting for a combination of economic and aesthetic reasons. This results in a patchwork rendition of a given location onscreen, marked by both the concreteness of place and its mutability through digital effects.

This collection demonstrates the pivotal role that location shooting has played in shaping Hollywood's production practices, aesthetics, and development as a global industry. Together, these chapters reconnect the history of location production from the silent era to the present and bring this mode of filmmaking from the periphery of Hollywood history toward the center. The peril and potential of location shooting both necessitated a studio system and beckoned Hollywood to venture far beyond the walls of the back lot.

NOTES

1. Peter Bart, "Where the Action Isn't," *New York Times*, July 31, 1966, D7.

2. See Tom Gunning, *D. W. Griffith and the Origins of American Narrative Film* (Urbana: University of Illinois Press, 1994); Richard Koszarski, *Hollywood on the Hudson: Film and Television in New York from Griffith to Sarnoff* (New Brunswick, NJ: Rutgers University Press, 2008).

3. David Cook, *Lost Illusions: American Cinema in the Shadow of Watergate and Vietnam, 1970–1979* (Berkeley: University of California Press, 2000).

4. David Bordwell, Janet Staiger, and Kristin Thompson, *The Classical Hollywood Cinema: Film Style and Mode of Production to 1960* (London: Routledge, 1991).

5. R. Barton Palmer, *Shot on Location: Postwar American Cinema and the Exploration of Real Place* (New Brunswick, NJ: Rutgers University Press, 2016).

6. Patrick Keating, ed., *Cinematography* (New Brunswick, NJ: Rutgers University Press, 2014); Lucy Fischer, ed., *Art Direction and Production Design* (New Brunswick, NJ: Rutgers University Press, 2015).

7. Lawrence Webb, *The Cinema of Urban Crisis: Seventies Film and the Reinvention of the City* (Amsterdam: Amsterdam University Press, 2014); Adam O'Brien, *Transactions with the World: Ecocriticism and the Environmental Sensibility of New Hollywood* (Oxford, UK: Berghahn, 2016).

8. See Greg Elmer and Mike Gasher, *Contracting Out Hollywood: Runaway Productions and Foreign Location Shooting* (Lanham, MD: Rowman and Littlefield, 2005); Vicki Mayer, Miranda J. Banks, and John T. Caldwell, eds., *Production Studies: Cultural Studies of Media Industries* (New York: Routledge, 2009).

9. Edward Dimendberg, *Film Noir and the Spaces of Modernity* (Cambridge, MA: Harvard University Press, 2004); Mark Shiel, *Hollywood Cinema and the Real Los Angeles* (London: Reaktion, 2012); Stanley Corkin, *Starring New York: Filming the Grime and the Glamour of the Long 1970s* (Oxford: Oxford University Press, 2011).

10. See, for example, Mark Shiel and Tony Fitzmaurice, eds., *Screening the City* (London: Verso, 2003); Andrew Webber and Emma Wilson, eds., *Cities in Transition: The Moving Image and the Modern Metropolis* (London: Wallflower, 2008).

11. Geoffrey Nowell-Smith, *Making Waves: New Cinemas of the 1960s* (London: Continuum, 2008), 68–79.

12. Annette Kuhn and Guy Westwell, *A Dictionary of Film Studies* (Oxford: Oxford University Press, 2012), s.v. "location."

13. Helen Morgan Parmett, "Space, Place, and New Orleans on Television: From *Frank's Place* to *Treme*," *Television and New Media* 13, no. 3 (2012): 193–212.

14. See chapters 3 and 6 in this volume.

15. For a detailed discussion of *Trader Horn*, see chapter 2 in this volume. For *Heaven's Gate* (1980), see Steven Bach, *Final Cut: Art, Money, and Ego in the Making of "Heaven's Gate," the Film That Sank United Artists* (New York: Newmarket, 1999).

16. For a detailed discussion of the Cinemobile, see chapter 5 in this volume.

17. Julie Turnock, "The Screen on the Set: The Problem of Classical-Studio Rear Projection," *Cinema Journal* 51, no. 2 (2012): 157–62.

18. See chapters 4 and 5 in this volume.

19. See chapters 1 and 5 in this volume.

20. See chapter 2 in this volume.

21. Darrin Scot, "Ride the High Country," *American Cinematographer*, July 1962, 410–11, 438–39.

CHAPTER 1

THE SILENT SCREEN, 1895–1927

Jennifer Peterson

The motion-picture maker sets up his whirring camera in the wilds and the crowded city alike.
—David S. Hulfish, *Cyclopedia of Motion-Picture Work*, 1911

When I went out one glorious morning . . . [to] take the first "stills," and actually began posing the artists, it felt to me, just like it must feel to a prisoner leaving solitary confinement for the open air. Imagine the horizon is your stage limit and the sky your gridiron. . . . Our perspective was the upper chain of the Rockies, and our ceiling was God's own blue and amber sky. I felt inspired. I felt that I could do things which the confines of a theatre would not permit. . . . Nature did the rest.
—Cecil B. DeMille, 1914

In an article published in the *New York Dramatic Mirror* in 1914, Cecil B. DeMille claimed to have shot his first feature, *The Squaw Man*, on location in the Rocky Mountains. As quoted in the epigraph, he explained, "I felt inspired. . . . Nature did the rest." But in fact, DeMille was not telling the truth when he said that "our perspective was the upper chain of the Rockies." While the film was indeed shot partly outdoors, its location work took place entirely in Southern California.[1] While the West may have seemed like a generalized geography to many people in the 1910s, it is certainly a stretch to conflate Southern California and the Rocky Mountains, which are located roughly a thousand miles apart. But as a struggling young filmmaker eager to make his mark, DeMille's fabrication is hardly surprising and rather less scandalous than some of the other tall tales of the early film industry. In fact, DeMille's self-promoting yarn reveals a contradiction at the heart of the concept of cinematic location. Although the term "location shooting" implies authenticity and strict fidelity of place, the actual practice of shooting on location often means simply shooting outside the studio in some place that more or less resembles where the story is set. Location shooting is one of the core cinematic practices used to shore up film's celebrated sense of realism. But more often than not, filmmakers have used one location to stand for another. "Good enough" is the rule of location shooting, not "exactly" or "precisely." "Stunt locations" (as they are often called today) are extremely common, and as this example demonstrates, the practice of substituting one location for another dates from the silent era.[2]

DeMille's claim reveals a second timeworn concept at the heart of cinematic location: the idea that "nature" itself is a coauthor of films shot on location. For films set in the wilderness, exact coordinates were less important than the location's ability to signify nature's grandeur. What makes the outdoor scenes in *The Squaw Man* feel particularly "real" is not the specific geographical location in which it was shot but the materiality of nature, including real mountains, trees, rivers, and rocks. Nature, it seems, composed a generic theatrical outdoor space in the silent era. Indeed, it is around the time of *The Squaw Man* that the concept of "location" emerges in film history. As this chapter will show, there was already a well-established tradition of shooting films outdoors before the studio era, but the concept of location shooting as we think of it today emerged as a by-product of the studio system.

Finally, as DeMille's statement indicates, one particular kind of location bears a special relationship to American cinema: western scenery for western films. Western scenery is more than just a setting, according to DeMille; rather, wilderness landscapes add a sublime pathos that is, in this and other westerns, inextricably connected to American national identity. At the same time, "the West" was a particular kind of location in which particular kinds of stories could be told—about settlement, conquering nature, or the conflict between "civilization" and "savagery" that propels so many westerns. While this chapter does not focus specifically on westerns, it should be noted at the outset that the western is one of the genres most inextricably bound up with location shooting in American film history. Quite literally, the film industry's move west in the silent era echoed the nation's settlement of the West in the previous century. In this way, silent-era films dramatize a logic of settlement not just in many of their stories but in their evolving visualization of real, material landscapes.

The practice of shooting films on location is fundamental to cinema and can be traced back to the earliest films ever made. Well-known examples such as *The Arrival of a Train at La Ciotat* (Auguste and Louis Lumière, 1895) and *Rough Sea at Dover* (Birt Acres and R. W. Paul, 1895) make this point plain. But what does it mean to shoot a film on location? As it so often does, the history of early cinema reveals a complexity at the heart of this seemingly straightforward filmmaking practice. The technological and industrial idiosyncrasies of early cinema underscore the necessity of defining what location shooting meant in different historical periods. The concept of location shooting as it came to be understood by Hollywood did not develop until the consolidation of the narrative/feature-film-oriented studio system in the late 1910s. Before that, cinema was characterized by a set of competing ideas about the significance of outdoor shooting and the use of specific, identifiable real-life locations in film.

This chapter presents an overview of the predominant location shooting practices of U.S. film companies during the silent era. It also sketches a series of definitions for the different meanings of location work from 1895 to 1927. As this chapter demonstrates, silent cinema's phases of industrial development created different horizons of possibility for location work. Although its meaning changed, some form of shooting "on location" was always a prominent practice even as filmmaking developed from a minor and undercapitalized set of competing small businesses into a large, highly capitalized, vertically integrated industry. What changed was both the meaning of what was once called outdoor shooting and the range of places that came to signify realistic locations on film. Early cinema was characterized by a variety of outdoor shooting practices. In the so-called transitional era, various nomadic filmmaking practices were common. By the time the film industry had shifted (mostly) to Southern California, a new and more efficient set of location practices emerged that would remain dominant for much of the studio era. Location shooting gives the illusion of what Walter Benjamin called "the equipment free aspect of reality." But in fact, as Benjamin further explained, this representational trope is actually "the height of artifice."[3] In order to create the illusion of pristine nature and unfettered reality, film-makers on location shoots relied on many of the same concepts and technologies they used in the studio.

EARLY CINEMA: OUTDOOR SHOOTING AND SCENIC FILMS

Beginning with the first moving pictures made in the 1890s, every American film company shot films outside, and every kind of early film subject was filmed outdoors, including news stories, scenic views, sports, and comedies. Although studio filmmaking began with Edison's Black Maria studio in West Orange, New Jersey (in use from 1893 until its demolition in 1903), outdoor shooting was the more common practice for at least the first five years of American cinema history. The reasons for this are both aesthetic and technological. Outdoor shooting was immediately appreciated for its verisimilitude, but more importantly, the idea of the film studio as the primary site of production had not yet emerged. Shooting outdoors was easy and required no expensive construction of structures or sets. Most importantly, moving pictures needed bright illumination, and artificial lighting was not yet available, which meant that sunlight had to be used until studio-grade artificial lighting was developed (the first artificial lights were

Cooper Hewitt lamps installed in the Biograph Company's New York studio in 1903). Indeed, as Brian Jacobson has shown, "The search for favorable climatic conditions or, in their absence, substitutes for sunlight thus became one of the major driving forces in the development of early cinematic production."[4] Filmmakers began constructing glass-enclosed studio buildings using sunlight for illumination as early as 1897, but shooting outdoors remained the default practice for a great deal of filmmaking in the earliest years of cinema.[5] This was not yet location shooting as it later came to be understood; rather, at first, outdoor and studio shooting were not rigidly distinguished. A decade later, however, the difference was clear. David S. Hulfish wrote in a section on "pictures without studios" in his 1911 *Cyclopedia of Motion-Picture Work*, "A prominent film manufacturing company operated for years without a studio and without painted scene sets, releasing a reel each week."[6] What had been common in the 1890s and early 1900s was now remarkable in 1911.

The history of location shooting is both a history of cinema technologies and a history of cinematic realism. Film history textbooks typically contrast the French Lumière films, known for their "documentary" qualities and outdoor shooting, with the American Edison films, known for their fairground/vaudeville subject matter and for having been shot inside the Black Maria. But this distinction has as much to do with these companies' respective technological devices as it does with national/cultural differences. While the Lumière Cinématographe camera was lightweight and portable (thus enabling the Lumières to produce and exhibit outdoor views six months before Edison), the Edison Manufacturing Company's first Kinetograph camera was bulky and limited to shooting within the Black Maria and its immediate environs. The Edison Company soon developed a more portable camera, however, and began shooting street scenes in New York City. *Herald Square*, shot by Edison cameraman William Heise on May 11, 1896, is considered the first film shot on location in New York.[7] A reviewer from the *Buffalo Courier* described the film in this way: "A scene covering Herald Square in New York, showing the noonday activity of Broadway at that point as clearly as if one were spectator of the original seems incredulous, nevertheless is presented life-like. The cable cars seem to move in opposite directions and look real enough to suggest a trip up and down that great thoroughfare, while at the same time the elevated trains are rushing overhead, pedestrians are seen moving along the sidewalks or crossing to opposite sides of the street, everything moving, or as it is seen in real life."[8] As this description makes clear, it was the detailed realism of this moving picture of a real location that was so impressive to early audiences. Not only was the urban bustle of New York accurately captured by the film, but the materiality of objects and people moving through space was also remarkable in its own right. This discourse of realism has continued to define our notion of location shooting ever since, although the styles of realism have shifted over time.

Outdoor shooting was also more common in early cinema because film was not yet seen as a predominantly narrative medium; rather, nonfiction subjects were more frequently produced than fiction films in the first decade of film history. For example, a 1902 catalog from the American Mutoscope & Biograph Company lists about twice as many films shot outdoors as indoors, and this breakdown occurs across fiction and nonfiction lines.[9] After a list of comedy, vaudeville, and trick film titles, the catalog presents a long list of films shot outdoors with generic categories such as sports and pastimes, railroads, scenic, fire and police, military, parades, marine, and expositions. The few remaining subjects in other categories may or may not have been shot outdoors—notable personages, children, educational, machinery, miscellaneous—but the point is that in the early years of cinema, moving pictures were not just a medium for representing fictional stories. Rather, early moving pictures were more often understood as a recording device.

Clearly, we must distinguish between what we think of as location shooting today and what the film industry thought about outdoor shooting in the early cinema period. Generally speaking, outdoor shooting in early cinema was connected to an idea of nonfiction, even though terms such as "nonfiction" and "documentary" did not yet exist. As a 1909 article on "photographing outdoor subjects" explained, "outdoor" pictures meant nonfiction: "By outdoor subjects I mean those which are not specially rehearsed as in the dramatic pictures that are so popular just now. Take for example a procession, a street scene, or an athletic contest."[10]

But even in the realm of early nonfiction, some distinctions can be drawn. Although a film such as *President McKinley's First Campaign* (Biograph, 1902) was necessarily shot outdoors (in Canton, Ohio), its classification in the 1902 Biograph catalog under "Parades" indicates that it did not function as a film connected to a specific location, but rather its significance was the famous person it documented.[11] Scenic films such as *Washington Bridge and the Speedway* (Biograph, 1902), pictured in figure 1.1, are more clearly about specific places, and scenic films can be understood as an early form of location shooting. On the other hand, even though a surviving scenic film such as *Waterfall in the Catskills* (Edison, 1897) names a specific place in its title, the extant film presents little visual information about this specific place; indeed the waterfall is so tightly framed that we cannot even verify if it was actually shot where the title claims.[12] Although the film's location is not in doubt, the generic nature of such waterfall imagery suggests that it was the falling water that mattered more than the place. In sum, although outdoor shooting was a dominant practice in early cinema, it had not yet taken on its primary function as a setting for narrative.

Early and silent-era cinema can help us better understand the varied nature of location shooting, which has always been more complex than the term would suggest. I argue that scenic films (or travelogues, as they were also called) func-

SCENIC

UNDER this head come many pictures of strong local interest;— street scenes, along the great water highways, in the mountains, and on the plains. Our Niagara Falls series is particularly strong, embracing views of the giant cataract from all of the more interesting points, with several turning panoramas covering the whole extent of this wonderful phenomenon of nature, from the beginning of the upper rapids, across the Canadian and American Falls and as far down as the cantilever bridge. It will be noted also that the foreign subjects include most of the places visited and admired by tourists. The Chinese Philippine views are all very fine pictorially and photographically. The New York street scenes are without exception very typical of Metropolitan bustle and activity.

ALONG THE SPEEDWAY. NEW YORK

Figure 1.1. Scenic films as a prototype for location shooting. American Mutoscope & Biograph Company, *Picture Catalogue* (New York: AM&B, 1902), 130.

tioned as a prototype for what later became location shooting. In a taxonomy of early cinema location practices, scenic films stand as the limit case of an indexical notion of place. One of the most popular early film genres, scenics were short nonfiction films depicting geographical and cultural points of interest around the world, rather like postcards come alive. While they depicted places in the present moment, they often reified exotic or nostalgic ideas about traditional people, cultures, and landscapes that were perceived as fading away.[13]

In contrast, early fiction films often used outdoor settings as generic exterior non-places. The early British film *How It Feels to Be Run Over* (Hepworth, 1900), for example, was shot outdoors, but its indistinct diegesis (a dirt road flanked by hedges and trees) does not signify any specific place.[14] Here we can locate a second category of early cinema location work on the other end of the spectrum, a practice we might simply call "outdoor shooting." This descriptive term was used in the trade press, although it was not applied systematically and could be used to describe both fiction and nonfiction films. Reviewers frequently praised fiction films shot outdoors for their pictorial beauty, as in this review for a 1910 film: "as much as the picture has been taken outdoors, amid beautiful scenery, the general effect is very pleasing, and the photographic quality of the film leaves nothing to be desired."[15] Outdoor shooting was concerned to show generic exterior scenery rather than any specific location; it was not bound to an indexical sense of place as it was in scenic films.

Outdoor shooting bears resemblance to the painting term *en plein air*, or open-air painting, in that it was generically applied to any manner of subjects rendered outside rather than inside. In art, the term connotes the practice of representing things that appear as they are before the eye; this concept clearly bears resemblance to the idea of cinematic realism. *Plein air* painting became popular in the nineteenth century with the rise of landscape painting and the related emergence of impressionism. Portable field easels were developed at this time, which were used by painters both professional and amateur as they ventured outdoors to find suitable subjects; the practice is depicted in Winslow Homer's painting *Artists Sketching in the White Mountains* (1868). Early outdoor camera operators, with their cameras, tripods, and gear, resemble these fine-art practitioners outdoors with their apparatus of easel and paint. One commentator wrote in 1909, "Pictorial photography of the stationary kind is best done *en plein air*, as photographers know, and the same rule should hold good with regard to moving pictures."[16] Early comedies and chase films regularly utilized outdoor shooting. In these films, the actual location is not significant; rather, a general sense of being in the open air is what matters.

In between these two practices—scenic films and generic outdoor shooting— we can locate what eventually became the dominant, aspirational idea of location shooting in the studio era: fiction films shot in the actual location in which the story is set. At first, this involved a juxtaposition of actuality footage with staged footage. Edwin S. Porter's film *Execution of Czolgosz with Panorama of Auburn Prison* (Edison, 1901) is an important step toward this concept of cinematic loca- tion.[17] The four-shot film begins with two panoramic shots of the exterior of the prison taken on location the morning of the execution, shifting in the third and fourth shots to an interior reenactment of the execution. Thus, even though the film is a reenactment of a real event, the location shots add verisimilitude to the subject. Significantly, exhibitors could choose whether to purchase the film with or without the two opening actuality shots.[18] In its full-length version, this film begins to develop a unified sense of space in which inside and outside, actual and staged, signify a single diegesis. The location work on *Execution of Czolgosz* is faithful to the extreme—not only is the actual prison of the execution shown, but the exterior footage was also taken the morning of the actual execution (Por- ter had been denied permission to film inside the prison). Porter used a similar technique combining actuality footage with staged footage in his tourist parody film *European Rest Cure* in 1904.[19]

A fourth category of location work, which might be called the "substitute location"—the practice of using one location to stand for another—was also developing in the early years. One of the best-known early American films, *The Great Train Robbery* (Edwin S. Porter, 1903), is a good example of this practice. Like so many early films, this one was modeled after a popular stage play of the same name. Shooting a film outdoors was a way for cinema to distinguish itself from the theater, and early promotional efforts made note of this fact: "It has been posed and acted in faithful duplication of the genuine 'Hold Ups' made famous by various outlaw bands in the far West," proclaimed an Edison promotional pamphlet.[20] The film's exterior shots contain an element of indexical realism simply because they were shot outdoors in the woods, although the film's diegetic setting in "the West" was shot in Passaic County, New Jersey, just a few miles north of Edison's original Black Maria studio in West Orange. In *The Great Train Robbery*, the film's diegetic setting is not arbitrary but produces narrative meaning: it is important that this railway robbery story takes place in the West. But rather than a strong indexical sense of a specific place, we find a weak indexical sense of a generic "western" outdoors. We might then characterize the practice of the substitute location as a kind of weak indexicality. Numerous early westerns were shot in the East; Scott Simmon has called this tradition the "eastern Western," writing, "The overall stylistic conventions of filmmaking in these first years reinforce the landscape's theatricality: The camera is generally fixed in place, actors' bodies are filmed full length, and each shot is held for a relatively long duration."[21] This practice illustrates early cinema's debt to nineteenth-century landscape painting and illustration traditions, but the theatricality is also an effect of the imprecision of these landscapes: a generalized outdoor forest or lake only fifty miles inland from the Atlantic Ocean could evoke the western frontier.

In the first decade of film history, locations served as attractions in their own right (in scenic films), as arbitrary settings with better available lighting than early studios could provide (as in the outdoor shooting of *How It Feels to Be Run Over*), as actuality footage framing a staged drama (as in *Execution of Colgosz*), or as substitute locations (as in early westerns set in the West but shot in the East, such as *The Great Train Robbery*). As moving pictures shifted from the cinema of attractions to a cinema of narrative integration, location work became more integrated into narratives, and its landscapes came to signify not so much actually existing places or a generic outdoors but fictional settings. Locations continued to function as visual spectacle, however, and were often foregrounded as establishing shots or pauses between narrative events.

CONSOLIDATING THE NARRATIVE USES OF LOCATION

As narrative films developed in complexity and length, location shooting practices began to coalesce around a stable set of meanings—namely, the merging of

diegetic story space and extradiegetic geographical space. Much has been made
of the historical shift to more tightly framed shots in the early 1910s—film history
textbooks cite the advent of the "9-foot line" as an important development in
1910, a closer camera distance that allowed for a more subtle presentation of the
human figure. At the same time, however, a new deliberateness with the framing
of extreme long shots was emerging, which enabled a more complex presentation
of landscapes and exterior locations.

D. W. Griffith is one of the most important figures in the early history of location shooting, for his techniques signaled a new integration of naturalistic setting
with narrative. First of all, the development of continuity editing, self-promoted
by Griffith (though not invented by him as he claimed), allowed for a more seamless unification of exterior and interior spaces. The climactic canoe chase in *The
Red Man and the Child* (Griffith, 1908), shot on location on the Passaic River
(near the shooting location of *The Great Train Robbery*), creates what Tom Gunning describes as "a coherent geography which extends over five shots of the
eighteen-shot film," creating a synthetic space through shots of canoes entering and exiting the frame.[22] These continuity editing strategies had been used in
the popular chase film genre in preceding years, but in this and other films for
the Biograph Company, Griffith merged a consistent exterior story space into a
larger and more emotionally engaging melodramatic narrative.

Griffith's one-reeler *The Country Doctor* (1909), shot partly on location in
Greenwich, Connecticut, is a landmark film for its presentation of landscape in
the service of narrative, pushing Porter's innovative location techniques for *The
Execution of Colgosz* further toward narrative integration.[23] The film opens and
closes with two panning shots that stand apart from the main narrative but that
use location to create a powerful sense of rural setting. These two pans inaugu-
rate the use of sweeping landscape panoramas as lyrical establishing shots, a tradition that continues to this day—think of *Brokeback Mountain* (Ang Lee, 2005),
for example. As Gunning writes, "What is immediately striking about this pair
of pans is their difference from all of Griffith's previous pans and from how pans
were used in early narrative cinema. These pans do not follow the action of any
of the film's characters, although in most early narrative films that was the case.
In the opening shot of *The Country Doctor*, however, the camera itself initiates a
movement through a landscape to introduce the film's characters and begin the
narrative action."[24] The film's final shot reverses the path of the opening shot,
returning to the opening image of a pastoral landscape. Griffith uses the peaceful
setting as an ironic contrast to the tragic events of the film's plot, which heightens
the emotional devastation of the narrative, in which the doctor's own daughter
dies while he is away curing another sick child. By evoking the specificity of this
larger rural diegetic world, these two shots harness the power of location shooting to add both realism and poetic resonance.

Griffith continued to develop the dramatic potential of what he called "distant views" in films shot on wintertime trips to California with Biograph, including *The Last Drop of Water* (1911), *The Massacre* (1912), *The Sands of Dee* (1912), and *The Battle of Elderbush Gulch* (1913), each of which uses location in interesting ways. But while Griffith's Biograph films developed a rhetoric of location that was more fully articulated than previous directors', he still relied on an extremely generic notion of regional location in his films. Indeed, when Griffith chased down "realism" to a fetishistic degree, he was inspired by famous paintings—as in the "Historical Facsimiles" in *The Birth of a Nation* (1915)—rather than actually existing landscapes or places. It was not until the American film industry moved west for good that the term "location shooting" came to be used. The emergence of this concept was shaped by both geographic and industrial factors.

THE NOMADIC EARLY FILM INDUSTRY

The history of location shooting is also a geographical history of the American film industry as it moved from its East Coast origins to a range of locations around the country, eventually settling on the West Coast in the mid-1910s. In 1909, American film production was centered predominantly in and around New York City and Chicago. But as the industry grew and more films were needed year-round to satisfy the growing audience of moviegoers in the nickel theaters, production companies began sending stock companies to warmer climates in order to continue filming during the winter months. The Essanay Company's history serves as an exemplary case study: production that began in Chicago expanded to include itinerant filmmaking for a few years while remaining anchored in the Midwest, and eventually shifted entirely to California. Founded in April 1907, Essanay first specialized in producing split reels containing a comedy and an educational subject. In a 1918 *Photoplay* article, the comedian Ben Turpin remembered the early years at Essanay: "They didn't use automobiles to go on locations then. . . . They sent us out in street cars. Every actor had to carry part of the scenery. Out of gallantry we let the ladies carry the tripods of the camera while we carried chairs and screens and office furniture. Of course we had to go in all our make-up and we used to have some strange adventures. They didn't think much of picture folks in those days."[25] Essanay produced numerous comedies and westerns in and around Chicago and on location in Berrien Springs, Michigan, but when winter came, they needed to maintain their fast-paced release schedule of one film a week.

In order to continue production through the cold winter months, the company sent a few key players out to make films in California's warmer climate. Gilbert M. "Broncho Billy" Anderson, soon to become one of the first cowboy movie stars, was one of the founders of Essanay, and at this time, he was writing, directing, acting in, and editing most of Essanay's productions. In December 1908, Anderson and Turpin, along with cameraman Jess Robbins, traveled to San Francisco and Los Angeles, making several westerns and a few educational films along the way.[26] After returning to Chicago, they ventured west again, this time to Golden, Colorado, in March 1909; there they continued to produce westerns, along with the occasional travel or local-color subject. Anderson and his crew returned to Chicago again and made more films at Essanay's new studio on Argyle Street but returned to Colorado in September 1909 to shoot more westerns, then headed back to Southern California by way of El Paso, Texas, in January 1910. In February 1910 alone, Essanay released four films made by Anderson and his crew—two dramas and a nonfiction film—shot during this trip in locations ranging across Colorado, Texas, and California. These titles include *The Mexican's Faith* (a western drama shot on location in Santa Barbara, California, released February 26, 1910) and *Aviation at Los Angeles, California* (a nonfiction film shot on location at the Dominguez Airfield in Los Angeles, released February 16, 1910), both of which survive today.[27]

Essanay's practices at first resembled the old scenic production method of sending a few filmmakers out to find the most picturesque landscapes, only now the production unit had grown to include actors and the priority had shifted to fictional narratives. Other companies followed a similar model: while shooting dramatic films on location, many traveling production units shot scenic and topical subjects on the side. As an increasing number of films were produced, itinerant film production also grew in scope and scale. By the late 1910s, as we shall see shortly, location shooting had come to take on many of the trappings of studio production, with the goal of efficient scheduling and as much control as possible over the natural environment. But in the early 1910s, itinerant film production was still fairly haphazard with regard to destination and low-tech in its production costs and techniques.

By 1910, ambulatory filmmaking was becoming common. As Eileen Bowser explains it, 1910 was a turning point because that year film companies could "afford to rent private railroad cars to transport large groups of players, directors, and cameramen across the continent, or to send stock companies overseas by ship. . . . The idea of trooping around the United States to make moving pictures probably seemed natural to those who once spent all their days with touring stock companies."[28] Around this time, filmmaking moved south and west to a few key locations such as Florida and Colorado, as well as California (both Northern and Southern). A few regular film-production units were established in "distant" locations such as Golden, Colorado (Selig, Essanay); Niles, California (Essanay); and especially Jacksonville, Florida (Kalem, Lubin, Selig, and more). At the same time, companies such as Kalem, Vitagraph, and Selig sent still more itinerant production troupes to New Orleans, San Antonio, Oklahoma's "101 Ranch," Arizona, Mexico, Cuba, Jamaica, Ireland, Germany, and even Egypt.

Although many early film companies sent production units out on location, the Kalem Company made location work a particular focus of its marketing strategy. Kalem sent a troupe to Ireland in 1910 and again in 1911, advertising this production unit in the trade press as the "O'Kalems." Its first release, the one-thousand-foot *A Lad from Old Ireland* (Sidney Olcott), was promoted with great fanfare in November 1910. The film stars Kalem's most famous player at the time, Gene Gauntier, who filmed numerous additional scenes in the studio after returning to New York, which allowed the company to promote the film as "the first production ever made on two continents."[29] The company also shot nonfiction footage on this first trip, but it was not until after the troupe's second trip abroad in 1911 that nonfiction films were released, such as *The O'Kalem's Visit to Killarney* (released January 5, 1912).[30] Vitagraph sent a production unit to Jamaica in early 1910, releasing *Between Love and Honor* four months before *A Lad from Old Ireland*, in July 1910. An advertisement for the film boasts that the film was "photographed amid the beautiful scenery of Kingston, Jamaica."[31] The Independent Moving Pictures Company (IMP) sent a production unit to Cuba in late 1910 / early 1911, and the Yankee Film Company soon followed suit, sending a troupe to Bermuda, Jamaica, and Cuba in early 1911.[32]

The trade press demonstrates that 1910 was a turning point in the film industry's expansion of its location shooting efforts. Film companies can be seen trying to one-up each other in stories and advertisements about their traveling production troupes in the fall of 1910 and winter of 1911. One perceptive writer in *Moving Picture World* claimed that all this traveling production was evidence of a new stability for the industry and also characteristic of the global cross-currents of the new modern world:

> To our mind this [far-flung production] is one more proof, if proof be needed, of the stability of the moving picture business as a whole. Shrewd business men have satisfied themselves that the demand for the picture instead of diminishing is likely to expand with the growth of the population. . . . Of course, there is nothing remarkable to this fact of manufacturers being located hundreds of thousands of miles from New York City. The apple that we ate this morning was probably from Oregon; there is no reason why the moving picture that we looked at last night should not also have been made in the same distant State. The telephone, the telegraph, the aeroplane, as well as the fast railroad are, to modern business economics, rapidly annihilating time and space.[33]

The O'Kalem unit was sent out for a third trip in 1912, but this time it made a longer production tour, beginning in Egypt and the Middle East and then moving north through Europe. This time, the troupe was dubbed the "El Kalems." The trip lasted nearly a year, and numerous films were produced, including *Down through the Ages* (Olcott, 1912), along with several scenic and educational films including *Luxor, Egypt* (released May 29, 1912) and *Palestine* (released August

28, 1912).[34] *Moving Picture World* featured a photo showing the construction of a portable Kalem "Airdome" studio in Jerusalem, demonstrating how traveling production units aimed to replicate studio practices while on location.[35] The highlight of the trip was Kalem's most ambitious film, *From the Manger to the Cross* (Olcott, 1912), a multireel extravaganza with a large cast and color tinting shot in Jerusalem, Nazareth, Galilee, and the Egyptian pyramids. The film was well received and became one of Kalem's most profitable titles.[36]

Despite this expansion of shooting in far-flung locations, production outside the main hubs continued to be perceived as the exception rather than the norm in the early 1910s, and many filmmakers returned to New York and Chicago during the summer months. That began to change by 1912, as Southern California became increasingly popular as a permanent destination for film companies. By the mid-1910s, the geographical center of the film industry had shifted: what had formerly been understood as "remote" filming in California was transformed into a permanent central hub for the industry. A story in the *Los Angeles Times* explained as early as 1910, "The coming to Southern California by the picture firms is not a winter engagement, but will be an all-year enterprise. At first, they came here to avoid the snow and ice, but the bright quality of the sunshine and the number of clear days in which they may work, together with the variety of scenery, has all been found ideal and their making here is now permanent."[37]

The American film industry relocated from the East to the West for several reasons, and this territorial shift had important consequences for the development of location shooting as a standard industry practice. Most film histories explain the move west as a result of four factors: (1) the mild climate of Southern California enabled the film industry to shoot year-round; (2) the varied topography of Southern California (from ocean to forest to desert) enabled the production of many different genres; (3) filmmakers wanted to be as far away from the Motion Picture Patents Company as possible (it took at least four days to travel from New York to Los Angeles by train); and (4) labor unions were weak in California at this time, which was appealing to the undercapitalized and frequently exploitative young industry. What seems symptomatic (but rarely commented on) about this list of factors is the ideology of manifest destiny and settler colonialism that undergirds it. It is time to acknowledge the ways in which the film industry's move west and the stories it was able to tell using western locations rendered empire one of the dominant strands of Hollywood narratives.

By the end of the 1910s, there was a veritable gold rush of scenery afoot as filmmakers and studios sought to find ever-new landscapes to colonize with their cameras. The trade press spoke of "prospecting" for locations, envisioning landscapes as a natural resource to be exploited by the cinema. In a 1914 article for *Moving Picture World*, Jesse Lasky wrote, "We acquired a lease of a ranch of about 20,000 acres. Here is to be found some of the finest scenery in California.

Mountains rise to a height of 6,000 feet. On the top we can get snow, while at the base there is an abundance of tropical foliage. Included in this property are three or four acres of remarkable desert and cactus. . . . This setting has been available for 'Cameo Kirby.'"[38] The photo accompanying this story shows Lasky and DeMille (probably Cecil B. and not William C., though it is hard to discern faces) "prospecting for locations" on horseback in the mountains, presumably at the ranch Lasky is describing.[39] However, the story of *Cameo Kirby*, based on a play of the same name, takes place in antebellum Mississippi, which makes this a substitute location and thus an odd title to brag about for its desert and cactus.[40] It seems possible that Lasky might be describing a location at Mount Palomar instead, where Cecil B. DeMille shot scenes for *The Squaw Man* in 1914.[41]

Regardless of whether Lasky was speaking accurately, this was a moment when the idea of location shooting took on one of its predominant functions: to visualize nature and natural scenery. Location shooting also takes place in urban locations, of course, as underscored by the first epigraph of this chapter. But audiences have long singled out location shooting for particular praise when it presents sweeping vistas of nature. The grandiosity of location shooting in the landscapes of the American West proved to be a marketable commodity when contrasted with the constricted vision of films shot inside the studios. Location shooting was not just a strategy for realism but a marketing concept.

THE YOUNG HOLLYWOOD STUDIOS: A DIVERSITY OF LOCATIONS

Studio location work had the potential to range across the globe; but in practice during the silent era, much location shooting took place in the Southwest, and most of that occurred within driving range of Hollywood. Wherever it took place, the operating principle of a location shoot was to control exterior locations as much as possible. This concept of "location" is not so much a realistic depiction of natural landscapes but a theatricalization of actually existing places. As Lou Strohm, location manager for Metro Pictures, wrote in 1922, "There are, in California, locations that because of their peculiar topography, are admirably adapted to the filming of scenes depicting far-distant places and lands. Carpenters and scene makers build sets out in the open location and bring to the place the appearance of the native soil or surroundings that are to be depicted."[42] By 1917, as the studio system began to settle in as the dominant mode of production in American film, the history of location shooting shifted into a new phase. No longer can we break location shooting into the four-part taxonomy of early cinema: scenic, outdoor shooting, narrative integration, and substitute locations. While travel films continued to be produced throughout the silent era (they were now shown as part of the shorts program before the feature film), they were no longer one of the primary cinematic experiences of place. Instead, location shooting became further embedded into narrative filmmaking practices, and it was transformed by its new California landscapes, where the substitute location came to be institutionalized.

While the studios were building increasingly large and more expensive indoor studios, they also walled off plots of land adjacent to their buildings for more controlled outdoor shooting on the back lot. Back lot filmmaking does not qualify as location shooting, but it does help to define what location shooting was not: by this time, location film shooting meant more than just shooting outdoors. At the same time, the entire city of Los Angeles and its surrounding municipalities became one giant outdoor set for filmmakers, and this use of the rapidly industrializing city must be seen as the first and most common form of location shooting in the early studio era. In addition, the studios began to purchase or lease land on the far borders of Los Angeles for shooting westerns and other genres in the ranches, ravines, and mountains of the area. These peripheral studio properties, known as "movie ranches," should be understood as a gray area between studio filmmaking and location shooting. Movie ranches and location shooting farther afield also demonstrate the pervasiveness of the substitute location, as California's diverse regions were used to stand for a range of global settings. The studios soon formed location departments to scout locations in an efficient manner that fit within newly regimented modes of production. Production units were sent to far-flung locations around California and the Southwest, but these trips were now prescouted and planned ahead. Finally, although location shooting in foreign countries was still unusual in the late 1910s and early 1920s, there are some high-profile examples. I conclude this chapter with a brief consideration of *Ben-Hur* (Fred Niblo, 1925), a runaway big-budget feature shot mostly on location in Italy and perhaps the most high-profile example of silent-era location shooting in a foreign country. These practices—shooting in the streets of Los Angeles, movie ranches around the greater Los Angeles periphery, California as a double for the world, and foreign location shooting—are discussed in the remainder of this chapter.

IN AND AROUND LOS ANGELES: THE STUDIO ZONE

Thanks to mild weather and the often slapdash methods of early filmmaking, early Hollywood utilized a wide range of interior and exterior filmmaking spaces, often setting up shoots in makeshift open-air stages, in the road, or in whatever park or empty lot that seemed suitable. Indeed, some of the earliest companies such as Selig made films entirely outdoors upon their initial arrival in Los Angeles. From the start, filmmakers used the city of Los Angeles and its environs as their open-air movie studio. Slapstick comedies made by the Mack Sennett Studios and the Mutual Film Corporation were frequently shot on the streets. Films starring Charlie Chaplin, Roscoe "Fatty" Arbuckle, Buster Keaton, and Harold

Lloyd made great use of Los Angeles cityscapes in the late 1910s and early 1920s. These comedies, including *Tillie's Punctured Romance* (Sennett, 1914) and *Cops* (Keaton, 1922), are among the most famous films of the silent era, and numerous books and documentaries have traced their shooting locations.[43] Mark Shiel has discussed at length how silent comedy shaped the world's vision of Los Angeles as a place. He argues that the city's emergent sprawl was well suited for slapstick chase narratives in which characters traveled between two or more places. "In this way, the process of narrative integration found a city especially conducive to it because of its exceptional horizontality."[44]

At what point did the temporary and remote location work in Los Angeles (perceived as such by the home office in Chicago or New York) become reimagined as studio work conducted within the heart of the industry? While it may be impossible to locate a precise date for this shift from the perception of Los Angeles as a faraway location to the epicenter of the moviemaking universe, one development—the formation of the so-called studio zone—can illustrate how things changed along the way. Today the term "studio zone" or "thirty-mile zone" (TMZ) refers to the so-called thirty-mile zone in which most studio filmmaking occurs; outside this zone, permitting is different and production costs are higher. The mythology of the studio zone has yet to be thoroughly analyzed by film historians, and there is a great deal of imprecise information that circulates.[45] The first official version of the studio zone—initially inside a six-mile radius centered at Fifth and Rossmore Streets in what is now the Mid-Wilshire district—was established in 1934 in order to establish pay rates for extras.[46] By the 1970s, its expansion to a thirty-mile radius was ratified by all the industry's labor unions. Today the zone is centered on the corners of Beverly Boulevard and La Cienega Boulevard in West Hollywood (three and a half miles west of its original location), and it is used to establish per diem rates and driving distances for union crew members.[47] But a brief zoning incident in 1917 demonstrates that in the silent era, the "studio zone" could have quite a different meaning. As the growing city of Los Angeles issued zoning ordinances in the 1910s, the location of the movie studios was examined by the city from the perspective of property values. While many residents and businesses tolerated or even appreciated the film industry, some property owners felt that the movie studios were an unwelcome presence that should be moved to the periphery of the city.

In March 1917, *Moving Picture World* noted, "Establishment of a moving picture studio zone in Hollywood may be recommended by the City Council. The residents of East Hollywood and of the Sunset Boulevard and Western avenue districts have petitioned the council to forbid the moving picture people from operating in the residential districts to the deterioration of property values, and the peace and attractiveness of the district."[48] The next week, the same journal explained that the residents of Hollywood found that "motion picture studios are more or less of a nuisance and should be restricted in a zone by themselves."[49]

In other words, some locals were fed up with studios located in their neighbor-hoods and movies being made on city streets.

This first "studio zone" proposed in Los Angeles was envisioned as a film-making sector specifically relocated away from the Hollywood district and moved off the city streets. The Association of Hollywood Property Owners suc-cessfully lobbied the Los Angeles City Council to consider an ordinance creating a Moving Picture Zone outside the city limits. A March 1917 article in *Motion Picture News* explained, "It is the claim of the property owners that studios have caused a depreciation of the values of real estate adjoining the film companies' plants."[50] For a couple of months, it was unclear if the city would pass or enforce the ordinance. A May article in *Motion Picture Magazine* explained that "the Los Angeles film colony is all agog because the City Council has passed an ordinance creating a Moving Picture Zone," listing eight studios that might be forced to move.[51] But the ordinance was not universally supported, and the *Los Angeles Times* reported on a citizens' protest against the ordinance as early as February.[52] The ordinance was evidently not passed or never enforced, for the Hollywood studios did not move, and the issue disappears from the press after spring 1917.

This brief episode—and the failure of property owners to forcefully relo-cate the film studios outside the city limits—would have probably contributed to a sense of permanence for the fledgling film industry. By the mid-1920s, the whole debate seems to have been forgotten, and the concept of a "studio zone" had become a term of pride rather than opprobrium.[53] Indeed, most business leaders and residents in the 1910s and 1920s welcomed the movie industry, and many moved there expressly to work in it. While the changing perception of Los Angeles as a center rather than a periphery was certainly gradual (and indeed it continues to this day), this 1917 studio zone episode can serve to mark a turning point for the idea of Los Angeles as a home for the film industry.

SILENT-ERA STUDIO LOCATION DEPARTMENTS AND PRACTICES

The standard idea of "location shooting" began to emerge as an industrial con-cept in the mid-1910s, and by the 1920s, location shooting had been thoroughly absorbed into studio production practices. In a 1918 filmmaking manual entitled *How Motion Pictures Are Made*, Homer Croy described the newly emergent job of the "location man" and his professional tasks:

> If an exterior is chosen . . . it has been selected in advance by the "location man" and the director. To the former falls the duty of familiarizing himself with all spots in his territory that may have the least photographic appeal. This he accomplishes by riding around, often on a motorcycle, with a camera slung over his shoulder, making photographs of possible locations. Picturesque spots

form only a small part of the locations he must bring back; he has to have on his finger-tips ravines, brick-yards, gnarled trees, railroad stations and crossings, oil-wells, palm-trees, alkalai, and dead men's curves. The photographs are filed away alphabetically, so that when the director is ready to cast his exteriors he has but to turn through the photographs instead of having to go out himself and spend hours looking up suitable locations.[54]

Studio location departments began to form in the early 1920s as a key component of the regularized, compartmentalized work flow of the studio system. Fred Harris was appointed location director at Famous Players–Lasky in January 1921, and Lou Strohm began working as location manager for Metro Pictures in June of that same year.[55] Strohm published an article describing the job of location manager in 1922. He explained, "In bygone days the director was wont to ride about in a fast automobile seeking his own locations. This necessitated the spending of much valuable time. Today, whenever the location man is on tour, and he comes across a spot that appears to hold valuable possibilities for future location for a given purpose, it is immediately photographed. . . . Modern methods of motion picture producing demand that locations all be kept in elaborate index files."[56] As these accounts attest, suitable locations were photographed, organized by category, and placed into file cabinets. What these descriptions do not tell us is how a location was determined to be potentially valuable for location shooting and how these photographs were organized.[57] We can infer that the location man chose sites on the basis of pictorial elements as well as budgetary concerns. Availability and permissions would also have been taken into account, although the legal barriers to shooting on location were unstandardized at this time. The professionalization of the "location man," like the professionalization of many other studio jobs in the 1920s, is an effect of the studio system's industrial mode of production, which operated on then-new principles of efficient business management.

Although we lack location managers' cataloging metadata today, it is clear that by the early 1920s, they were attempting to systematically gather photos and information for every imaginable type of location. A 1927 article on "the unsung location man" explained that a location manager "must think of—and have plenty of pictures of—probably half a dozen different locations, for different directors, at the same time. He must have sufficient knowledge of the country to be able to tell one director where he can find a Japanese fishing village, another a Zulu village from the heart of Africa, another a typical Long Island estate, and whatnot for the rest of them."[58] These kinds of grab-bag lists emphasizing the variety of locations used in film are common in promotional accounts of moviemaking in the 1920s (and beyond). What these lists of exotic locations mask, however, is the way the studio standardized and organized its potential locations into generic categories in order to make efficient use of them in its work flow.

Figure 1.2. "How They Pick Those Beautiful Locations," *Picture-Play*, September 1925, 97.

A 1925 promotional photo in *Picture-Play* magazine shows how location managers such as Fred Harris were essentially cataloging locations by type and place (see figure 1.2). The photo, captioned "How They Pick Those Beautiful Locations," shows Harris standing before dozens of location photos pinned up on a wall. As the photo implies, the location manager's job was not just to organize and systematize the world's geographies but also to maintain a running inventory of architecture, cityscapes, small towns, parks, and other potentially cinematic views. These locations could be used as primary shooting locations or filmed as B-roll for later use as stock footage. In this way, the location manager resembles not only a cataloging librarian but also the actuality filmmakers of early cinema, who also attempted to film and categorize locations around the world. By 1927, there were enough location managers in place to establish a Motion Picture Location Managers' Association. Although not a guild, the small group (which had just over a dozen members) met monthly to discuss matters of business. The Location Managers' Association officers were R. C. Moore of the DeMille Studios (president), Jack Lawton of Universal Studios (vice president), and Fred Harris of the Lasky Studios (secretary-treasurer).[59] According to one article, this organization "was formed primarily to establish a better contact between the property owner, the public official and the motion picture studio."[60]

The general operating principle of location shooting in the studio era was to ensure a smooth, efficient, and cost-effective shoot by controlling the location and reproducing studio conditions as much as possible. Indeed, Jacobson's notion of the Hollywood back lot as "the studio beyond the studio" can be extended to all location work undertaken by film studios during the studio era.[61] As Croy explained in his 1918 filmmaking manual, "For the photographing of so simple a scene as an exterior often half a dozen men are needed" (see figure 1.3).[62] The photo accompanying this caption reveals the elaborate apparatus necessary to shoot Douglas Fairbanks on location, including a camera crew on a raised platform with a light-reflecting white canvas. It is important to understand that location shooting—particularly in wilderness locations—frequently required that substantial alterations be made to the site. Location work often involved the building of sets on location, as well as the trimming back and/or enhancement

Figure 1.3. "For the photographing of so simple a scene as an exterior often half a dozen men are needed. Douglas Fairbanks is shown on horseback." Homer Croy, *How Motion Pictures Are Made* (New York: Harper, 1918), 135.

of plants on the site. "Carpenters and scene makers build sets out in the open location and bring to the place the appearance of the native soil or surroundings that are to be depicted," one 1922 filmmaking manual explained.[63] It was not enough just to *go* to a location; paradoxically, a location typically needed artificial enhancement to make it look like itself.

Significant studio resources were devoted to transporting equipment, props, costumes, crew, actors, food, and drink to off-studio locations. Already in the 1910s, transportation was becoming an essential component of the studio location shoot. In 1917, the Ince Culver City studio announced the addition of "two large carry-all automobiles" to its equipment for the express purpose of transporting cast and crew to exterior locations.[64] As productions grew in size and scope, studios formed transportation departments to organize this component of production labor. For example, in 1935, Ward Rawlings, the head of transportation at Columbia Pictures, estimated that his studio vehicles covered an average of 250,000 miles annually in the transportation of materials to off-studio locations within driving range across town or within Southern California.[65] Throughout the silent era and beyond, however, trains were still used as the primary means of transporting cast, crew, and equipment to more distant locations. When Raoul Walsh shot his location extravaganza *The Big Trail* in seven different western states in 1930, his giant cast, crew, and equipment apparatus traveled by train.

Depending on the picture and the place, location shooting could be cost-effective, or it might add a sizeable percentage to a film's budget. Indeed, it is difficult for the historian to generalize about location shooting costs in the early studio era because itemized budgets rarely survive for many of these films. Some people claimed that location shooting was a cost-saving measure, as in a 1927 article boasting that a location shoot "often means the saving of thousands of dollars which would otherwise have to be spent for sets. In this, a good location man can often save his company many times his salary every month."[66] On the other hand, location shooting was clearly an expensive practice. A 1935 *Los Angeles Times* article marveled at the huge fees for location shooting (from $750 to $1,500 per day) that were regularly paid out by the studios to local businesses and residents in towns all over California to cover costs such as lodging, food, lumber, and local transportation. The article's subtitle proudly trumpeted the boon to local economies, proclaiming, "Sonora, Bear Valley, Kernville, Jacumba Benefit from Recent Films; $1,000,000 to Be Spent Outdoors Next Year."[67] There was no guarantee that each location shoot would bring a return on this kind of investment, but by this time, it was an accepted practice. Within the highly capitalized, mature studio system, each film was simply one component of a larger annual slate of titles. Location shooting for particular subjects was considered necessary to create "authenticity," and these expenses could be absorbed by the studio as a whole. The fact that the practice was so common indicates that the studios considered it worth the expense.

CALIFORNIA AS THE WORLD

By the 1920s, location shooting in Los Angeles, on the movie ranches, and across Southern California was a regular component of studio filmmaking. The substitute location—in which California settings were rendered in such a way that they could stand for locations around the world—became a regularized part of the industry. More distant location work was reserved for films with bigger budgets and stars. Many of the most famous films of the 1920s rely heavily on location shooting, including *The Covered Wagon* (James Cruze, 1923), *The Iron Horse* (John Ford, 1924), *The Gold Rush* (Charlie Chaplin, 1925), *The General* (Clyde Bruckman and Buster Keaton, 1926), and *The Wind* (Victor Sjöström, 1928). Many of the most famous silent-era documentaries also depended on foreign location work, including *Nanook of the North* (Robert Flaherty, 1922), *Grass* (Merian C. Cooper and Ernest B. Schoedsack, 1925), *Chang* (Cooper and Schoedsack, 1927), and *Tabu* (F. W. Murnau, 1931). Many less famous films were also shot on location in this period, of course, and scenic films continued to be made, including a series called "Rothacker Outdoor Pictures" that included titles such as *Bad Men and Good Scenery* (1918).[68] While a complete filmography of silent-era films shot on location lies beyond the scope of this chapter, an informal survey of titles demonstrates that most of the films shot on location in this period used the western United States, and specifically California, as a substitute location. As one filmmaking manual put it, "There are, in California, locations that because of their particular topography, are admirably adapted to the filming of scenes depicting far-distant places and lands. . . . Do you imagine a company would care to send its players to that distant location [Banff, Canada] when a similar one might be found in the closely lying Sierra Nevada mountains?"[69]

Indeed, more than one map circulated in which California was overlaid with names of other places it could represent. For example, a 1920s Paramount studio location map shows that the Mojave Desert could be used to represent the Sahara Desert, the Sacramento River could be used for the Mississippi River, and the canals of Venice on the west side of Los Angeles could be used to depict Venice, Italy (see figure 1.4).[70] More surprisingly, the map suggests that the Central Valley could be used for the Swiss Alps and that Sacramento could stand in for New England. These suggestions feel almost like boasts from the California Chamber of Commerce; but they were certainly not jests, for these kinds of place combinations were used with regularity by the resourceful studio location managers. The goal was to keep costs low while still aiming for authenticity of place, and the practice of the substitute location fit the bill on both counts. Location "doubles" were a cause for praise and wonder; it was not a problem to reveal this technique but instead just another instance of movie magic at work.[71] In sum, studio practices institutionalized the substitute location in the 1920s.

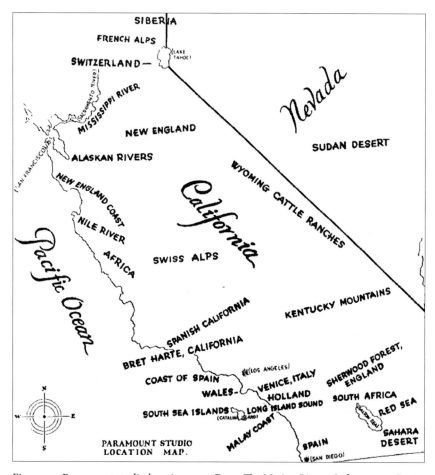

Figure 1.4. Paramount studio location map. From *The Motion Picture Industry as a Basis for Bond Financing* (Halsey, Stuart, 1927), 10; reproduced in Tino Balio, ed., *The American Film Industry* (Madison: University of Wisconsin Press, 1976), 202.

While location shooting was mostly confined to domestic geographies in the early studio era, as the industry grew, so did its foreign location shooting ambitions. *Ben-Hur* was not the only production shot on location in Europe in the 1920s, but it is perhaps the most famous. The film's disastrous production history and ultimate box-office triumph can dramatize some of the difficulties and contradictions of foreign location shooting in the silent era. *Ben-Hur* was initiated in 1922 but not completed until 1925. Its location shoot in Italy stalled out repeatedly due to studio mismanagement and Italian labor disputes and eventually stretched out over two years, resulting in endless expenditures and poor-quality footage, much of which had to be reshot after the production returned to Hollywood. During the shoot in Italy, the Goldwyn company, which had originated the project, was purchased by Metro Pictures Corporation, and after one more merger, the newly formed Metro-Goldwyn-Mayer (MGM) company took over the production in 1924. MGM replaced much of *Ben-Hur*'s cast and crew and sent over Fred Niblo as the new director and Ramon Novarro as the new star, but little of the footage shot on location in Italy was used in the final cut of the film.

Ben-Hur has been much written about, and accounts differ on why the decision was made to shoot it on location in Italy. Kevin Brownlow's classic account in *The Parade's Gone By* attributes the decision to June Mathis, the film's initial screenwriter and one of the most powerful figures in Hollywood in 1922 when the project was initiated.[72] However, as a recent article by Thomas J. Slater argues, "Mathis became a scapegoat for her failed production of *Ben-Hur*."[73] While in Italy, Mathis was sidelined (she was not even allowed on the set), and she was fired from the production when MGM took over. Moreover, archival records indicate that the Goldwyn company originally thought it would be cheaper to film on location in Europe than at home in the studio. The producer J. J. Cohn discussed in an oral history many years later what happened after his initial location scouting trip in Europe: "I came back, and I said, 'There are only two ways,' and I was inexperienced, I was a kid almost, then, and I said, 'Make the picture one of two ways. Let it be made in a hurry, in Vienna, or some such place for 300 thousand, 400 thousand, or spend a million two [$1.2 million] here [in California]."[74] A page in the MGM *Ben-Hur* archival materials itemizes numerous early production developments in June 1922, including these two items listed one after the other:

> Made budget at studio for American production—$1,500,000, conservatively $1,300,000.
> Numerous wires regarding producing abroad and possibility of picture being made in Italy for $500,000.[75]

Whatever the reason for going on location (and there seem to have been multiple factors), the Italian shoot quickly spiraled out of control and became an unmitigated disaster. Even after Mathis was fired and Niblo was put in charge, the shoot continued to suffer from technical problems and an ongoing Italian labor dispute, which resulted in months of shooting delays, which were logged into the daily production records. A cable from Niblo to Louis B. Mayer soon after his arrival in late June captures some of the desperation on the shoot: "Condition serious must rush work before November rain; no sets or lights available before August 1st. 200 reels film wasted; bad photography terrible action; send Seitz Gaudio or Edeson quick; also best miniature and trick effect cameraman available."[76] Between August 13 and December 9, 1924, almost every entry in the daily production records contains some "reason for delay" logged into the account, ranging from "fascisti trouble" to "set not satisfactory" to "big delay on account of power off owing to outbreak of fire" to "generators not working," along with many public holidays listed.[77] In short, the American studio personnel could not gain control over the Italian labor force, and the studio did not want to give up on the money it had already invested in the production. The cast and crew were not recalled to Los Angeles until January 1925. In the end, only a few scenes from the two-year Italian shoot that ended up in the final film convey an authentic sense of place—the sea battle in particular, although the difficulties encountered during the shooting of that sequence necessitated the use of miniature models. The film's most famous sequence, the chariot race, was shot on a specially built outdoor set near the MGM studio lot in Culver City in spring 1925.

Ben-Hur became a huge hit and ended up grossing millions of dollars worldwide. But millions had been spent on the film's runaway location shoot in Italy, and the most noteworthy scene had been shot on a Hollywood set. While location shooting was a necessary tool for the silent era's style of realism, in the end, it seems that authenticity of place often functioned as just another spectacle, easily rivaled by other cinematic tricks such as action sequences and special effects. Ben-Hur's crowning, excessive, and even ironic example of cinematic location seems an appropriate place to end this account of location shooting in the silent era. As Ben-Hur demonstrates, within the studio system, realistic spectacle often proved easier to achieve on the back lot than in the authentic location. When distant location shoots were undertaken for specialty features, the effort and difficulty involved became a part of the film's publicity, marketing strategy, and legend.

By the mid-1920s, Hollywood had regularized methods of production in which believable locations could be most efficiently recreated locally or just a little farther afield. In subsequent decades, new technologies for representing locations were developed and new styles of realism emerged, but the basic idea of using artifice to enhance nature and render "realistic" locations remained the bedrock of the Hollywood mode of production throughout the studio era. Although audiences have understood all along that filmmakers use technology to produce "equipment-free" images of cinematic location, audiences also quickly became familiar with repressing that knowledge. Indeed, of all the location shooting practices established in the silent era, one of the most important may have been an audience practice: the pleasure of playing along with artifice in the service of realism.

NOTES

For their help obtaining research materials and tracking down countless tips for this chapter, I would like to thank Ned Comstock at the USC Cinematic Arts Library and the staff of the Academy of Motion Picture Arts and Sciences' Margaret Herrick Library. *Epigraphs*: David S. Hulfish, *Cyclopedia of Motion-Picture Work: A General Reference Work* (Chicago: American Technical Society, 1911), 7; Cecil B. DeMille, "First Experiences before the Camera," *New York Dramatic Mirror*, January 14, 1914, quoted in Simon Louvish, *Cecil B. DeMille: A Life in Art* (New York: St. Martin's, 2007), 66–67.

1. Scott Eyman, *Empire of Dreams: The Epic Life of Cecil B. DeMille* (New York: Simon and Schuster, 2010), 69. Robert S. Birchard writes, "Stories in the trade paper *Moving Picture World* told of the Lasky company's travels to Utah, Arizona, and Wyoming in search of authentic scenery, but DeMille and company never left Southern California." Birchard, *Cecil B. DeMille's Hollywood* (Lexington: University Press of Kentucky, 2004), 8.

2. For a useful account of place substitution in a very different context (the 2007 film *The Kite Runner*), see Mark B. Sandberg, "Location, 'Location': On the Plausibility of Place Substitution," in *Silent Cinema and the Politics of Space*, ed. Jennifer M. Bean, Anupama Kapse, and Laura Horak (Bloomington: Indiana University Press, 2014), 23–46.

3. Walter Benjamin, "The Work of Art in the Age of Its Technological Reproducibility," trans. Edmund Jephcott and Harry Zohn, in *"The Work of Art in the Age of Its Technological Reproducibility" and Other Writings on Media* (Cambridge, MA: Harvard University Press, 2008), 35.

4. Brian R. Jacobson, *Studios before the System: Architecture, Technology, and the Emergence of Cinematic Space* (New York: Columbia University Press, 2015), 99.

5. Jacobson has traced the development of early glass-walled film studios, which began in France with Georges Méliès's glass-and-iron studio in 1897. In the United Kingdom, R. W. Paul built a glass studio in 1898, followed by G. A. Smith in 1899 and Cecil Hepworth in 1900. Edwin S. Porter built the first American glass-and-iron studio in 1901, and Ferdinand Zecca built a glass studio for Pathé in France in 1902. Jacobson, *Studios before the System*, 68.

6. Hulfish, *Cyclopedia of Motion-Picture Work*, 35.

7. This film, like all Edison's early output, was deposited as a paper print for copyright purposes at the Library of Congress, which is why we have the remarkable ability to view it today at www.loc.gov/item/00694124.

8. *Buffalo Courier*, June 7, 1896, 10, quoted in Charles Musser, *Edison Motion Pictures, 1890–1900: An Annotated Filmography* (Washington, DC: Smithsonian Institution Press, 1997), 203.

9. American Mutoscope & Biograph Company, *Picture Catalogue* (New York: AM&B, 1902).

10. Thomas Bedding, "Photographing Outdoor Subjects," *Moving Picture World*, May 22, 1909, 666.

11. AM&B, *Picture Catalogue*, 189.

12. *Waterfall in the Catskills* is available for viewing on the Library of Congress website at www.loc.gov/item/00694329/.

13. See Jennifer Lynn Peterson, *Education in the School of Dreams: Travelogues and Early Nonfiction Film* (Durham, NC: Duke University Press, 2013).

14. *How It Feels to Be Run Over* can be readily found on YouTube, for example at www.youtube.com/watch?v=m6F1VAPzvkU.

15. H. Kent Webster, "Little Stories of Great Films," *Nickelodeon*, August 15, 1910, 96.

16. Thomas Bedding, "The Modern Way in Moving Picture Making," *Moving Picture World*, March 27, 1909, 360.

17. *Execution of Czolgosz with Panorama of Auburn Prison* is available for viewing on the Library of Congress website at www.loc.gov/item/00694362/.

18. Charles Musser, *The Emergence of Cinema: The American Screen to 1907* (Berkeley: University of California Press, 1990), 320.

19. *European Rest Cure* is available for viewing on the Library of Congress website at www.loc.gov/item/00694197/.

20. *The Great Train Robbery*, Edison promotional pamphlet no. 201, 1903.

21. Scott Simmon, *The Invention of the Western Film: A Cultural History of the Genre's First Half-Century* (Cambridge: Cambridge University Press, 2003), 15.

22. Tom Gunning, *D. W. Griffith and the Origins of American Narrative Film: The Early Years at Biograph* (Urbana: University of Illinois Press, 1991), 70.

23. *The Country Doctor* can be readily found on YouTube, for example at www.youtube.com/watch?v=ks2e22FeNhg.

24. Gunning, *D. W. Griffith*, 215.

25. Harry C. Carr, "Looking Backward with Ben," *Photoplay*, December 1918, 61.

26. For the definitive account of Essanay, see David Kiehn, *Broncho Billy and the Essanay Film Company* (Berkeley, CA: Farwell Books, 2003).

27. Kiehn, *Broncho Billy*, 302–6. A print of *The Mexican's Faith* is held at the National Film and Television Archive in London, and a print of *Aviation at Los Angeles, California* is held at the George Eastman House.

28. Eileen Bowser, *The Transformation of Cinema: 1907–1915* (Berkeley: University of California Press, 1990), 149.

29. Ad for *The Lad from Old Ireland* in *Film Index,* November 12, 1910, 34.

30. Today, *A Lad from Old Ireland* is sometimes said to be the first American film shot on location in a foreign country. However, this claim, like many "firsts," is off base, not only because of the many scenic films shot on location around the world since the 1890s but because even in the realm of fiction film production, this claim is untrue. Among the many scenic films shot on location since the 1890s, we might separate out a subcategory of films showing tourists, such as *Tourists Starting for Canton* (Edison, 1898), made when traveling American camera operators filmed English tourists abroad. See the entry for this title in Musser, *Edison Motion Pictures*.

31. Ad for *Between Love and Honor* in *Film Index*, July 19, 1910, 32.

32. IMP advertisement, *Moving Picture World*, January 21, 1911, 168; "Of Interest to the Trade," *Nickelodeon*, February 4, 1911, 140.

33. "The 'IMP' Company Invades Cuba," *Moving Picture World*, January 21, 1911, 146.

34. Other scenic and educational releases by Kalem shot on this same trip include *Egyptian Sports, Ancient Temples of Egypt, from Jerusalem to the Dead Sea, The Ancient Port of Jaffa*, and *Along the River Nile*. For a filmography of travelogues released in the United States between 1910 and 1914, see Jennifer Peterson, "World Pictures: Travelogue Films and the Lure of the Exotic, 1890–1920" (PhD diss., University of Chicago, 1999), appendix A, table 1.

35. Photo of Kalem's portable "Airdome" studio in Jerusalem in *Moving Picture World*, July 6, 1912. Also see Jacobson, *Studios before the System*, 175–76, for a brief description and another photo of Kalem's "Airdome" studio. The term "airdome" was also used to describe open-air theaters in this period. One writer in *Motography* explained, "An airdome is simply an outdoor moving picture show that is run on practically the same lines as the old summer garden, and is therefore essentially a fair-weather show." John B. Rathbun, "Motion Picture Making and Exhibiting," *Motography*, July 26, 1913, 70. See also Hulfish, *Cyclopedia of Motion-Picture Work*, 31.

36. John J. McGowan, "The 'O'Kalems' and the 'El Kalems,'" in *J. P. McGowan: Biography of a Hollywood Pioneer* (Jefferson, NC: McFarland, 2005), 33–56.

37. "In the Motion Picture Swim," *Los Angeles Times*, February 1, 1910, 14.

38. "Jesse L. Lasky Returns from Coast," *Moving Picture World*, December 12, 1914, 1501.

39. Photo of "Lasky and De Mille Prospecting for Locations," in *Moving Picture World*, December 12, 1914, 1501. This photo is reproduced in Jacobson, *Studios before the System*, 186.

40. The 1914 version of *Cameo Kirby* appears to be lost; John Ford directed a 1923 version, which does not make much use of landscape or location.

41. Further research is needed on Lasky's lease of this particular movie ranch, for it may have been temporary or it may have been merely apocryphal. Lasky eventually came to own two other, more famous movie ranches in the San Fernando Valley and the Santa Monica Mountains, neither of which contains a six-thousand-foot mountain.

42. Lou Strohm, "The Location Man: What You Must Know to Become One," in *Opportunities in the Motion Picture Industry* (Los Angeles: Photoplay Research Society, 1922), 86.

43. See for example John Bengston, *Silent Echoes: Discovering Early Hollywood through the Films of Buster Keaton* (Santa Monica, CA: Santa Monica Press, 2000); and Bengston, *Silent Traces: Discovering Early Hollywood through the Films of Charlie Chaplin* (Santa Monica, CA: Santa Monica Press, 2006).

44. Mark Shiel, *Hollywood Cinema and the Real Los Angeles* (London: Reaktion Books, 2012), 85.

45. See for example this online article, which uses one archival source but interprets it incorrectly: Zelda Roland, "Studio Labor and the Origins of Hollywood's Thirty-Mile Zone, or TMZ," KCET website, March 10, 2016, www.kcet.org/shows/lost-la/studio-labor-and-the-origins-of-hollywoods-thirty-mile-zone-or-tmz.

46. "The rules establish a normal working day of eight hours. . . . Other rules . . . define the Los Angeles studio zone as all territory within a radius of six miles from the intersection of 5th and Rossmore Sts., Los Angeles." "Discover NRA Rules on Extras Already Approved," *Motion Picture Daily*, October 4, 1934, 6.

47. California Film Commission, "Locations: Studio Zones, Permit Offices & Fees," accessed July 25, 2018, http://film.ca.gov/locations/studio-zones/.

48. "Los Angeles Film Brevities," *Moving Picture World*, March 3, 1917, 1365 (noncapitalization of "avenue" in the original).

49. "Biggest Industry of Southern California," *Moving Picture World*, March 10, 1917, 1608.

50. "West Coast Studios," *Motion Picture News*, March 31, 1917, 2004.

51. "Little Whisperings from Everywhere in Playerdom," *Motion Picture Magazine*, May 1917, 124.

52. "Citizens Protest. Oppose 'Movie' Zone," *Los Angeles Times*, February 15, 1917, 6.

53. For example, in a *Photoplay* story from 1927, Carl Laemmle is shown with some chickens at his "model chicken ranch at Universal City, in the heart of the studio zone." The story is meant to present a humorous contrast, thus demonstrating that barnyard animals have no place in the glamorous world now conjured up by the term "studio zone." Terry Ramsaye, "Little Journeys to the Homes of Famous Film Magnates," *Photoplay*, June 1927, 33.

54. Homer Croy, *How Motion Pictures Are Made* (New York: Harper, 1918), 120–21.

55. "Lasky Studio Has New Location Director," *Motion Picture News*, January 15, 1921, 716; Fred Schader, "Coast Film Notes," *Variety*, June 24, 1921, 35.

56. Strohm, "Location Man," 86.

57. Surviving location photos from the Fox Film Corporation Picture Background Stills Collection at UCLA (from the post–World War II era) have been organized by the studio into general categories such as "Cabins—Mountains," "Desert Mountains and Trees," "Residential backyards" and "Skyline Roof Tops." Some specific locations are also listed, such as "African Homes" and "Ottawa—snow"; but the categories are not systematic, and the collection is probably not representative of all the materials at the location manager's disposal. Moreover, these Fox location photos are from the 1950s (although I was able to positively identify at least one location still from a 1945 production). Nonetheless, it seems likely that similar categorizations were in use well before that time. Collection of Motion Picture Background Stills, 1950–1960, Collection 1188, Fox Film Corporation, UCLA Special Collections, UCLA Library, Los Angeles, CA.

58. H. M. Ayres, "The Unsung Location Man," *Hollywood Vagabond*, September 22, 1927, 8.

59. In addition to Moore, Lawton, and Harris, ten other members are named in this article. Ayres, "Unsung Location Man," 9. A listing in the 1928 *Film Daily Yearbook* lists four officers, twelve members, and two honorary members. *Film Daily Yearbook, 1928* (New York: John Alicoate, 1928), 524.

60. Ayres, "Unsung Location Man," 8. According to this article, the Location Managers' Association also fostered "a spirit of camaraderie" that resulted in the sharing of locations between managers at different studios, established a system for charitable payments to help persuade owners of "finer locations" to allow the use of their properties, and held frequent banquets for public officials to straighten out misunderstandings and pave the way for future location shoots (8–9).

61. Jacobson, *Studios before the System*, chap. 5, "Studios beyond the Studio," 168–200.

62. Croy, *How Motion Pictures Are Made*, 135.

63. Strohm, "Location Man," 86.

64. J. C. Jessen, "In and Out of West Coast Studios," *Motion Picture News*, March 10, 1917, 1539.

65. Fanya Grahame, "Efficiency of Columbia's Transportation Department Is Tested by Many Simultaneous Locations," *Motion Picture Studio Insider* 1, no. 1 (1935): 47.

66. Ayres, "Unsung Location Man," 8.

67. Philip K. Scheuer, "California Towns Get Rich as Hollywood 'Locations,'" *Los Angeles Times*, October 13, 1935, A1.

68. Numerous trade-press stories describe this series. See for example "Rothacker 'Outdoors' by Exhibitors' Mutual," *Motion Picture News*, December 14, 1918, 3555.

69. Strohm, "Location Man," 86–87.

70. Another of these California-as-the-world maps was published in the *Los Angeles Times* in 1934. See "Around the World in California," *Los Angeles Times*, March 4, 1934.

71. "'Doubles' Found for Locations in Many Places," *Los Angeles Times*, January 26, 1930.

72. Kevin Brownlow, "The Heroic Fiasco—*Ben-Hur*," in *The Parade's Gone By* (Berkeley: University of California Press, 1968), 389.

73. Thomas J. Slater, "June Mathis's *Ben-Hur*: A Tale of Corporate Change and the Decline of Women's Influence in Hollywood," in *Bigger than "Ben-Hur": The Book, Its Adaptations, and Their Audiences*, ed. Barbara Ryan and Milette Shamir (Syracuse, NY: Syracuse University Press, 2016), 119.

74. Rudy Behlmer, "Oral History with J. J. (Joe) Cohn" (1987), unpublished manuscript, 51–52, *Ben-Hur* Production Information, MGM Collection, University of Southern California Special Collections, USC Libraries, Los Angeles, CA (hereafter MGM Collection).

75. Studio record itemizing early production developments in June 1922, n.p., MGM Collection.

76. Fred Niblo to Louis B. Mayer, cable, July 4, 1924, MGM Collection.

77. Days in Production, August 13–December 9, 1924, n.p., MGM Collection.

CHAPTER 2

THE CLASSICAL HOLLYWOOD STUDIO SYSTEM, 1928–1945

Sheri Chinen Biesen

The industrial, technological, and aesthetic transformation of the Hollywood studio system between 1928 and 1945 ushered in an array of contradictions that affected filming on location. The coming of sound and later World War II presented new production considerations and logistical challenges that mitigated against filming on location in lieu of a more easily controlled filmmaking environment on a studio "soundstage" or back lot, which was frequently less costly. Nonetheless, a number of ambitious and innovative films such as *The Big Trail* (Raoul Walsh, 1930), *Trader Horn* (W. S. Van Dyke, 1931), and *Mutiny on the Bounty* (Frank Lloyd, 1935) were shot primarily outside the studio, paving the way for the expansion of location shooting during and after World War II. Drawing on these case studies, alongside films such as *The Adventures of Robin Hood* (Michael Curtiz / William Keighley, 1938), *Northwest Passage* (King Vidor, 1940), *Shadow of a Doubt* (Alfred Hitchcock, 1943), *Sahara* (Zoltan Korda, 1943), *Air Force* (Howard Hawks, 1943), and *Memphis Belle* (William Wyler, 1944), this chapter investigates how Hollywood employed location filming in the studio era. Primarily because of the coming of sound, comparatively constrained shooting practices evolved in distinct contrast to the silent period, in which location filming flourished. Yet, as these case studies show, Hollywood filmmakers worked to overcome the logistical challenges of location work and the constraints of synchronized sound in the early to mid-1930s. Later, World War II offered both constraints and opportunities for location filming. Though wartime rationing and regulation curtailed filming practices, the conflict also catalyzed technological innovation and helped establish a production and reception climate that enabled location shooting to become firmly embedded in Hollywood filmmaking practice.

STUDIO SYSTEM SHOOTING ON LOCATION:
CHALLENGES AND CONSTRAINTS

Location shooting was potentially disruptive both to the efficient operation of the studio system and to the classical mode of storytelling. Yet a number of high-budget pictures in the early 1930s attempted to integrate location shooting into the studio mode of production. Why was location shooting valuable and worth this risk on big pictures? Was it more feasible as a smaller percentage of a bigger production than an overwhelming expense on smaller pictures? By the 1940s, a fascinating shift had taken place: the advent of new filming strategies changed location filming from being a cost multiplier to a potential cost saver. However, some executives thought it was worth the risk, while others did not.

With the transition to synchronized sound technologies in the late 1920s to early 1930s and restrictions during World War II in the early to mid-1940s, the ensuing material, industrial, technological, and aesthetic constraints on film-makers led to more enclosed, soundstage-bound production methods, which offered greater convenience and efficiency, saving time and money compared to filming outside the studio. An array of factors affected studio system film-ing during this time. Early "coming of sound" conditions added new challenges that inhibited location shooting. These included bulky cameras; the logistical constraints and expense of adapting to filming with new technology (such as microphones); and huge, cumbersome soundproofing "blimp" enclosures that covered cameras to reduce noise (especially wind, rain/stormy weather, and traffic out on location) while filming for sound. Further, the financial impact of the Great Depression had placed economic constraints on studios, filmmakers, and theater chains and curtailed extravagance. Such factors largely constrained film production to soundstages in the early sound era. Sound technology was thus a key limiting factor in filming and especially mitigated against shooting in an uncontrolled environment on location without the benefit of soundproof production and audio recording.

These production conditions fostered a greater reliance on soundstages by filmmakers and studio executives who recognized their importance and economic value as the primary mode of film production. When locations were used for filming during this period, studios and filmmakers would turn to smaller remote crews or "second units" for additional shooting to supplement principal photography. Second units were primarily used to film backgrounds more efficiently and capture atmospheric images for remote cinematic locales, which would frequently be combined with studio close-ups placed in the foreground through "rear projection" or process shots. They also replaced the need to send the full cast and crew to distant locations for principal photography. Filmmakers would typically shoot exteriors with second unit crews on location while saving close-ups and interiors to be filmed on studio soundstages, which were a less expensive and more controlled production environment. This enabled better lighting, sound recording, and image quality. Moreover, when film crews did go out on location, they frequently encountered logistical challenges and grueling, disastrous experiences, including lost or damaged equipment, technological problems resulting in poor sound recording or unusable footage, bad weather delays that disrupted production and prevented filming, communication disruptions, sickness, injury, and in some cases death. Nonetheless, there were numerous remarkable films shot on location in the studio era, with full production units and casts shooting in the vicinity of Los Angeles, across the United States, and even overseas. As filming conventions evolved during the Great Depression and World War II, these films began to spur changes in production techniques that were only fully realized in the postwar period.

Original production correspondence provides insights into the practice of Hollywood location filmmaking during this period. Studio moguls made no bones about weighing in to convey their preference to avoid the challenges and huge expense of location shooting. By September 1938, 20th Century-Fox vice president of production Darryl Zanuck expressed concern about location shooting on the western *Jesse James* (1939). In a memo to the film's director, Henry King, who was filming in Missouri, Zanuck wrote, "After reviewing everything that has been shot to date, I am definitely convinced that the entire location trip was, to a great extent, a financial mistake." Film crews were "molested and hampered by crowds and other difficulties" that placed the picture "six days behind schedule with no prospects of improvement." Zanuck continued, "I always opposed the entire idea of extended location trips. . . . There is nothing in the way of scenery or backgrounds that we could not have photographed near here at far less expense and trouble." Expressing his regret that the picture was shot on location rather than on a studio soundstage using rear projection, he emphasized "the waste of time and money shooting closeups . . . which should have been done with process [rear projection] background." Like many Hollywood executives during this period, Zanuck insisted, "We will cancel all further interiors and will concentrate on long shots of . . . essential things that you cannot do in the studio. You will take your second camera crew and have them get process background shots to cover all other episodes that are necessary. . . . We will duplicate and fake everything that we possibly can at the studio." He further instructed, "Bring the main company and main camera crew back to the studio as quickly as possible. . . . Episodes like the long shot of the jump off the cliff should be left for second unit to be done with doubles and to be covered for background [rear projection] plates, as it is ridiculous and completely out of proportion for us to contemplate holding the entire company for sequences which are strictly second unit stuff. At the rate we are going, this picture will never break even, no matter how successful it is, because of the expenditure."[1]

As these lengthy comments suggest, Zanuck concluded that economic necessity outweighed the desire for shooting authentic locations. "The Universal western [back lot] street or our own [studio] street could have served just as well as what I have seen on the screen, and photographed twice as fast," he complained, detailing how the film could have been shot more efficiently in Hollywood than on location: "The railroad station is very interesting and effective, but could have been built anywhere in the Southern Pacific between here [Los Angeles] and San Bernardino. Certainly the farm exteriors were nothing in the way of scenic beauty to justify the transportation and living expenses that we are being penalized with, to say nothing of what you are going through with an effort to try and get a full day's work." Summing up his logic about location shooting, Zanuck concluded, "In the history of our industry there has never been a successful location trip that lasted longer than two weeks."[2] Years later in an August 9, 1952, memo, Zanuck insisted that realistic locations were a secondary concern and maintained, "Nobody buys tickets to see authenticity; they go in to be entertained."[3]

Likewise, MGM executive Joe "J. J." Cohn admitted that he "evaluated" whether it was worth shooting on location during the studio era. "Even in those days, if you went to Sherwood Forest . . . immediately when you left the studio you spent $1,800. In addition, if you had bad weather the day was lost. In the studio, if you had bad weather—and a day's shooting meant $25,000 or $30,000—you could move into a stage." He recalled, "when David Selznick made *Notorious* [Alfred Hitchcock, 1946] . . . he did it so wisely. The setting was Buenos Aires, Argentina. They used doubles, photographed down there, and they took background shots against which they put Cary Grant and Ingrid Bergman. At the New York office everyone thought they had gone to the Argentine." Cohn explained, "when I suggested building a park on the [MGM] lot, they said, 'Build a park—with trees? You're crazy.' Anyway, I spoke to [set designer] Cedric Gibbons and we laid it out. The initial cost, I believe, was $8,000. Well, C. B. DeMille decided he would use the park instead of going to Pasadena for three days. So the park paid for itself immediately."[4]

This kind of logic was also in evidence at Warner Bros., where studio chief Jack Warner complained in 1938 about a park sequence in the film *Four Daughters* (Michael Curtiz, 1938), "[It] could have been shot on our lot here. We have a better looking park and it is all in close shots so why go on location. . . . We spend a fortune building a park in the studio and then everybody wants to go on location. The other fellow's grass seems the greenest."[5] Warner Bros. production executive Hal Wallis instructed film crews in 1939 to shoot the historical drama *The Private Lives of Elizabeth of Essex* (Michael Curtiz, 1939) on soundstages and the back lot so that sets could be recycled for the Errol Flynn swashbuckler *The*

Sea Hawk (Michael Curtiz, 1940) and thus save the studio enormous time and money in cost efficiency. Wallis instructed production managers, "please plan" to film using sets "on stages where they can be saved after this production as we will be able to use practically every set over again for *The Sea Hawk* and this will save a fortune."[6]

However, despite the considerable challenges these accounts identify, several films featured striking examples of shooting on location in a variety of ways.[7] In the early sound era, as the industry made the transition to new technology and filmmakers adapted to cumbersome sound-recording equipment, a number of sound pictures were shot with innovative location footage. For example, *Hell's Angels* (Howard Hughes, 1930) began filming as a silent picture but was later reshot for sound and included stunning aerial footage of flying planes and aerial battles; Universal's *Broadway* (Paul Fejos, 1929) included second unit night shots of New York's Broadway theater district; and MGM's African American musical drama *Hallelujah* (King Vidor, 1929) was filmed on location in Memphis, Tennessee, and Arkansas. Other films such as *Trader Horn* featured impressive, experimental forays into overseas location work.

Synchronized sound, proper amplification, and recording quality were challenging to achieve in early sound films, as action revolved around (nondirectional) microphones and noisy cameras needed soundproofing. Filming for sound was especially difficult when shooting on location. One transitional film, *Trader Horn*, was an extreme example of these early struggles. The production began as a silent film with extensive location shooting but abruptly had to adjust to the spiraling difficulty and expense of sound filming with new (or adapted) equipment.

TRADER HORN

One attraction of location shooting for the Hollywood studios was that it could be used to showcase exotic locales and create onscreen spectacle with travelogue appeal. A fascinating example of early studio system location shooting is MGM's *Trader Horn*. MGM production executive Irving Thalberg acquired screen rights for the 1927 book *Trader Horn* by Alfred Aloysius Horn and Ethelreda Lewis, about nineteenth-century adventures on safari in Africa. *Trader Horn* began shooting in Africa as a silent film, directed by W. S. Van Dyke and shot by the cinematographer Clyde DeVinna (with additional filming by Robert Roberts and George Nogle). The cast, including Harry Carey and Edwina Booth, and crew for *Trader Horn* left Hollywood's MGM Culver City studio in February 1929 and arrived in Africa to start shooting on location in March.[8]

Trader Horn was viewed by MGM and Thalberg as a follow-up to *White Shadows on the South Seas* (W. S. Van Dyke, 1928),[9] a silent picture that had been shot on the South Pacific island of Tahiti (MGM was still producing silent films in

1928). *Trader Horn*'s cast and crew would travel twenty-five thousand miles. After winning an Oscar for the all-talking sound film *The Broadway Melody* (Harry Beaumont, 1929), MGM decided that *Trader Horn* would be shot as a sound picture. Van Dyke and DeVinna had to convert to sound production after location filming was under way overseas in Africa. MGM story files show the transformation of *Trader Horn* from silent 1928 treatments (with intertitles) to sound (with dialogue) in 1930. Once filming of *Trader Horn* began in March 1929, it was an arduous location shoot lasting nine months as cast and crew traversed an expansive range of geography across fourteen thousand miles of African jungle and wild plains. *Trader Horn* was shot with cooperation from the (colonial) governments of Tanganyika, Uganda, Kenya, the Anglo-Egyptian Sudan, and the Belgian Congo. The epic location shoot included the large MGM cast and crew, with hundreds of locals headquartered in Nairobi (where MGM built its own film lab to develop footage) and many remote location sites. DeVinna used radio transmissions to communicate between remote sites while filming.

Trader Horn was Hollywood's first nondocumentary film shot in Africa. From the film's opening, images of Africa—sunsets, treetops, rivers, wildlife, and native tribes—have an ethnographic quality as many shots bear the traces of originally being filmed as a silent picture (with more mobile equipment). *Trader Horn*'s ethnographic documentary style is seen in a series of close-up shots of tribespeople in villages with their traditional garb and earrings against the dense jungle terrain, capturing the location setting of Africa. The crew built their own crane to enable high camera angles and moving camera shots framed through the leaves and trees of the jungle and against the steep cliffs of waterfalls. The images of Africa filmed on location for *Trader Horn* also included an effective sequence of the sound of the roaring waterfall audibly drowning out dialogue, combined with shots of Murchison Falls.

The shoot was difficult and beset with disasters of various kinds. The cast and crew immediately became sick from mosquitoes spreading diseases, and the MGM location company turned to heavy drinking to survive the rigors of the harsh filming conditions. Sound equipment eventually arrived in Africa from the studio. However, a sound truck fell off a boat into the river, which resulted in lost and damaged equipment. Moreover, two new (albeit cumbersome) Mitchell sound cameras sent from the studio to film for sound never arrived. As a result, DeVinna, Van Dyke, and the remote MGM crew had to resort to creating their own makeshift soundproofing for their existing cameras to try to mute camera noise when filming. The shoot was dangerous and deadly. Wildlife scenes were plagued by accidents, flash floods, insects (even an invasion of camp by locusts), sunstroke, and malaria; and the shoot became deadly when crew members were killed in crocodile and rhino attacks (both of which are shown in the film).[10]

Meanwhile, back in the United States, the 1929 stock market crash ushered in the Great Depression, which hurt studios, theaters, and moviegoers. As a result of this drastically altered economic climate, after months of filming *Trader Horn* overseas, Thalberg and MGM brought Van Dyke's cast and crew back to the studio. Thalberg and MGM spent most of 1930 reshooting close-ups and dialogue because the sound quality of the location footage was determined to be inferior and unusable. Thalberg almost scrapped the footage and considered canceling the entire production but instead salvaged the film and rewrote and reshaped the Africa story for sound. MGM sent a second unit to shoot additional footage of animals killing each other in Tecate, Mexico (to avoid animal cruelty laws in the United States). Cast members Mutia Omoolu and Riano Tindama were brought to Hollywood to reshoot sequences for sound and dialogue. *Trader Horn* was the beginning and end of star Edwina Booth's career: she suffered a mysterious illness for six years following the rough conditions of the African location shoot (she eventually sued and settled with MGM). As a result of the overseas shooting (and additional filming), the final cost of *Trader Horn* rose into the millions, though the film was nominated for an Academy Award and enjoyed box-office success when it was released in January 1931.[11] MGM promoted *Trader Horn* as "filmed in the wilds of Africa" and billed the film as "The Greatest Adventure Picture of All Time!"[12] Moreover, *Trader Horn* provided the studio with ample stock location footage for future productions: MGM continued to reuse footage shot for *Trader Horn* in later films. The impact of *Trader Horn* resonated in the sound era as MGM abandoned extensive location shooting after this production in favor of soundstage filming combined with second unit and rear projection sequences.

Ultimately, was sound, or the trouble with these early sound pictures, the defining factor in quashing extensive location shooting? Despite conventional wisdom, primary archival evidence surprisingly reveals that it was not sound. Sound initially precluded location shooting, but Hollywood eventually developed sound trucks that allowed for location shooting. Nevertheless, it drove up costs, and location shooting was a risk overall. In spite of the many challenges of location shooting in the early sound era, an Academy of Motion Picture Arts and Sciences book for industry professionals, *Recording Sound for Motion Pictures*, describes how, by 1931, location shooting was possible with early recording equipment, using a sound truck and a suitcase-sized sound system to overcome the challenges of cumbersome filming equipment. The 1931 Academy publication instructs filmmakers on how to shoot on location, to film in remote areas, and even to record sound on a plane, on a barge, or with underwater camerawork, as seen in the social realist film *I Am a Fugitive from a Chain Gang* (Mervyn LeRoy, 1932).[13] After 1932, technological advancements such as directional microphones, "looping" rerecording in postproduction, and RCA's improved "ultraviolet" recording system aided the filming of sound pictures and made it easier to shoot on location and correct problems in postproduction.[14] Thus, eventually sound got easier, as other studios and gutsy filmmakers were willing to take on the risks of ambitious location shooting, but other challenges, such as filming on location with 70 mm widescreen, were a problem, as seen in *The Big Trail*.

THE BIG TRAIL

While *Trader Horn* illustrated the obstacles that filmmakers faced when shooting overseas in Africa, another early sound-era film, *The Big Trail* (Fox Film Corporation, 1930), a western starring a young John Wayne, revealed the challenges of filming using 70 mm widescreen on location in wilderness across the American West. John Wayne and widescreen location shooting in the West became a staple of cinematic screen fare during the 1950s in films such as *The Searchers* (John Ford, 1956). However, *The Big Trail* was an innovative, underrecognized film that was ahead of its time in 1930, when widescreen processes and location shooting were less frequently used. Unfortunately, it was a huge box-office flop. Nevertheless, *The Big Trail* (originally *The Oregon Trail*) used spectacular location filming on a grand scale to tell its story of early pioneers and their arduous "wagon train" journey traveling from Missouri across the plains, desert, and mountains to settle in Oregon. A remarkable feat of location shooting, *The Big Trail* was filmed with thousands of extras over four months and thousands of miles. The shoot spanned seven states in remote areas of the American West, from Jackson Hole, Wyoming, to Idaho, Montana, Oregon, Utah, the Yuma, Arizona, desert, and Sequoia National Park in California. It was Wayne's first film in a leading role; the former USC football player Marion "Duke" Morrison, renamed John Wayne, was a youthful newcomer recruited from the prop department. Work on *The Big Trail* began in 1929 (some sources cite production beginning in 1929; others note filming the following spring–summer, from April to August 1930), and the film was released in October 1930.[15]

The extraordinary location photography for *The Big Trail* was shot by the silent-era cinematographer Arthur Edeson.[16] The film was backed by the influential early Hollywood studio mogul William Fox of the Fox Film Corporation (prior to its 1935 merger with Twentieth Century Pictures), who wanted to promote his new widescreen 70 mm Grandeur system, a forerunner of the Todd-AO 70 mm widescreen system (introduced in 1955). Walsh and Edeson shot an enormous amount of film (nearly five hundred thousand feet), and a key difficulty was filming on location without the benefit of seeing dailies or rushes of their developed film, since they sent it back to the studio for processing.

Location filming for *The Big Trail* was especially difficult because it was a sound film using new recording equipment and cumbersome 70 mm cameras and was simultaneously shot in multiple formats—70 mm widescreen Fox Grandeur process (twice as wide, double the size of a standard screen image, with hulking, unwieldy equipment) and standard 35 mm—and also shot in multiple languages with different casts. Fox's Grandeur process required new technology, such as larger widescreen/sound-era cameras to film in both 70 mm and 35 mm formats and new special equipment to project in widescreen 70 mm format, which showcased the spectacular landscapes and vistas of the American West.

The Big Trail includes incredible scenes shot across the West, as wagons full of hefty equipment, livestock, and people precariously descend steep cliffs and horses and caravans make their way through dangerous river crossings. Like the crew being killed by wild animals in *Trader Horn*, such rough production conditions are actually shown in the film. The production's massive scale is evident in its impressive opening scene of wagons, settlers, livestock, and mountainous panoramas of natural wilderness landscape sweeping across the horizon. As with *Trader Horn*, *The Big Trail* encountered difficulties filming on location. The immense cast (featuring New York stage actors who were not accustomed to arduous shooting in remote wilderness), crew, and thousands of extras traveled thousands of miles across seven states, facing thunderstorms, torrential rain, blizzards, and buffalo stampedes as they made their way through mountains and scorching deserts. In the vast expanse of extras and scenic vistas of the West, oxen pulled wagons; tribes of Native Americans, settlers, and wildlife roamed; pack mules carried huge loads of filming equipment, lowered down rock faces with pulleys; hydraulic pumps diverted millions of gallons of water from the Colorado River to create mud holes from parched desert; and stuntmen and cowboys rode horses, crossed treacherous rapids, mountains, and hazardous canyon precipices. Hal Evarts's production log recalls twenty mules pulling double-decker sleds with six (70 mm/35 mm) cameras; film jammed, camera motors burned out. In a similar way to *Trader Horn*, *The Big Trail*'s harsh location filming took its toll on cast and crew, including sickness. Wayne, who was young, fit, and athletic, was sick for days, losing nearly twenty pounds on the rough location shoot.[17]

Like *Trader Horn*, location filming for *The Big Trail* was an immense, ambitious undertaking on an epic scale, which resulted in high costs. *The Big Trail*'s huge expense contributed to its financial failure when the film bombed. William Fox, who backed *The Big Trail*, owned the impressive 70 mm widescreen Grandeur process (and the sound technology Fox Movietone) and the famous Grauman's Chinese Theatre in Hollywood, where the film premiered, had influential ownership of a studio, and tried unsuccessfully to acquire the rival company Loews MGM. However, 1929–30 was a difficult time for Fox, who had overexpanded, lost his fortune in the stock market, and was in debt; he was forced out, losing control of his company in 1930 as the industry felt the aftershocks of the Wall Street crash. The economic reality was that only two theaters in the country could show *The Big Trail* in all its 70 mm widescreen glory, and as studios, theaters, and moviegoers were hit hard at the height of the Depression, there was no appetite for theaters (and studios), whose owners had just spent an enormous amount converting to new sound technology, to invest in new 70 mm projectors and equipment. Thus, in the end, *The Big Trail* was for the most part shown in a subpar 35 mm version and did not find an audience. However, a few people, such as Mordaunt Hall of the *New York Times*, were able to see *The Big Trail* in the Grandeur format when it opened in October 1930 and praised its spectacular natural landscapes.[18]

It was unfortunate that theater owners did not want to invest in Fox's Grandeur process, and ultimately *The Big Trail* was a failure. "If anyone had, a few months ago, told me that I would not only be photographing a big picture on wide film, but also rabidly enthusiastic over its artistic possibilities, I would have thought him crazy," Arthur Edeson wrote in *American Cinematographer* in 1930. "I have spent more than six months photographing the 70 millimeter version of Raoul Walsh's *The Big Trail*. In this time I have shot hundreds of thousands of feet of Grandeur film, and the results have convinced me . . . that I shall find it difficult, indeed, to return to the cramped proportions of our present-day standard film." He explained, "70 millimeter photography has given me an entirely new perspective. Instead of regarding things in the light of the old, cramped, Movietone frame, I now see them, photographically, as my eye naturally perceives them—in much the same proportions as the low, wide Grandeur frame."[19]

American Cinematographer later reflected on *The Big Trail*'s advances and how it benefited from 70 mm widescreen compared to the standard Academy ratio 35 mm version. "It was the movie that made John Wayne a star—and nearly ruined his career. It was the most ambitious Western of its time—and nearly ended the genre for good." Observing the contradictions of the film's incredible innovation for its time in 1930 but also noting that it was a flop that initially set back its lead actor, filmmaker, studio, and technology, Jason Apuzzo opined in 2015, "It's a movie about which everything was genuinely big, from its 70 mm Grandeur cameras, to its payroll of 20,000 extras and five separate casts, to its epic behind-the-scenes tales of Prohibition-era carousing. It was director Raoul Walsh's sprawling, rambunctious 1930 feature, *The Big Trail*, and nothing about it was small—including its legacy."[20]

The financial failure of *The Big Trail*, not to mention its enormous cost, potentially contributed to the reluctance of the industry to adopt widescreen, 70 mm, Grandeur, and extensive location shooting, because cinematic images of the scenery were not as impressive in standard 35 mm-format aspect ratio. It also hurt the Fox studio, the careers of Walsh and Wayne, and the western as an A-picture film genre, although, for cheap B westerns, as Brian Taves astutely notes, location shooting was inexpensive, and filming outdoors to visually recreate the open spaces of the American West made more sense than spending money building and filming expensive sets at the studio.[21] After the failure of *The Big Trail*, for example, Wayne was mostly relegated to B westerns. However, a 1932 Warner Bros. advertisement promoted Wayne as "He-Man of *The Big Trail*," prior to his (and the A western's) comeback a few years later in *Stagecoach* (John Ford, 1939). Walsh later directed productions on a smaller scale than the epic

70 mm locations and expense of *The Big Trail*, including a number of successful crime films at Warner Bros.[22] Ultimately, *The Big Trail's* widescreen 70 mm location shooting was twenty years ahead of its time and anticipated the postwar Hollywood era. A few years after *The Big Trail*, cinematographer Arthur Edeson filmed another remarkable location project, *Mutiny on the Bounty*.

MUTINY ON THE BOUNTY

In the wake of the sweeping landscapes of *The Big Trail*, Hollywood filmmakers achieved incredible scale at great expense in an acclaimed, innovative film that was notable and important for its ambitious location work, much of which was shot on the water of the Pacific Ocean and across miles on the islands of Catalina, San Miguel, and Tahiti: Irving Thalberg's Oscar-winning MGM production of *Mutiny on the Bounty*, starring Clark Gable, Charles Laughton, and Franchot Tone. Director Frank Lloyd acquired the screen rights to the novel and sold it to MGM and Thalberg with the understanding that he would direct the picture. The 1935 version of *Mutiny on the Bounty* is a brilliant example of creative geography by Lloyd and Thalberg, who create a seemingly seamless cinematic tapestry by blending shooting locales and location landscapes to resemble Tahiti and the historic voyage of the *Bounty*. The production included full sailing replicas of the *Bounty* and used second unit location crews in Tahiti, in the South Pacific, and in San Miguel Island, near Santa Barbara, California, to heighten realism.

Like *Trader Horn* and *The Big Trail*, *Mutiny on the Bounty* was an extravagant prestige production shot on location; no expense was spared. According to location filming reports for *Mutiny on the Bounty* in the MGM Collection,[23] cinematographer Arthur Edeson shot principal photography for *Mutiny on the Bounty* from May to September 1935 on Santa Catalina Island and aboard ships sailing on the Pacific Ocean off the California coast. MGM created whole villages and ships in Tahiti and Catalina with thousands of South Pacific extras, erected elaborate replica sets on the islands, and added extensive set dressings such as coconut palms to Catalina foliage to resemble Tahiti. Thalberg flew by sea plane from MGM to Catalina Island locations off the coast of Southern California near Los Angeles to oversee production and settle disputes.

Mutiny on the Bounty suffered disastrous tragedies while filming on location. An assistant cameraman, Glenn Strong, was killed; several technicians were injured; and expensive camera equipment was lost while filming second unit photography when a barge overturned in rough seas off San Miguel Island near Santa Barbara. Another replica ship of the *Bounty* with several crew aboard disappeared in bad weather for days until they were rescued. Filming on Catalina Island was hampered by dense fog on a daily basis, necessitating use of interior sets as soundstages until fog cleared for outdoor shooting of exteriors on the *Bounty* ship. Lloyd traveled great distances on a "second unit" trip, sailing thousands of miles to Tahiti for background shots, which resulted in fifty thousand feet of unusable film, so another second unit had to be sent back to Tahiti for additional filming.[24] Actor Charles Laughton was seasick during most of the production's location filming. James Cagney, who was on hiatus from Warner Bros., and David Niven also played seamen extras in the film.

The results of this laborious location shoot were remarkable. *Mutiny on the Bounty*, which cost a hefty $1.95 million, was the most expensive motion picture of 1935 and one of the last big productions made by Thalberg at MGM before the talented producer's sudden death in 1936 at the age of thirty-seven.[25] But the cinematic, artistic, and technological achievements of the arduous location filming of *Mutiny on the Bounty* did not go unrecognized, as film reviewers and screen audiences praised its success. When the film opened, critics were impressed with its realistic, atmospheric, swashbuckling sea locales. Ads for the film noted the huge crowds of filmgoers flocking to theaters in massive droves to see the movie. Ads for *Mutiny on the Bounty* in a 1935 issue of *Motion Picture Daily* clamored, "help! police! 'mutiny,'" noting that police were "vainly trying to handle Broadway crowds which have been storming" the theater, calling the film's stars Laughton, Gable, and Tone "box-office mutineers," and claiming it was MGM's biggest picture since the grand silent-era epics *Ben-Hur* and *The Big Parade*.[26] On November 12, 1935, *Variety* heralded the production of *Mutiny on the Bounty*, admitting, "Technically, and going by precedents, this is no women's picture; but Clark Gable and Franchot Tone are in the cast and the likelihood is that they'll atone for any weakness in that part of the business end. And with that one possible vulnerable point covered up, there's nothing to stand in the way of 'Mutiny' qualifying for box office dynamite rating. At the Capitol on Broadway, and with no cutting since the Coast previews, 'Mutiny' is running 131 minutes."[27]

On November 17, 1935, Andre Sennwald of the *New York Times* commended the film's artistic achievement and its extravagant accomplishment. In assessing *Mutiny on the Bounty*, Sennwald wryly observed, "Say one thing for Hollywood: when a studio spends $2,000,000 on a film, you can see where the money went." He went on to praise the film's sweeping artistry, noting,

> On those occasions when a fabulous budget is fortified by genuine skill and imagination, Hollywood can silence her critics with a picture like "Mutiny on the Bounty," which is playing to tumultuous crowds at the Capitol Theatre. Probably the film could have been made with complete success for a quarter of the sum which Irving Thalberg is reported to have spent on it. But there is a prodigal air about it, that gives it a special attractiveness which the economy of pure art would lack. When a film is as good as "Mutiny on the Bounty" it is not heretical to compare the fortune that Mr. Thalberg requires to tell a great story with the 1,000 pages that Dickens needed for the same purpose.[28]

By November 17, 1935, Louella Parsons of the *Los Angeles Examiner* wrote that "some of the scenes were actually taken [shot] in Tahiti" and remarked that "they are beautiful," noting that *Mutiny on the Bounty* was "destined to become a box office gold mine."[29] *Mutiny on the Bounty* was nominated for several Academy Awards and won the Oscar for Best Picture of 1935. Nevertheless, as seen in the perilous shooting circumstances of *Mutiny on the Bounty, Trader Horn,* and *The Big Trail,* accidents, expense, and unpredictable production conditions were typically a deterrent to filming on location. Thus, many filmmakers opted to shoot in safer conditions on soundstages during the studio era.

However, despite the deadly incidents and challenges of location shooting demonstrated by pictures such as *Mutiny on the Bounty, Trader Horn,* and *The Big Trail,* there were other pictures such as 1930s social realist documentaries that relied on location filming to reveal grim Depression-era realities. In the wake of the human suffering of the Great Depression, grittier social realism, location photography, and even the term "documentary" became more prevalent during the 1930s. This trend is seen in Pare Lorentz's social realist documentary films made for President Roosevelt's Resettlement Administration (RA): *The Plow That Broke the Plains* (1936), which documents the environmental ravages of the Dust Bowl; and *The River* (1938), which depicts flooding along the Mississippi River and impoverished farmers.[30] Social realism was also seen in the RA's Depression-era still photography. The stark images of poverty, starvation, the Dust Bowl, and migrant farming conditions are shown, for example, in Dorothea Lange's iconic image *Migrant Mother* (1936) and in the photography of Walker Evans, which also influenced Hollywood's social realist film style during the period.

After the success of *Mutiny on the Bounty,* as well as the topical social realism of Lorenz's documentaries, by the late 1930s and early 1940s, there were also a number of prestige productions in Hollywood with extensive sequences shot on location. These included Ford's *Stagecoach,* with its striking landscapes of Monument Valley (reviving Wayne and westerns as A pictures in the process), and *The Grapes of Wrath* (1940), shot with Gregg Toland to capture the plight of the Dust Bowl; *Under Two Flags* (Frank Lloyd, 1936); *The Adventures of Robin Hood*; *Gunga Din* (George Stevens, 1939); *Northwest Passage*; and *High Sierra* (Raoul Walsh, 1941), as well as documentary newsreels such as *The March of Time* and numerous travelogues. On a more escapist note, Hollywood travelogues, such as MGM's *Fitzpatrick Travel Talks* short subject films (which began in the 1930s and continued through the 1950s) were Technicolor location documentaries. These travelogues showcased location filming of exotic locales. For instance, one 1930s short featured the wonders of Japan, highlighting its beautiful scenery, ancient temples, and cherry blossoms for prospective tourist cinemagoers to vicariously enjoy remote travel sights onscreen.

As the cases of *Mutiny on the Bounty, Trader Horn,* and *The Big Trail* show, films shot on location under the studio system were typically expensive and had higher costs. For example, as a comparison to other well-known, average-budgeted films of the era, RKO's *Top Hat* (1935) cost $600,000, and *Bachelor Mother* (1939) cost $500,000. Warner Bros.' *Angels with Dirty Faces* (1938) cost $600,000, and *The Roaring Twenties* (1939) cost $725,000. MGM's *Babes in Arms* (1940) cost $748,000, and *The Philadelphia Story* (1940) cost $900,000. However, films shot on location were considerably more expensive: *Mutiny on the Bounty* and *Gunga Din* both cost over $1.9 million, *The Adventures of Robin Hood* cost over $2 million, and *Northwest Passage* cost nearly $2.7 million, as Technicolor location filming was costly.[31]

Three-strip Technicolor, which required more light and special equipment to film images, was particularly expensive for location filming. Even MGM's 1939 *The Wizard of Oz*, which was filmed entirely in studio with Technicolor, cost $2.7 million.[32] However, several ambitious pictures, including *The Adventures of Robin Hood* and *Northwest Passage*, were shot on location with three-strip Technicolor cameras and equipment, which was especially cumbersome for shooting far away from the studio in remote locales.

TECHNICOLOR: *THE ADVENTURES OF ROBIN HOOD* AND *NORTHWEST PASSAGE*

As films such as *Mutiny on the Bounty, Trader Horn, The Big Trail,* and later color productions illustrate, studio executives often considered location shooting a huge gamble and an unnecessary expense. This was especially evident when filming in Technicolor. Such a costly endeavor was certainly the case with the swashbuckling Technicolor Warner Bros. production *The Adventures of Robin Hood*, which began shooting on location with a large cast (including Errol Flynn, Olivia de Havilland, Claude Rains, and Basil Rathbone) and crew in Chico in Northern California (some four hundred miles from Hollywood) for six weeks from September through November 1937. Initially directed by William Keighley and shot by Tony Gaudio (with an additional second unit filmed by B. Reeves Eason in late October), the production encountered difficulties and weather delays that slowed and hampered filming of the Sherwood Forest sequences, which were shot in Chico's Bidwell Park and used tall oak trees by the Big Chico Creek.

Back in Los Angeles, production managers and studio executives at Warner Bros. had serious reservations about potential difficulties and sluggish progress on location. "I wonder if we are wrong in allowing *Robin Hood* to be shot at Chico," Warner Bros. production manager Tenny Wright wrote to executive producer Hal Wallis, concerned that filming on location precluded getting much shooting done due to rain. Wright continued,

> From all indications now *Robin Hood* will not start until the later part of this
> month, September, and the rains generally set in around the first of October. If

it rains one day, it will take another day to dry out, particularly in the woods, under the trees. . . . Do you think that the locations there are so vastly superior to the ones we can secure down here in Sherwood. I mean by this—is it worth gambling on the weather? . . . We must consider the additional costs of transportation, etc., that we will be burdened with. I think that you should give this very careful consideration before you make up your mind, as truthfully I am a little worried about weather conditions during the month of October up and around Chico.[33]

By October, Wallis sent a missive to Keighley on location: "I don't want to start worrying you . . . but while the first three days' dailies are gorgeous . . . it has taken three days to shoot the meeting between Robin and Little John, and it was not yet complete at the end of three days' work." He warned, "I don't have to tell you that at this rate we will be on location until it snows, and naturally change in backgrounds will be so great as to make the difference marked." He then added, "Don't know what you can do about it except to cut down angles and not spend so much time on this sort of stuff, but believe you will agree that at the rate of three days to shoot one little sequence we have cause for worry."[34]

As the leaves began changing color with autumn foliage, the crew began dressing up the trees in the forest sets and spraying leaves green so the shots would match in the Technicolor images. (This problem of changing fall colors in filming the location was less of a problem with black-and-white film.) The Warner Bros. film crew had also added rocks, artificial grass, and plaster tree trunks to the natural location for *The Adventures of Robin Hood*. Later in October, star Errol Flynn wrote a handwritten letter to Wallis to complain about the unpleasant location filming. "I feel like one of the oldest inhabitants of Chico now—we all do. And we're all rather sick of it but consoling ourselves with the report or rather rumour that you like the stuff down there. Is it so?"[35] By November, Wallis was already looking to cut sequences from the picture and wrote to the film's associate producer, Henry Blanke: "I imagine we are about two weeks behind schedule on *Robin Hood* so far. . . . You know what this will amount to in dollars and cents."[36]

Eventually, Warner Bros. replaced the director with Michael Curtiz (who had filmed *Captain Blood*) and a different cinematographer, Sol Polito. They began filming on soundstage sets of the medieval castle at the studio and on various locations near Los Angeles, such as an archery scene at Pasadena's Busch Gardens, additional shots of Robin and his Merry Men climbing up and swinging across vines hanging from trees for an ambush in Sherwood Forest, and Sherwood Lake. Curtiz filmed for several weeks from December 1937 to January 1938 to fix and finish the shooting with brisk scenes of swashbuckling swordplay and stunt work filmed in the studio. In the end, despite the challenges of location filming, *The Adventures of Robin Hood* was an important example of a successful and spectacular Technicolor studio system production. By keeping location shooting under control and avoiding disasters, Warner Bros. earned nearly $4 million for *The Adventures of Robin Hood*, making it the studio's top-grossing film that year.[37]

Another example of Technicolor location filming is MGM's historical adventure film *Northwest Passage* (1940), shot far away from the studio in the remote mountainous wilderness of McCall and Payette Lake in Idaho and near Glacier National Park. In contrast to the success of *Robin Hood*, the film became a massive, difficult, and expensive production that was not a success. Based on Kenneth Roberts's 1937 novel *Northwest Passage: Book One, Rogers' Rangers*, it starred Spencer Tracy as Major Rogers leading a huge cast of rangers, troops, and Native Americans across the wilderness of pre–Revolutionary War North America. In 1938, MGM scouted locations and began remote filming, sending a large (sixty-eight-member) second unit crew to McCall, Idaho. However, it was a long, arduous, and futile exercise that was costly and resulted in considerable losses. In particular, the early 1938 McCall location filming for *Northwest Passage* included the loss of a Technicolor camera, which fell into rough river rapids and had to be sent back to Technicolor. It also led to a lawsuit for the studio over location filming land use, permissions, and ownership, which was finally settled with MGM but delayed principal photography. Finally, an enormous amount (sixty thousand feet) of Technicolor footage was filmed, including a water-rapids sequence, but ultimately not used after Technicolor changed and improved its film stock and earlier footage would not match later footage shot the following year with the new film.[38]

Northwest Passage illustrated how resolving problematic script issues was more difficult and challenging to accomplish on location, where going over schedule limited potential story fixes while far away from the studio. Originally, MGM planned to film two parts of the story, but it ended up filming only the first part and had to throw together an abrupt ending for the film later when back at the studio. It was the antithesis of MGM's earlier commitment to strong cohesive storytelling, as seen in *Mutiny on the Bounty* during the Thalberg era.

Initially, *Trader Horn* director Van Dyke was to film *Northwest Passage* with principal photography on location in Idaho beginning in August 1938. However, Van Dyke had a filming conflict and was committed to another picture when MGM postponed shooting until after winter, with plans to start in spring 1939. *Northwest Passage* finally began filming in July 1939 in Payette Lake, Idaho, and near Glacier National Park, with King Vidor at the helm of the lavish Technicolor production.

Northwest Passage was a vast production with extensive use of locations and impressive scenes of remote forests, waterways, and mountainous landscape. However, it was a rough, exhausting shoot. Star Spencer Tracy even complained to MGM about the unreasonably difficult location filming experience. Notably, studios had a strategic interest in cultivating the idea of arduous and exotic loca-tion shoots, for the sake of art, for the sake of majestic splendor, and as a market-ing ploy—such publicity was part of the hyperbole of the industry in general. With this in mind, MGM also made a short subject, *Northward, Ho!* (Harry Loud, 1940), about the *Northwest Passage* production and its location shooting process. The short promotes the filming as an immense labor involving the cast and crew spending six months in the remote wilderness swinging "giant 600 pound Technicolor cameras" to get the right shot in the best light. The huge cast (with thousands of extras) and the studio's location crew had massive resources and literally transformed the Idaho wilderness for *Northwest Passage*. They cut down trees, built their own remote MGM studio (complete with departments, dormitories, cabins, and equipment run on generators), built dams to deepen river/lake waterways, and built large and elaborate flaming sets from the ground up, even building an entire village and then burning it down (using copper pipes that sprayed gasoline and were lit afire). Another highlight of the film was the treacherous river crossing by Major Rogers and his rangers, which was shot in part on location, though much of it was actually filmed back at MGM in a huge studio tank with professional swimmers as stunt extras.[39]

And it was all extravagantly shot in three-strip Technicolor. However, the look of the Technicolor location shots of MGM's *Northwest Passage* contrasted with the vibrant colors of Warner Bros.' *The Adventures of Robin Hood*. To strive for a realist aesthetic in *Northwest Passage*, MGM crews tried to tone down the col-ors in the Technicolor film dyes so the leaves would not look so green, which at times resulted in muted, muddy hues. However, the bright-colored flames of the burning village were impressive. Unfortunately, *Northwest Passage* was the most expensive MGM picture (costing $2.687 million) and biggest financial loss ($855,000) for the studio that year.[40]

WORLD WAR II ON LOCATION AND HITCHCOCK'S *SHADOW OF A DOUBT*

By 1939–40, Hollywood's earlier trend of showcasing lavish, exotic locales for prospective tourist-travelers to enjoy vicariously—as seen in *Trader Horn*'s Afri-can safari, *Mutiny on the Bounty*'s idyllic Polynesian South Pacific, and MGM's *Fitzpatrick Travel Talks* travelogues (visiting locations such as Japan)—shifted drastically as previously glamorous, enticing overseas travel locales in Europe, Africa, Asia, and the South Pacific rapidly became dangerous combat zones embroiled in World War II. With the onset of the deadly global conflict and widespread catastrophic destruction overseas, the studio system produced many films featuring American settings (*The Grapes of Wrath*, *High Sierra*) or historical settings (*The Adventures of Robin Hood*, *Gunga Din*) or both (*Stagecoach*, *Gone with the Wind*, *Northwest Passage*), with location shooting.[41] Contemporary documentary newsreels such as *The March of Time* reported current events abroad and included news about the escalating world war.

World War II brought a set of constrictions to the Hollywood studio system. With Los Angeles suddenly designated a potential war zone by the U.S. Army, Hollywood studios faced tremendous restrictions on shooting locations beyond the back lot or soundstage. These constraints prevented studios from filming vital transportation facilities essential to the war effort, such as coastlines, railroads, trains, planes, and bridges, and manufacturing facilities, especially outdoors in broad daylight. Los Angeles locations could be filmed at night, though nocturnal filming beyond the studio often encountered unexpected production interruptions or disturbances due to mandatory blackouts and dim-outs that cloaked the city in darkness and made it difficult to shoot without essential light, as well as air-raid drills and noise from planes flying overhead patrolling the coastline. Further production constraints due to security concerns and rationing included travel restrictions and shortages of gasoline, rubber tires, and automobiles. Wartime rationing also made filming more difficult at studios, including limits on film stock, set construction material, electricity, and lighting equipment. Nails to build sets were salvaged, sets were recycled, costumes were reused, film was rationed, and soundstages became scarce and less available because of increased demand. Thus, as the United States was drawn into the conflict overseas in the immediate aftermath of the Pearl Harbor attack, filming in Hollywood was more difficult and precluded extensive location shooting, as the Los Angeles production environment was abruptly, unexpectedly transformed.[42]

In stark contrast to the lavish resources, travel, and Technicolor seen in *Northwest Passage*, studios across Hollywood eliminated extravagant travel plans, which were discouraged unless they were deemed essential for the war effort. In this frugal, constrained, and austere filmmaking environment, few color films were made, as three-strip Technicolor was expensive, needed more light, and also used three times as much film due to its three-color separated film strips (during the shooting and developing process). Film stock was rationed and pared down to essentials, and with increasingly severe restrictions in 1942 and 1943, war-related limitations affected filming in the Hollywood studios and location shooting in Los Angeles and elsewhere.

In response to these constraints, Alfred Hitchcock's *Shadow of a Doubt* was filmed on location in Santa Rosa, California, to avoid wartime restrictions. Producer Jack Skirball (who worked with Frank Lloyd on Hitchcock's *Saboteur*) began work in spring 1942, signing a one-picture deal with Universal, with Hitchcock directing. *Shadow of a Doubt* (based on Gordon McDonell's *Uncle Charlie*) was scripted by Thornton Wilder, fresh off his stage success after penning *Our Town*, and coadapted by Sally Benson and Alma Reville. Like Wilder's *Our Town*, Hitchcock's *Shadow of a Doubt* is set in a small American town. Unlike typical soundstage-bound productions, Hitchcock left Hollywood studios in Los

Angeles and instead innovatively filmed *Shadow of a Doubt* on location in Northern California, an unusual practice at the time. Significantly, Hitchcock took a more minimalist approach and staged the film's action simply using the town and plain main-street ambiance in Santa Rosa to serve as a natural, realistic set rather than constructing the more grandiose and artificial sense of cinematic glamour on Hollywood soundstages. In stark contrast with sweeping classic Technicolor historical romance such as *The Adventures of Robin Hood*, Hitchcock's modest black-and-white Gothic thriller has a contemporary setting and involves a teenage girl, Charlie (played by Teresa Wright), and her charming, beloved uncle Charlie (Joseph Cotten), who turns out to be a serial killer.

Hitchcock and cinematographer Joseph Valentine avoided war-related set-construction limits by filming *Shadow of a Doubt* outside Hollywood's constrained production environment. Hitchcock chose instead to shoot on location in Newark, New Jersey, and Santa Rosa, California; however, he ended each day early in the evening to avoid filming night scenes because of dim-out lighting restrictions. A *Life* magazine feature reported on the location shoot with the headline, "$5,000 Production: Hitchcock Makes Thriller under WPA Order on New Sets," and observed in January 1943,

> Alfred Hitchcock has already proved himself ingenious in creating suspense-filled melodramas. As a director of one of the first movies to be produced under the Government restriction placing a $5,000 ceiling on new materials used for sets, he has shown he has more than one trick up his sleeve. Accustomed to spending more than $100,000 on sets alone for one picture, Hitchcock made *Shadow of a Doubt* by reverting to the "location shooting" of early movie days. . . . Instead of elaborate sets he used the real thing. To shoot scenes supposed to take place in New Jersey, he traveled cross-country and shot them in New Jersey. Instead of building a studio version of a typical American city, his main setting, he searched for a ready-made one. Selecting Santa Rosa, Calif. (pop. 13,000), Hitchcock with his cast and crew took over the entire city for four weeks, converted it into a complete motion-picture studio. The result is an exciting and highly realistic film whose new set cost, mainly for studio replicas, was well under the imposed limit.[43]

Shadow of a Doubt was filmed from August through November 1942 and shot in a house and on everyday streets on location in Santa Rosa, while a second unit shot background shots in Newark, New Jersey, and near the New York waterfront for a parking lot sequence early in the film. Production records and location files for *Shadow of a Doubt* in the Alfred Hitchcock and Universal Collections reveal the considerable expense and logistical considerations involved in arranging for the production to be shot away from a Hollywood studio—from renting rail cars to moving cast, crew, heavy equipment, cables, generators, and all the necessary essentials for transforming Santa Rosa's small town into a functioning movie set

Figure 2.1. Alfred Hitchcock filming *Shadow of a Doubt* (Universal, 1943) in Santa Rosa.

on location (figure 2.1). However, Hitchcock's new sets cost a mere $2,979, which was below the wartime requirement.

As Pare Lorentz's social realist films of the Depression demonstrate, a new documentary realism was increasingly evident in U.S. film before World War II. Cinematographer James Wong Howe discussed what would become known as a "semidocumentary" style prevalent during the war. He noted the influence of newsreel documentary-style filming in response to Hollywood's rationing and the film industry's war restrictions in *American Cinematographer* in June 1942 and observed that "visual suggestion can enhance 'rationed' sets."[44] Howe articulated how visual suggestion was employed in filming and noted its impact as a strategy for shooting in a restrictive wartime production environment that restrained locations. He observed how realistic "newsreel style" filming on remote locations could more simply and efficiently create cinematic artistry during wartime. "Unaware of the documentary method before the war began," he explained, "audience[s] saw newsreels, *March of Time* . . . but real awareness grew only when nations began to record on film the history of their countries at war. We began to see documentaries from England and Russia and . . . Germany. Magazines like *Life* and *Look* acquainted us with the documentary 'still.' . . . Film taught us what war looked like." Recalling powerful images of combat from newsreels shot overseas, Howe observed, "Despite the hundreds of thousands of feet of battle shots being shown, we are not accustomed to seeing such an intimate picture of a man's death. . . . Equipment now in use by the Army and Navy, developed from the necessity of wartime expediency, offers a new and vital opportunity to the motion picture industry, a new and much-needed mechanical flexibility and simplicity."[45] Howe's observation anticipated the demand for more realistic overseas location shooting after the war.

Paradoxically, while wartime restrictions frequently curtailed location filming in the Hollywood studio system, as Howe suggests, World War II was nevertheless an important catalyst for technological innovation that enhanced and enabled greater location filming. In response to the necessities of filming the combat front, technological advances—including more mobile equipment such as lightweight 16 mm handheld cameras, better lenses that allowed deep-focus cinematography, and "faster" light-sensitive film stock that enabled shooting in natural light and darker settings—aided location filming.[46] Films such as *Five Graves to Cairo* (Billy Wilder, 1943), *Double Indemnity* (Billy Wilder, 1944), *Casablanca* (Michael Curtiz, 1942), and *Mildred Pierce* (Michael Curtiz, 1945) featured striking filmed locations despite war-related blackouts, rationing, and constraints on studio production as Los Angeles was declared a "theater of war." Newsreels about the war influenced location-shot combat dramas such as *Wake Island* (1942), *Sahara* (1943), and *Air Force* (1943).

The combat film *Sahara* was shot in the U.S. Southwest desert and drawn from wartime incidents in Africa. *Sahara* included impressive cinematography in shots of its desert locations filmed from January through April 1943 in Brawley, the Imperial Valley, and Chatsworth, California, and Yuma, Arizona. Stark cinematography in *Sahara* emulated the unvarnished style of news from the front, made possible by faster stock for low-light filming and portable lightweight cameras, which were used to capture military action using available light to expose better high-contrast images in darker settings. Cinematographer Rudolph Maté was nominated for an Oscar for his location camera work on *Sahara*. James Agee recognized *Sahara*'s stunning realistic visual style, which was filmed remotely like a newsreel: "It borrows chiefly from the English, a sort of light-alloy modification of realism which makes the traditional Hollywood idiom seem as obsolete as a minuet."[47] Like *Sahara*, *Five Graves to Cairo* was shot on location in the desert in Yuma, Arizona, and near the Salton Sea and Indio, California; cinematographer John Seitz captured striking newsreel-style images of the desert locations.

Filming on location during the war also presented challenges. For instance, James Wong Howe shot Warner Bros.' *Air Force* (1943) at Drew Field in Tampa, Florida, and Randolph Field in San Antonio, Texas, because wartime restrictions prevented the Warner Bros. studio production crew from shooting aerial footage of flying planes in Los Angeles (particularly filming planes resembling Japanese bombers). Howe and Hawks faced production difficulties when filming was significantly delayed by heavy rain while shooting in Florida. The film also included actual combat footage as well as miniatures and water-combat scenes shot in Santa Monica Bay.[48]

Documentary newsreels and nonfiction filming techniques on location were enhanced by filmmakers in Hollywood joining the effort to photograph military combat from the front. Hollywood creative talent that contributed to filming on location for the war effort included directors Frank Capra, John Ford, William Wyler, George Stevens, and John Huston. President Roosevelt lifted military restrictions on photographing of actual combat in late 1942, and the ensuing combat documentaries such as *The Battle of Midway* (John Ford, 1942), *Memphis Belle* (William Wyler, 1944), and *The Battle of San Pietro* (John Huston, 1945) captured stunning overseas footage of the conflict. John Ford landed on Omaha Beach on D-Day, filming the battle (figure 2.2). This documentary filming of military combat from the front lines was visible in newsreels and nonfiction news reports covering the war and added realism to narrative genre films (especially crime films) during this time. Émigré directors such as Hitchcock and Billy Wilder left Hollywood to make documentaries on location overseas about the horror of Nazi atrocities and genocide as the Allies liberated Europe in 1945.[49] John Ford's short subject *The Battle of Midway* and the British documentary *Desert Victory* (1943) received Academy Awards.

William Wyler shot the combat documentary *Memphis Belle* (U.S. War Department / Paramount, 1944) in cooperation with the Army Air Forces First Motion Picture Unit over Europe in 1944. Filmed in color, *Memphis Belle* opens with a statement explaining the nature of the extremely hazardous, even deadly shooting conditions: "All aerial combat film was exposed during air battles over enemy territory." *Memphis Belle* is the nonfiction story of the first B-17 Flying Fortress bomber to complete twenty-five aerial missions in Europe and return intact after leaving England to fly over France. The crew faced enemy fire while shooting on location, and the footage includes attacks by enemy fighter planes and flak from German antiaircraft guns. Wyler initially wanted to film *Memphis Belle* with standard 35mm cameras and sound equipment, which would have been heavier and bulkier for filming on location. However, like the cameras that never arrived in Africa for *Trader Horn*, the 35mm cameras and sound equipment were shipped but never arrived in England. Thus, the film was shot on 16mm color stock with handheld cameras. In March 1944, the *New York Times* noted that special electric devices covered and heated cameras to keep equipment from freezing at high altitudes (since the planes were not pressurized or heated and temperatures in the aircraft dropped to forty degrees below zero). *Memphis Belle* was filmed by three camera operators with over sixteen thousand feet of film shot during thirteen flights. Conditions were dangerous: Wyler lost his hearing in one ear while filming an aerial bombing run, and cameraman Harold Tannenbaum was killed in action while filming, losing his life when the

Figure 2.2. John Ford lands on Omaha Beach on D-Day, filming the battle.

plane he was in was shot down during a bombing mission flying over France in April 1943.[50]

Memphis Belle and other combat documentaries of the war years (including those shot in color) are significant not only because of their remote location filming but also because of their verisimilitude, conveying a gritty, unvarnished view of the conflict, with its graphic horror and violence. The war catalyzed location filming and heightened cinematic realism with its more authentic, rough-and-tumble newsreel style of shooting. The technological filming innovations advanced by the war—lightweight production equipment, better "coated" camera lenses, and faster, light-sensitive film stock—enhanced location filming and made it possible to shoot in deep focus with available light and carry out "night-for-night" shooting with more natural light.[51] Cinematically, the complex circumstances of the war contributed to a starker visual style and narrative content in some wartime Hollywood productions, especially those shot on location. Moreover, "stock" newsreel footage shot on location was added to narrative feature films and combined with studio soundstage shots (made to emulate the gritty look and style of the newsreel images) in classical Hollywood montage sequences that were edited together to add realism to studio system films. This was evident in the flashback sequence in *Casablanca*, which includes newsreel location shots of combat tanks and troops marching on the front line of the war to show the fall of Paris to the invading Nazis.

Figure 2.3. Billy Wilder's *Double Indemnity* (Paramount, 1944), Jerry's Market location set.

The war restrictions, blackouts, and newsreels also influenced the visual style and location shooting of film noir. For example, Wilder noted that cinematographer John Seitz simulated the stark realism of newsreel style when shooting *Double Indemnity*, which was shot on several locations, including the Bradbury Building in downtown Los Angeles, Jerry's market, Kingsley Drive, Sunset and Hollywood Boulevards, Western Avenue, a Rossmore Avenue apartment building, an Olvera street café, and art director Hans Dreier's Beachwood Canyon home (figure 2.3).[52] The crew nearly canceled night shots due to wartime blackouts but instead filmed at Glendale train station, at an East Los Angeles rail yard, and in Phoenix, Arizona, to avoid dim-out restrictions. *Mildred Pierce* was shot in Glendale and Malibu (at director Curtiz's beach house) at night despite bans on filming the coastline; the Navy allowed the filming but viewed the shot footage.

Conclusion: The Legacy of Location Filming in the Studio Era

As these case studies of location shooting during the studio system suggest, Hollywood films shot on location—especially the costly extravaganzas of the early sound era—reveal that producers were typically justified in avoiding location shooting since it so often spun out of control. Yet they also show how these ambitious productions had a lasting effect on Hollywood filmmaking, establishing practices that were later picked up, such as semidocumentary style and integrating second unit footage with soundstage work. These films' use of locations was frequently enhanced through their pairing with other technologies such as widescreen and Technicolor. In short, these exceptional cases reveal the larger paradigm of the studio period, particularly for first unit location shooting. As the case studies of extravagant, big-budget films of the 1930s show, studio filmmakers and producers would promote filming locations for their prestige value or, in the cases of *The Adventures of Robin Hood* and *Mutiny on the Bounty*, use California locations to make the film more spectacular for audiences.

Following these ambitious and extravagant films, Depression-era social realism and wartime newsreel documentaries heightened cinematic realism and set the stage for an explosion of semidocumentary-style location filming in the postwar era, both in the United States and abroad (as seen in the example of Italian neorealism). What emerged after the social realism of the Depression and the combat newsreels of the war was a stark newsreel style of semidocumentary realism that sought to emulate front-line news coverage shot on location with available lighting and to render it more pervasive on the Hollywood screen.[53]

Semidocumentary style relied extensively on location shooting, which grew out of newsreel style and capitalized on wartime production constraints, technological possibilities, and available lighting. Following the social realism of the 1930s, World War II filmmaking trends coincided with the massive production of documentary newsreels and burgeoning newsreel-style screen realism, which showcased location filming and encouraged cinematic conventions such as shooting with available light. The growth of documentary realism and technological enhancements enabled remote photography, despite combat, bad weather (rain, fog, sleet), shadows, or limited production resources.

As seen in social realism and documentary newsreels of the Great Depression and World War II, this emergent newsreel style relied on filming locations to achieve greater realism and verisimilitude. Like the grim realities of the Depression era, seen in the social realism of Pare Lorentz films and photography of Dorothea Lange, the experience of World War II and deadly bloodshed of combat as seen in *The Battle of Midway*, *Memphis Belle*, and *The Battle of San Pietro* changed the views of Hollywood filmmakers and audiences, especially those who served in the war. In the wake of the conflict, after being exposed to the striking images of harsh violence and the unvarnished brutality of wartime (and the genocide of the Holocaust), cinemagoers, filmmakers, and even studio executives now craved the authenticity that location shooting provided. The growing wave of semidocumentary films, which offered stark realism and abundant location filming, satisfied that need in the postwar era.

NOTES

1. Darryl Zanuck to Henry King, n.d. (ca. late September 1938), Cinematic Arts Library, University of Southern California, Los Angeles, CA (hereafter USC Cinematic Arts Library); Rudy Behlmer, *Memo from Darryl F. Zanuck: The Golden Years of Twentieth Century-Fox* (New York: Grove, 1993), 17–18.

2. Zanuck to King, n.d. (ca. late September 1938); Behlmer, *Memo from Darryl F. Zanuck*, 17–19. Zanuck was a proponent of location filming in the postwar era.

3. Darryl Zanuck, memo, August 9, 1952, USC Cinematic Arts Library; Behlmer, *Memo from Darryl F. Zanuck*, 216–17.

4. Philip K. Scheuer, "Cohn: Remembrances of Screens Past," *Los Angeles Times*, October 9, 1977, R1.

5. J. L. Warner, memo to Henry Blanke, May 25, 1938, Warner Bros. Archive, USC Cinematic Arts Library; Rudy Behlmer, *Inside Warner Bros.* (New York: Viking Penguin, 1985), 65.

6. Hal Wallis, memo to T. C. Wright, April 5, 1939, Warner Bros. Archives, USC Cinematic Arts Library; Behlmer, *Inside Warner Bros.*, 95.

7. MGM features prized high production values and spectacular production design. See Mark Shiel, "Classical Hollywood, 1928–1946," in *Behind the Silver Screen: Art Direction and Production Design*, ed. Lucy Fischer (New Brunswick, NJ: Rutgers University Press, 2014) 48–72. Thus, designing sets on soundstages often proved to be more valued as an efficient production strategy over filming on location. Even in the silent era, after filming in Rome, the MGM production executive Irving Thalberg moved *Ben-Hur* (1925) back to Hollywood and reshot the film with sets on the studio back lot to stop the expensive location shooting from spiraling out of control. When the MGM art director Cedric Gibbons complained to Thalberg in 1925 about having to design a beach for a scene in Hollywood's incarnation of Paris (despite the fact that there was no beach in Paris), Thalberg replied, "We can't cater to a handful of people who know Paris. . . . Audiences only see about ten per cent of what's on the screen anyway, and if they are watching your backgrounds instead of my actors, the scene will be useless." Samuel Marx, *Mayer and Thalberg* (New York: Random House, 1975), 82–83; Mark Vieira, *Irving Thalberg* (Berkeley: University of California Press, 2010).

8. Van Dyke was later known for *Tarzan*, *The Thin Man*, and *San Francisco*.

9. *White Shadows on the South Seas* was directed by Van Dyke, with DeVinna and the documentary filmmaker Robert Flaherty, with sound effects.

10. MGM production, location, and script file correspondence for *Trader Horn*, 1928–30, MGM Collection, USC Cinematic Arts Library.

11. MGM files cite a $3 million cost for *Trader Horn* (rivaling *Ben-Hur*'s $4 million); budgets cite a cost over $1.3 million. MGM Collection, USC Cinematic Arts Library; Eddie Mannix ledger, 1931, Academy of Motion Picture Arts and Sciences (AMPAS), Los Angeles, CA.

12. MGM *Trader Horn* publicity, 1931, USC Press Book Collection, USC Cinematic Arts Library.

13. Academy of Motion Picture Arts and Sciences, *Recording Sound for Motion Pictures* (New York: McGraw-Hill, 1931), 272–78.

14. For further reading regarding technological advances, see Tino Balio, *Grand Design* (New York: Scribner, 1993).

15. Fox production correspondence for *The Big Trail*, 1929–30, Fox Collection, USC Cinematic Arts Library.

16. A talented cameraman and veteran of the silent era, Edeson filmed *The Thief of Bagdad* (1924) and later shot *Casablanca* (1942).

17. Hal Evarts, log for *The Big Trail*, production files, 1929–33, Fox Collection, USC Cinematic Arts Library.

18. Mordaunt Hall, "The Big Trail," *New York Times*, November 2, 1930, X5.

19. Arthur Edeson, "Wide Film Cinematography," *American Cinematographer*, September 1930, 8.

20. Jason Apuzzo, "Visions of Grandeur," *American Cinematographer* 96, no. 4 (2015): 82.

21. Brian Taves, "The B Film: Hollywood's Other Half," in *Grand Design: Hollywood as a Modern Business Enterprise, 1930–1939*, by Tino Balio (New York: Scribner, 1993), 313–50.

22. Walsh later directed *The Roaring Twenties, They Drive by Night, High Sierra, Objective Burma!*, and *White Heat*.

23. Location filming reports for *Mutiny on the Bounty*, 1935, MGM Collection, USC Cinematic Arts Library.

24. Location filming and camera reports for *Mutiny on the Bounty*, 1935, MGM Collection, USC Cinematic Arts Library; Mannix ledger, 1935.

25. Mannix ledger, 1935. For further reading on the MGM producer Irving Thalberg and his death, see also Thomas Schatz, *Genius of the System* (New York: Simon and Schuster, 1988), 173–74.

26. *Mutiny on the Bounty* ad in *Motion Picture Daily* 38 (1935) n.p., Constance McCormick and Press Book Collections, USC Cinematic Arts Library.

27. "Mutiny on the Bounty [review]," *Variety*, November 12, 1935, 16.

28. Andre Sennwald, "Mutiny on the Bounty [review]," *New York Times*, November 17, 1935, 5.

29. Louella Parsons, "'Mutiny on the Bounty' A Hit," *Los Angeles Examiner*, November 17, 1935, n.p., Constance McCormick Collection, USC Cinematic Arts Library.

30. For further reading, see Charles Wolfe, "The Poetics and Politics of Nonfiction: Documentary Film," in Balio, *Grand Design*, 351–86.

31. Mannix ledger, 1938–40; C.F. Tevlin ledger, 1938–40, MGM Collection, USC Cinematic Arts Library; William Schaefer Collection, USC Cinematic Arts Library.

32. Mannix ledger, 1939.

33. T. C. Wright to Hal Wallis, September 7, 1937, USC Cinematic Arts Library; Behlmer, *Inside Warner Bros.*, 45–46.

34. Hal Wallis to William Keighley, October 6, 1937, Warner Bros. Archive, USC Cinematic Arts Library; Behlmer, *Inside Warner Bros.*, 48–49.

35. Errol Flynn to Hal Wallis, October 24, 1937, Warner Bros. Archive, USC Cinematic Arts Library; Behlmer, *Inside Warner Bros.*, 49.

36. Hal Wallis to Henry Blanke, November 10, 1937, Warner Bros. Archive, USC Cinematic Arts Library; Behlmer, *Inside Warner Bros.*, 50.

37. Production and budget files, 1938, William Schaefer Collection, Warner Bros. Archive, USC Cinematic Arts Library.

38. Rudy Behlmer, "To the Wilderness for *Northwest Passage*," *American Cinematographer* 68, no. 11 (1987): 38–47.

39. Ibid.

40. Mannix ledger, 1940.

41. *Gone with the Wind* locations included Chico, Pasadena, Malibu, Big Bear, and Triunfo, California. The *Adventures of Robin Hood* composer Erich Wolfgang Korngold immigrated to Hollywood from Europe.

42. Sheri Chinen Biesen, *Blackout: World War II and the Origins of Film Noir* (Baltimore: Johns Hopkins University Press, 2005); Thomas Schatz, *Boom and Bust: American Cinema in the 1940s* (New York: Scribner, 1997).

43. "$5,000 Production: Hitchcock Makes Thriller under WPA Order on New Sets," *Life*, January 25, 1943, 70–73; see also production correspondence in Alfred Hitchcock Collection, AMPAS, and, Joseph Cotten Collection, USC Cinematic Arts Library.

44. James Wong Howe, "Visual Suggestion Can Enhance 'Rationed' Sets," *American Cinematographer* 23, no. 5 (1942): 246–47; Joseph Valentine, "Using an Actual Town Instead of Movie Sets," *American Cinematographer* 23, no. 10 (1942): 440–62.

45. James Wong Howe, "Documentary Film and Hollywood Techniques," in *Writers' Congress: The Proceedings of the Conference Held October 1943 under the Sponsorship of the Hollywood Writers' Mobilization and the University of California* (Berkeley: University of California Press, 1944), 94–96, reprinted as "Documentary Technique in Hollywood," *American Cinematographer* 25, no. 1 (1944): 10, 32; Biesen, *Blackout*; Thomas Doherty, *Projections*

of War: Hollywood, American Culture and World War II (New York: Columbia University Press, 1993).

46. For further reading regarding technological advances, see Biesen, *Blackout*, 74–75; see also Thomas Schatz, *Boom and Bust: American Cinema in the 1940s* (New York: Scribner, 1997); and Balio, *Grand Design*.

47. James Agee, "Sahara," *Nation*, October 8, 1943; Biesen, *Blackout*; Fred Stanley, "Blast at Hollywood," *New York Times*, July 30, 1944, X1.

48. The University of California, Berkeley, and the YMCA wrote to Warner Bros. to protest the film's inaccurate depiction of Hawaiian-Japanese sabotage.

49. Wilder's family in Europe was sent to Nazi concentration camps during the war and died in the Holocaust.

50. Thomas M. Pryor, "Filming Our Bombers over Germany," *New York Times*, March 26, 1944, X3; "Memphis Belle," *Variety*, March 22, 1944, 18; see also American Film Institute catalog; Mark Harris, *Five Came Back: A Story of Hollywood and the Second World War* (New York: Penguin, 2014).

51. Biesen, *Blackout*, 74–75; see also Schatz, *Boom and Bust*; and Balio, *Grand Design*.

52. For Wilder's commentary on shooting *Double Indemnity*, see Biesen, *Blackout*, 107; see also Sheri Chinen Biesen, *Film Censorship: Regulating America's Screen* (New York: Wallflower, 2018).

53. See Biesen, *Blackout*; Howe, "Documentary Film and Hollywood Techniques"; Doherty, *Projections of War*; Schatz, *Boom and Bust*; Balio, *Grand Design*.

CHAPTER 3

POSTWAR HOLLYWOOD, 1947–1967, PART 1

DOMESTIC LOCATION SHOOTING

Joshua Gleich

The semidocumentary emerged as a genre in 1945 and all but disappeared by the end of 1948, ending Hollywood's postwar experiment in extensive location shooting. In 1967, films such as *Bonnie and Clyde* (Arthur Penn, 1967) and *The Graduate* (Mike Nichols, 1967) heralded New Hollywood's rapid shift to shooting largely on location by the early 1970s. During the two decades in between, the major studios favored a hybrid approach to filmmaking, shooting for a few weeks on location, followed by as many as a few months on the soundstages and back lots. While early semidocumentaries such as *The House on 92nd Street* (Henry Hathaway, 1945) reduced production costs by shooting on location, projects such as *Dark Passage* (Delmer Daves, 1947) and *The Naked City* (Jules Dassin, 1948) showed that extensive location work in the 1940s more often raised production costs and added greater unpredictability to budgets and schedules. Nonetheless, the semidocumentary style continued to influence later location shooting strategies in postwar Hollywood, ranging from noirish police procedurals to location westerns and touristic sequences in various genres. Through the lens of the semidocumentary, location shooting and realism became synonymous in trade-industry accounts; yet behind the scenes and onscreen, location shooting offered as much fantasy as actuality of place.

The reasons for Hollywood's hybrid approach were economic. Despite several technological and logistical developments, location shooting cost more than shooting on the lot, except for filmmakers willing to sacrifice accepted standards of Hollywood cinematography. Yet for early semidocumentaries, widescreen extravaganzas, and realist dramas such as *Anatomy of a Murder* (Otto Preminger,

1959), real locations added production value for audiences. Thus, every frame that filmmakers shot on location raised the implicit question, Was it more effective or more efficient than shooting the scene on the back lot? While this threshold varied for different studios and different filmmakers, a certain consensus arose. Second unit crews shot scenic locations whenever stars were absent from the shot or could not be covered by body doubles. First unit crews captured exterior shots of the stars in distinctive locations, particularly entrances and exits, establishing their physical presence within the location. Then crews returned to the studio to shoot nearly every interior setting and generic exterior, usually the lion's share of the film. Rather than supplanting studio filmmaking during this period, location shooting provided a supplement to preexisting production techniques.

Shooting abroad, Hollywood took advantage of frozen funds in Europe and coproduction deals that could compensate for the additional expenses of location shooting in historic locations. No such opportunities existed domestically. Local and state filmmaking incentives amounted to the willing support of local elected officials and starstruck residents. Outside of Los Angeles, New York, and by the mid-1960s, Miami, there were no professional-grade studios to provide equipment, personnel, or backup sets for visiting crews. Hollywood unions demanded standbys, members paid for the lost opportunity to work on location, and sought other forms of compensation for location shoots in the United States that they failed to secure abroad. Prior to an explosion of new technologies that reduced the cost of location shooting in the late 1960s and early 1970s, filmmakers working on location domestically could only defray additional costs through innovation in production practices. Here, semidocumentary techniques and other new shooting methods, including television production, allowed a handful of filmmakers to expand location work beyond the typical hybrid approach.

As B pictures faded in the 1950s, independent production companies working on modest budgets shot more extensively on location. Often lacking physical production facilities and rear projection capabilities, while having little room in the budget to build new sets, these filmmakers could more economically add production value by shooting exciting locations. Filming in Moab, Utah, *Canyon Crossroads* (1955) avoided set building entirely, shooting almost exclusively outdoors against a western mountainscape and otherwise relying on buildings left over from previous location productions.[1] *Cry Terror!* (1958), an inexpensive thriller, took advantage of New York City sites that producers could not afford to recreate.[2] Production companies with tighter budgets proved more inclined to sacrifice cinematographic quality for dramatic settings. Semidocumentary style helped to justify aesthetic compromises, from handheld camerawork to inadequate lighting, as markers of realism.

As for A pictures, Otto Preminger was the salient example of an independent producer-director who pushed the boundaries of shooting on location in the United States and Canada. At Fox, Preminger worked on an early CinemaScope feature, *River of No Return* (1954), shot in color in the Canadian Rockies to show off the new photographic capabilities of the widescreen process. He grew more ambitious by the late 1960s as an independent, shooting *Anatomy of a Murder* (1959) entirely on location in Michigan's Upper Peninsula. He continued to work extensively in domestic locations in Washington, DC, for *Advise and Consent* (1962) and New England for *The Cardinal* (1963). Preminger's success on location stemmed from his ability to take advantage of detailed location scouting, efficient production planning, local goodwill, and the various publicity opportunities provided through location work.

Preminger also exemplifies the inherent contradictions of location shooting and its associated realism during the postwar era. Rather than develop a new style or aesthetic for location work, Preminger and his crew relished the ability to creatively light and configure locations to function like studio sets. Ironically, this approach limited the scope and impact of location shooting. Matching the look of location footage to studio footage created a seamless diegetic universe, but it also subsumed real locations under the aesthetic dictates of a soundstage style. Preminger further demanded that real locations be altered to fit the story, rather than altering the scenario to fit the location. Preminger serves as a limit case for extensive location shooting in the postwar era, a practice that largely conformed real places to studio practices. In the second half of the 1960s, younger filmmakers began to offer a contrary approach to location shooting, allowing the practical and aesthetic demands of locations to dictate a new style of filmmaking.

FILMMAKING TECHNOLOGY ON LOCATION

A variety of technologies that facilitated location shooting gained industry acceptance in postwar Hollywood, including faster film stock, smaller lighting units, smaller cameras, and by the late 1960s, smaller sound-recording systems. Yet the adoption of these new tools not only suggested the growing importance of location shooting in postwar Hollywood filmmaking but also revealed how poorly equipped Hollywood was for extensive location shooting in the postwar era. Existing equipment designed for the soundstage often limited the effectiveness of new, more portable cameras and lights. As in later eras, technologies that reduced overall lighting requirements had the most substantial impact on location shooting, simultaneously offering time, money, and stylistic latitude to productions through quicker lighting setups and smaller crews.[3] Despite the development of portable cameras and lighting units, by the end of the semidocumentary boom in the late 1940s, rear-projected backgrounds still proved far more cost-effective than location shooting for a great majority of studio productions into the 1960s.[4]

At Fox, Louis De Rochemont, who produced and directed the *March of Time* newsreel series, pioneered the semidocumentary with *The House on 92nd Street* (1945), followed by *13 Rue Madeleine* (Henry Hathaway, 1947), both lensed by

Norbert Brodine. *13 Rue Madeleine* shot both exteriors and interiors entirely on location in New York, Boston, and Quebec, but the limitations were daunting. Setting up equipment in actual interiors for *13 Rue Madeleine* left barely enough room for the actors or camera operators. Meanwhile, each location required generators since professional lights demanded more power than household electricity could provide. Sound equipment designed for large studio stages proved just as cumbersome. All but one night exterior had to be shot day for night in order to get sufficient exposure.[5] Thus, Brodine's efficient and straightforward documentary style barely compensated for the large crew and massive equipment required to provide adequate lighting and sound.

More photosensitive film stock held the greatest potential for improving both the cost and aesthetics of location shooting by reducing the necessary light levels for every scene. However, Eastman did not offer significantly faster black-and-white stock until Tri-X debuted in 1953, and even this new stock produced a grainier image than the standard Plus-X.[6] Through the early 1950s, studios experimented with alternative film stocks and development processes, hoping to effectively shoot on location at lower levels of illumination, particularly at night. Universal tried shooting day-for-night scenes with infrared film to economize, rather than eliminate dark scenes from scripts due to location lighting expenses.[7] Paramount technicians found a less cumbersome solution, a development process known as latensification. Latensification could intensify lighting on exposed negative film, effectively adding up to two f-stops during development (similar to postflashing, a popular technique in the 1970s).[8] The studios realized the clearest benefits on location: "Production has been able to use many desirable locations which otherwise could not have been considered, either because of prohibitive lighting expense or because of restrictions which would have made it impossible to bring in the necessary lighting."[9]

Black-and-white stock continued to improve over the course of the 1950s. In 1961, Eastman Kodak's Film Department director, Don Hyndman, reflected on the key changes. While Tri-X greatly facilitated night-for-night shooting, "a tremendous boost toward ultimate realism,"[10] Kodak's Double-X rendered it obsolete in 1960. Double-X was twice as fast as Plus-X, the industry standard, yet with almost identical sharpness and far less grain than Tri-X. According to Hyndman, "light and speed problems were no longer a detriment in photographing a motion picture," resolving the primary challenges to location filmmaking for black-and-white films.[11] According to the director Jack Garfein, who shot *Something Wild* (1961) on location in New York, frequent sunlight, a fundamental reason why Los Angeles became the center of the American film industry, was no longer an asset. This was no consequence of smog but a result of faster film stock. For black-and-white filmmakers, the Southern California sun sometimes shined too bright to optimally shoot more light-sensitive negatives.[12]

Color film stock could not keep pace with black and white, although it improved dramatically in the late 1950s and early 1960s.[13] Following the debut in 1953 of Eastman's one-strip process, it steadily gained on the cumbersome three-strip process, becoming the industry standard by 1958. Yet the single-strip process came at a price, necessitating large, high-intensity tungsten lights; these behemoth units made sets unbearably hot, took up a great deal of room, and raised electricity costs.[14] The adoption of various widescreen formats in the mid-1950s also demanded more light, limiting the hours of day that locations could be captured effectively.[15] In 1962, the introduction of the faster Eastman 5251 color stock finally allowed filmmakers to switch to smaller lights and lower illumination levels in most situations.[16] Lights designed for soundstage production suffered from fluctuating color temperatures, which had to be carefully monitored to match daylight color temperatures on location.[17] With the introduction of the wide-angle Angénieux lens in the late 1950s, black-and-white filmmakers could reach exposure under almost any conditions.[18] Color did not reach that standard until the early 1970s. Hence the bright daylight New York locations for *West Side Story* (Robert Wise, 1961) stood in stark contrast to the shadowy locations for *The Hustler* (Robert Rossen, 1961); this technological disparity further reinforced the generic distinction between scenic color locations and less picturesque, "realist" black-and-white locations.

Large lighting units proved particularly costly and inefficient on location. Arc lights offered high-intensity light but required massive generators, operators for the generators, and trained operators for each individual light. They frequently smoked and flickered, halting the shoot while operators changed carbons and then waited minutes for them to fully ignite.[19] Many interior locations simply could not accommodate these units or, in doing so, left little room for actors, other personnel, and additional equipment. Such difficulties helped spur more efficient lighting units. Around 1948, Universal developed the quad light, a rectangular metal pan that held four photoflood bulbs. These lights, primarily used by amateur photographers, helped light small location interiors for *The Naked City* (1948). The new lighting units, which could be powered by utility lines, also reduced the need for generators. When William Daniels won the Oscar for Best Cinematography, he helped legitimize the application of these photofloods for Hollywood location shooting. Photofloods proved particularly handy for shooting night exteriors; Robert Surtees attached them to streetlights to capture night-for-night scenes in the film noir *Act of Violence* (Fred Zinnemann, 1949).[20]

A powerful new halogen light, the Sun Gun, debuted in 1962, and Hollywood quickly adopted it for location shooting. The three-pound, one-thousand-watt light provided five thousand watts of exposure and joined an array of photo lights as a staple of black-and-white location production. The cinematographer Hal Mohr called it the greatest improvement in lighting equipment in thirty years.

John Frankenheimer used Sun Guns to light the Madison Square Garden cat-
walks for *The Manchurian Candidate* (1962). On the television series *Shannon*,
D. P. Phil Tannura found another important application for the Sun Gun; using
two lights with a car-mounted 35 mm Arriflex, he captured two characters driving without using a process shot.[21] In 1964, the familiar, through-the-windshield
process shot still relied on a blue-screen process for color film; by 1962, black and
white could accomplish the same on location.[22]

Faster lenses also helped reduce lighting requirements. In the early 1960s,
Panavision developed new lenses that both captured more light and reduced
camera size. One of these, the Ultra-Speed Panatar, promised to revolutionize
35 mm filmmaking in color. During camera tests, cinematographers captured
night scenes with only a lighted store window as the key light. William Daniels,
who innovated low-intensity lighting on *Naked City* (1948), raved about the new
lens, capable of shooting long shots with light levels as low as forty foot-candles.[23]

Like lighting technology, new cameras with greater maneuverability opened
up new spaces to location filming. The first truly portable 35 mm cameras were
developed for World War II combat and had an immediate impact on the late
1940s semidocumentaries. *Dark Passage* (1947) relied on an early Arri, brought
back from Germany by a Warner Bros. employee, for its subjective location shots
of San Francisco through the eyes of Humphrey Bogart's character.[24] Unlike the
American Eyemo, the Arri offered direct reflex viewing, allowing the camera
operator to see a reflection of the image captured by the camera lens. For the
first time, professional cinematographers could see an accurate image while they
filmed, which proved particularly useful outside the controlled studio environment.[25] While undergoing periodic redesigns, the Arriflex camera remained a
staple of location filmmaking through the 1970s, facilitating camera movement
in cramped interiors, uneven ground, and other locations that prevented laying
dolly track.

Sound technology remained laggard in its adaptation to location work. The
Nagra, a thirteen-pound, sync-sound recording device, debuted in 1958; yet it
was slow to gain acceptance in Hollywood. When it received an Academy Award
in 1965, it primarily served as a tool for documentary and low-budget independent filmmakers.[26] The consequences are readily apparent in almost any film
shot on location from the mid-1940s to the mid-1960s. Scenes shot on location
involving dialogue are frequently static or recorded on a soundstage with rear
projection, except when wide shots allow for reasonable postsync dubbing. For
instance, *Vertigo* (Alfred Hitchcock, 1958), famous for its use of San Francisco,
features almost no dialogue captured on location in the city.

Although rear projection can appear staged to contemporary viewers, postwar
filmmakers described it almost synonymously with location realism, and thus it
remained a vital technology in their conception of location shooting. For example, Joseph LaShelle, who won an Oscar for shooting *Laura* (Otto Preminger,

1944), described the practice on *Under My Skin* (Jean Negulesco, 1950) as follows: "A majority of studio action was filmed against process plates provided by scenes shot on location, following the usual procedure of staging live action in front of translucent screens on which background scenes are projected by rear projection. Thus the authenticity of backgrounds was maintained throughout."[27] LaShelle suggests that photographic backgrounds of real settings added more realism than staged settings, regardless of the fact that the actors and real settings were never physically copresent. For LaShelle, "closer shots filmed in the studio must match the location quality as closely as possible while at the same time achieving the amount of technical finish one expects from Hollywood major studio cinematography."[28] Rather than adapting Hollywood standards to real locations, Hollywood cinematographers largely sought to adapt real locations to Hollywood's photographic standards, typical of the aesthetic balancing act that Patrick Keating describes in *Hollywood Lighting*.[29] Unrefined, "documentary" realism was relegated to low-budget features.

In fact, improvements in rear projection help explain the gap between technological innovations in location shooting between the late 1940s and early 1960s. In a 1958 *American Cinematographer* article, Joe Henry summarized the advances in process photography: "One of the most highly perfected of cinematic sciences is that of background projection and process photography, which is employed in nearly every major feature film production today."[30] While backgrounds shot on location remained the norm after the semidocumentary boom of the late 1940s, they could now be easily combined with foreground action shot at the studio. Widescreen and color increased the cost and complexity of location shooting at the same time that new technology lowered the cost of process photography.

Other minor technological developments suggest just how far Hollywood had to come to embrace extensive location shooting. In 1948, the cinematographer Robert Burks devised a mobile film lab that promised to save hours of work for assistant camera operators, who could spend up to three hours after shooting working in makeshift darkrooms and another two hours transporting equipment to and from locations.[31] This production vehicle anticipated the Cinemobile of the early 1970s, which neatly packaged feature-production equipment into a single van or truck; by contrast, Burks's seven-thousand-pound, twenty-two-foot trailer merely held equipment for a single production department.

Norbert Brodine described the first semidocumentary, *The House on 92nd Street*, as "an almost complete reversal of previously standardized studio techniques."[32] This suggests just how significant a technological overhaul was necessary to expand Hollywood's postwar location shooting practices. The late 1940s saw several innovations that jerry-rigged existing technologies, such as photofloods, to meet the demands of location shooting. Technologies developed specifically for location shooting, including faster stock and new lights, only began to arrive in the early 1960s. This raises the question of why studios embraced various forms of location shooting throughout this period, a question that ties the economics of specific location productions to the larger economics of studio planning.

The Hollywood studios thrived on building realistic settings within the confines of soundstages, back lots, and ancillary sites, such as the Warner Bros. Ranch. Thus, the decision to shoot a wave of semidocumentaries in various cities cannot be solely attributed to realist aesthetics or technological innovations, which proved inadequate in reducing production costs. Rather, as William Lafferty details, the postwar semidocumentary boom of 1945–48 directly responded to quickly rising set-construction costs and overhead expenses, as well as violent labor unrest.[33] While semidocumentary techniques persisted in films such as *Panic in the Streets* (Elia Kazan, 1950) and *The Sniper* (Stanley Kramer, 1952), this roughly three-year experiment with extensive location shooting revealed that the expense of semidocumentary-style location shooting was hard to predict (because of production delays) and often just as expensive as set building.[34] Instead, by the early 1950s, Hollywood pruned production budgets and production schedules, favoring careful planning and cost assessment over new production techniques. As a result, domestic location shooting became primarily a supplement to studio-based filmmaking rather than a viable alternative.

Prolonged location shooting, mainly centered in American cities, peaked between April 1946 and August 1947. *Variety* ran headlines such as "Studios Broaden Program of Filming Yarns in Real Locale" and "WB Scatters Units to 4 Winds: Locationing Hits Record High."[35] By August 1947, RKO had twelve pictures in production but only two shooting on the home lot.[36] While filmmakers and studios continued to cite realism as a reason for shooting on location, *Variety* made the economic incentives explicit in a June 10, 1947, headline: "Studio Is Saving Set Costs thru Location Lensing." The article begins, "Studios are shopping around for stories which can easily be filmed on actual locations, thus eliminating costs of set construction. During past six months this item has become so major an expense factor that plenty of story properties have been shelved." Prestigious realist films were no exception. For instance, "Mark Hellinger currently is filming 'The Naked City' in New York as direct outgrowth of upped set costs." [37]

While *Naked City* exemplified the economic incentives for location shooting, it also proved how this practice could be a false economy in the late 1940s. The production incurred $42,688 in travel expenses, including $5,958 for eighteen round-trip air tickets to New York and $4,455 for eleven round-trip rail tickets. Hotel meals and lodging for cast and crew totaled $22,735. Director Dassin and cinematographer Daniels needed hotel rooms for seventy-five days. Meanwhile, an additional $3,000 went to feeding New York crews and extras.[38] Mayor William O'Dwyer actively courted Hollywood filmmakers to shoot in New York, promising "full cooperation of [the] city."[39] Yet the *Naked City* expense report lists miscellaneous expenses of $10,000 for the New York Police Department Athletic Fund and $7,500 for "Gratuities and Entertainment for New York Police," suggesting that "full cooperation" came at a price.[40]

Variety noted Hellinger's flight to New York to begin *Naked City* on the front page of its August 18, 1947, edition. Yet the lead headline, "Slice Film Costs 30%," suggested that location shooting alone could not solve Hollywood's production-expense crisis. The imposition of a 75 percent tax in Hollywood's most important foreign market, Britain, was the final straw that motivated an industry-wide effort to reduce production costs by 30–40 percent.[41] While Hollywood continued its efforts to lower construction costs and, less successfully, star salaries, several studios decided to freeze production until scripts and budgets could be finalized to ensure continuous shooting. Executives also targeted wastefulness in scripts and shooting practices. In 1947, semidocumentaries appeared to be a cheaper alternative to expensive, set-bound pictures. By 1948, expensive productions such as *The Naked City* and *Dark Passage* suggested that extensive location shooting added as many new costs as it saved in set construction, including production delays caused by inclement weather and logistical problems that exacerbated "shooting waste."

Fox's production head, Darryl Zanuck, detailed these new economic restrictions on production in a series of late-1940s memos. In May 1947, he addressed Fox's directors, including Elia Kazan, Ernst Lubitsch, Joseph Mankiewicz, Otto Preminger, and John Stahl, with a point-by-point criticism of working methods, made "critically urgent" in light of the industry's economic struggles. First, he emphasized preplanning, noting that, "Even if *only one* superfluous angle per day is shot, this could easily add six to nine days to a schedule."[42] In a similar December 1949 memo accompanied by a detailed spreadsheet, Zanuck emphasized the 1,652 feet of footage per film that never reached the screen. Over the course of twenty-three pictures in 1949, this cost $2,226,000, or "the *physical cost* of approximately four feature 'A' productions."[43] By point of comparison, Dassin and Hellinger shot nearly 225,000 feet of film for *The Naked City*; this length was nearly equivalent to the first cut of all of Fox's twenty-three features combined![44] Dassin shot a less ambitious semidocumentary for Fox in 1949, *Thieves' Highway*, capturing real location footage in San Francisco's large produce market. Zanuck marked this picture's 2,820 feet of eliminated footage with an asterisk, noting, "These pictures, in respect of added scenes and retakes, are of special interest."[45] The unpredictability of partially controlled, actual locations made semidocumentaries particularly prone to overshooting and retakes. As Hollywood studios pursued more careful cost oversight, location shooting offered poor accountability compared to soundstage production.

Tighter budgets far from ended location shooting, but they helped bring an end to the extensive, first unit location shooting that defined the semidocumentary boom of the postwar era. Urban semidocumentaries such as *Panic in the Streets* (1950), shot in New Orleans, became more infrequent. A genre noted for blunt social critiques and left-wing filmmakers, it was particularly vulnerable to the political pressure of the House Un-American Activities hearings and the blacklist.[46] With that fact and the poor box-office showings for *Panic in the Streets* and *Asphalt Jungle* (John Huston, 1950), Zanuck largely abandoned the semidocumentary genre that Fox had pioneered.[47] By the 1950s, "semidocumentary" was more often a style than a genre, an unvarnished method of location shooting that was most prevalent in moderately budgeted crime films such as *Pick Up on South Street* (Sam Fuller, 1953) and *The Lineup* (Don Siegel, 1958).

Meanwhile, location shoots were strictly budgeted, allowing little room to add extra days for production difficulties. William Wellman shot *Across the Wide Missouri* in 1951 for MGM, a studio often synonymous with lavish productions. Amid rain and snow, Wellman's crew hurriedly switched between multiple alternative setups to match previously shot footage. His comment "No time for weather" headlined an *American Cinematographer* article on the production, a clear contrast to semidocumentaries such as *Dark Passage*, for which producers waited out several rainy days in San Francisco.[48] Through the 1960s, films shooting on location often returned to the studio before completing their location schedule, once the cost of additional sets appeared cheaper than the cost of remaining on location.

The development of widescreen processes in the mid-1950s provided a clear economic incentive for location shooting. As John Belton argues in *Widescreen Cinema*, new technologies briefly restored the novelty phase of film spectatorship.[49] Cinerama confirmed this thesis, relying on outdoor travelogues of spectacular European and American locations for its earliest hits, such as *This Is Cinerama* (Merian Cooper, 1952) and *Cinerama Holiday* (Robert Bendick / Philippe De Lacy, 1955).[50] Location shooting in the American West became a prominent part of widescreen, color, A westerns such as *River of No Return* (1954) and *How the West Was Won* (John Ford / Henry Hathaway / George Marshall, 1962). At the same time, widescreen formats added to the expense of location shooting. Shooting in Cinerama created major challenges for filmmakers, including lens distortion, high-intensity lighting requirements, and difficulty moving the three cameras during production without causing image distortion across the three screens in exhibition.[51] Even the less cumbersome CinemaScope added to the location lighting burden, particularly when Fox paired it exclusively with color during the first half of the 1950s. Despite these expenses, the technology had the unintended consequence of raising the standards for studio sets. In a 1956 *Variety* article on runaway production, one executive noted how widescreen processes "so cruelly show up any artificial note," pushing productions to shoot more scenes and backgrounds on location rather than shoulder the expense of more meticulously realistic sets.[52] In the early 1960s, 70 mm processes had a similar effect, adding to the scale and expense of set building while greater photographic clarity revitalized the production value of location footage.

The cost versus reward of shooting on location largely depended on the scale of the production. For a major Hollywood feature, location costs could be insignificant compared to the above-the-line costs for major stars and directors. "Semi-independent" producers such as Alfred Hitchcock, whose use of the Paramount lot was factored into his multipicture deal with the studio, could choose to shoot certain locations for aesthetic purposes and complete the rest of the picture under the technical control of a soundstage.[53] For example, the first unit shooting schedule for *Vertigo* (Alfred Hitchcock, 1958) called for eleven shooting days on location and twenty-nine days in studio.[54] Independent producers unaffiliated with a studio, who by 1957 produced 40 percent of Hollywood features, often preferred shooting on location to the often-exorbitant rental rates for studio space.[55] For instance, *The Indian Fighter* (André De Toth, 1955), the first film for Kirk Douglas's new independent company, Bryna Productions, shot entirely on location in Bend, Oregon, a rare feat for mid-1950s Hollywood.[56]

While European productions continued to dominate location shooting away from Hollywood, the early 1960s brought a renewed emphasis on domestic location shooting. *Variety* suggested that by the end of the 1950s, there were no longer clear economic benefits derived from shooting abroad or featuring foreign locales, as added expenses nullified the money saved through financial incentives.[57] The directors William Wyler and Robert Aldrich returned from making European-based epics abroad to make smaller-budget American films such as *The Children's Hour* (William Wyler, 1961) and the surprise hit *Whatever Happened to Baby Jane?* (Robert Aldrich, 1962). The growing clout of independent producer-directors and stars allowed them not only to pursue lucrative productions in Europe but also to produce dozens of dark, challenging story properties, the vast majority shot in black and white in American locations. A wave of early-1960s films shot in and around New York City, including *Butterfield 8* (Daniel Mann, 1960), *The Hustler* (1961), and *Long Day's Journey into Night* (Sidney Lumet, 1962), paired real locations with realist dramas that sought to challenge Hollywood "make-believe" in both aesthetics and theme.[58]

Throughout the postwar era, Hollywood unions fought to combat runaway production to foreign locations. While prompting two congressional probes, in 1962 and 1966, they saw few results, and unemployment continued to spike during Hollywood's periodic booms in European production. The unions' greatest achievement came in 1963 when they helped end the total-tax exemption for stars working abroad for eighteen consecutive months, which had helped drive Hollywood's foreign production glut.[59] Prior to 1963, a major star such as Elizabeth Taylor could insist that *Cleopatra* (Joseph Mankiewicz, 1963) shoot abroad to lower her tax burden, and relatedly, this distant location helped contribute to the film's exorbitant production costs.[60] But in large part, producers successfully argued that an audience demand for realism, not economics, drove European location shooting.[61] As a consequence, studios shied away from the contemporary practice of doubling cheaper foreign locations for American ones, which would contradict this public stance. Films set in America almost exclusively featured footage shot in America. But without foreign financial incentives to compensate for additional costs and inefficiencies working on location, filmmakers had to employ new, more flexible production methods in order to compete with films shooting extensively abroad or on the studio lot.

LOGISTICS ON LOCATION

Pragmatically, Hollywood emphasized locations that could not be replicated on the studio lot. This largely eliminated suburban locations outside of Southern California, where studios avoided the major location expense of housing and transporting the cast and crew, as well as the need to pay standby workers in Los Angeles due to union contracts.[62] The most ambitious location shoots concentrated on urban and rural locations, whose respective architectural and landscape scales would be expensive to reproduce on the back lot. Crowds and cramped interiors were the most formidable obstacles to working in cities. Remoteness and lack of infrastructure created major difficulties in rural locations.

The semidocumentary again illustrates of the scope of challenges that Hollywood needed to overcome in order to shoot efficiently (and thus economically) on location. *The Naked City*'s ambitious semidocumentary strategy was a logistical nightmare. Producer Mark Hellinger had to airmail all the dailies to Los Angeles for screening. New York had no procedure for approving so many location shoots at one time, requiring individual permits for each of the 107 locations at least a day in advance. Meanwhile, thirty-four exterior locations drew large crowds. At one point, the crew hired a juggler to draw onlookers away from the set. In order to grab street scenes without alerting pedestrians, Daniels used a camera hidden behind a mirrored-glass window of a van. This concealment proved effective but reduced exposure by at least two f-stops.[63] Two decades later, films such as *The Graduate* still relied on hidden cameras, which allowed for Dustin Hoffman and Katherine Ross, then unknown actors, to mingle with unsuspecting hippies at a Sunset Strip music venue while the camera rolled from across the street.[64]

The difficulty of shooting in a major city was profound in 1961, when John Frankenheimer shot *The Young Savages* in Spanish Harlem. Indeed, *American Cinematographer* reflected the colonialist bravado of location shooting, describing a neighborhood where "even the police tread lightly, . . . a jungle loaded with ominously restless 'natives.'"[65] In order to infiltrate a crowded neighborhood,

Frankenheimer had to coordinate both offscreen and onscreen strategies. Local actors cast as gang members helped negotiate a payment to two youth gang leaders, who controlled their turf to facilitate shooting. The dynamic opening sequence, in which several actors rush through the streets toward the scene of a stabbing, spreads across several unbarricaded city blocks. Using battery-powered handheld cameras on luggage trucks, one cameraman trailed the actors; once a crowd of onlookers formed around the camera, a second camera wheeled after the actors, while the initial camera served as a decoy. Frankenheimer would continue to steal shots with handheld cameras in difficult situations, particularly in *Seven Days in May* (1964). He managed to capture a staged protest and fight in front of the White House, while grabbing a shot of Kirk Douglas entering the Pentagon without a permit.[66]

While urban location shooting necessitated aesthetic compromises to manage people, rural location shooting could represent a fight against nature itself. *The Palomino* (Ray Nazarro, 1950), Columbia's first feature shooting on Technicolor's new Monopack system, searched to find both mountains and green grass at the wrong time of year. This sent them to the Santa Susana Mountains, a beautiful but undeveloped location only twenty-five miles from Hollywood. In order to shoot there, the studios had to construct ten miles of mountain road. At the end of this road, pack mules carried the camera equipment. The grass did not prove green enough for Technicolor, so the crew deployed fifteen thousand gallons of paint to cover grass and fire-damaged trees. On a fourteen-day shoot, the filmmakers saw only a single clear day. Meanwhile, they waited up to four days to view dailies.[67] The price to photograph a beautiful natural location could quickly outstrip the price of recreating it on the lot.

Unpredictable weather remained a greater factor in remote locations, not just because of a lack of transportation infrastructure but because the entire photographic field could change. Early snow completely transformed the look of *Ride the High Country* (Sam Peckinpah, 1962), whose tight budget precluded waiting out the weather or changing locations. *The Defiant Ones* (Stanley Kramer, 1958), while eschewing its southeastern story setting, shot 80 percent of its location work in frigid rain throughout Southern California, building a "stark, cold and unfriendly atmosphere."[68] It went on to win the Academy Award for best black-and-white cinematography, but perhaps scarred by the experience, Stanley Kramer shot *Ship of Fools* (1965), which took place at sea, entirely on the studio lot.[69] Night exteriors proved particularly difficult, especially in color, with the need to rely on natural light to capture backgrounds. *American Cinematographer* marveled that the 1959 western *They Came to Cordura* (Robert Rossen, 1959) featured no studio interiors.[70] But the film had to rely on blue-filtered day for night, which also appears throughout Anthony Mann's ambitious location westerns such as *The Naked Spur* (1953) and even late-1960s westerns such as *The Professionals* (Richard Brooks, 1966), which shot extensively in Nevada and

Death Valley.[71] In short, real locations often necessitated less natural lighting schemes than those captured at the studio.

LOCATION STYLE AND SEMIDOCUMENTARY AESTHETICS

Between 1947 and 1967, Hollywood employed several variations of the formative location style of the postwar period, the semidocumentary. Originally, this genre featured stories based on real events shot primarily in real locations.[72] Flattened lighting schemes and newsreel techniques, such as occasional handheld shooting, gave the imprimatur of realism while sidestepping the economic and logistical impossibility of matching Hollywood cinematography standards on location. Nonetheless, Fox was the only studio capable of producing popular semidocumentaries at a lower cost than studio production, with successful semidocumentaries such as *13 Rue Madeleine* and *Call Northside 777* (Henry Hathaway, 1948). Not coincidentally, these productions skewed closest to newsreel aesthetics.

The only unassailable element of semidocumentary style became shooting exteriors on location. These needed not be the actual place depicted: *13 Rue Madeleine* used Quebec as a stand-in for France. Interiors were overwhelmingly captured on soundstages, even for hallmarks of realism such as *The Naked City*. Generic interior spaces such as police stations, offices, and apartments could be affordably doubled by inexpensive studio sets, while avoiding the physical constraints of cramming studio equipment into interior locations. Soundstages allowed for a more realistic lighting scheme and a more natural staging of actors than real sites did.

As an A-picture genre, the semidocumentary largely disappeared by the 1950s, doomed by an industry-wide reduction in production expenses and a shrinking market for the downbeat, ripped-from-the-headlines stories that best suited this style of production.[73] As a production method, it was more sustainable for low-budget pictures with lower aesthetic standards, including a wave of "city confidential" films that appeared in the mid-1950s.[74] But certain techniques gleaned from these early location efforts proved effective for a rather different form of semidocumentary: the travelogue. Widescreen processes, particularly Cinerama, revived the attractiveness of location footage by producing it in full color on a grander scale. The "America the Beautiful" number in *This Is Cinerama* (1953) employed dazzling airplane and helicopter footage spanning the natural landmarks of the continent. Other popular, high-budget films, such as *On the Town* (Stanley Donen / Gene Kelly, 1949) and *North by Northwest* (Alfred Hitchcock, 1959), incorporated travel narratives into their plotlines, and through location panoramas and montages, interludes of pure scenic beauty momentarily supplanted the narrative progression.

While achieving a much-different tone than the sobering semidocumentaries of the late 1940s, these productions nonetheless employed similar strategies to maximize the value and efficiency of location shooting. Location work predominantly favored wide shots to capture the scale of landscapes and cityscapes. In keeping with classical Hollywood style, wide shots also minimized dialogue, which remained a challenge to capture on location. Aside from distinctive locations, such as the actual FBI grounds and offices featured in *The FBI Story* (Mervyn LeRoy, 1959), filmmakers continued to avoid interior locations in favor of the more conducive shooting environment of the studio.[75] On set, a "wild wall" could be easily removed to set up a camera angle that might require the wholesale destruction of a real building.

Semidocumentary techniques also expanded the range of location shooting for lower-budgeted film noirs. As the major studios produced more color features, independent producers often distinguished their products by promoting dramatic realism while taking full advantage of the economies of black-and-white location shooting. A husband-and-wife production team, Andrew and Virginia Stone, made headlines when *The Night That Holds Terror*, produced for $76,000, became a sleeper hit in 1955. The Stones shot and recorded sound entirely on location, never building a set or using a process shot.[76] Their style of quick location filmmaking became more common for many low- to medium-budget films, although it was not without jarring disadvantages. Shooting in the Holland Tunnel for *Cry Terror!* (1958) demonstrated the sensitivity of black-and-white film, but the fumes from generators running the lights sent the lead actress, Inger Stevens, along with several crew members, to the hospital for exhaust inhalation. Undeterred, the Stones kept shooting with Rod Steiger; as they emerged to a clutter of emergency vehicles attending to the crew, they shot the chaos to use for the film's closing image.[77]

Clearly, "the Stone method" was not suitable for star productions. And their ad hoc approach suggests that Hollywood location work remained an unpredictable, experimental practice throughout much of this era. Nonetheless, moderate-budget noirs such as *On Dangerous Ground* (Nicholas Ray, 1951), *Kiss Me Deadly* (Robert Aldrich, 1955), *The Lineup* (1958), and *Odds against Tomorrow* (Robert Wise, 1959) all went on location to gain production value without incurring the expense of elaborate set building. The speed of black-and-white film stock made this possible, although notably, all of these films feature extensive daylight location work. With some notable exceptions in each film, the high-contrast lighting of film noir proved more difficult to capture on location or required creative shot selection, such as the sea of headlights on the freeway that Mike Hammer overlooks in *Kiss Me Deadly*.

By 1960, the semidocumentary style began to incorporate other elements of documentary filmmaking, exemplified by the early work of John Frankenheimer. On *The Young Savages*, he deployed portable equipment and improvised, multi-camera shooting in order to shoot in Spanish Harlem. Like Blake Edwards and Sam Peckinpah, who would also shoot extensively on location, Frankenheimer came out of television, where shoestring budgets and immutable deadlines trained filmmakers to adjust their style to their immediate situation.[78] The film featured fluid camerawork and jarring compositions that were absent from the semidocumentaries of the 1940s and 1950s. Rather than the film newsreel, this style mimicked the run-and-gun technique of the television news exposé.[79] Shooting interiors on location also revealed urban realities beyond Hollywood's darkest fantasies. After working inside an actual railroad-style tenement, the art director realized that, as Herb Lightman recounted in *American Cinematographer*, "sets which had heretofore been considered sufficiently squalid were found to be vastly understated when compared to the real thing."[80] This experience of crossing the threshold of location facades not only provided more realistic location footage but also augmented the realism of the soundstage reproductions.

In the second half of the 1960s, filmmakers not only adapted the tools of cinema verité to narrative features but also brought a similar ethos of unadulterated realism. They faced a new challenge when Hollywood rapidly abandoned black-and-white film in the mid-1960s. Realist dramas such as *The Hustler* featured crisp, shadowy black-and-white location cinematography; now stark realism had to be achieved on color film, a format still strongly associated with less serious stories and more highly saturated hues. One solution was to desaturate color, as Burnett Guffey did on *Bonnie and Clyde*, which won the award for Best Cinematography.[81] Another solution involved shooting extensively on location, while employing the imprecise framings, camera movements, and lighting associated with late-1960s documentary and avant-garde filmmakers. This lack of polish became a badge of realism by comparison to the traditional Hollywood aesthetics that persisted in many Hollywood features.

Shooting *You're a Big Boy Now* (1966) for Francis Ford Coppola, Andrew Laszlo noted a "sharp turn" in Hollywood cinematography. Viewing the early camera tests, Coppola complained that they looked "too good." Rather than landmark sites, the film occurred in everyday New York locations, such as "a drug store or a meat market," and Coppola wanted his footage to "come as close to the actual look of these places as possible."[82] Laszlo credited these instincts to Coppola's background in student filmmaking. While old-guard filmmakers cautioned against certain techniques popularized by younger directors, they all faced the same paradigm shift. The growing scope and prominence of location shooting favored a new semidocumentary style, in which cinema verité techniques suggested greater realism and a stronger sense of place.

The same technological improvements that made interior lighting appear less stage bound also made interiors less stage based. *Bonnie and Clyde* shot almost entirely on location in Texas, spending ten weeks in small towns outside of Dallas. With the ability to shoot in actual building interiors, the crew could take advantage of a number of towns that had hardly changed their appearance since the 1930s. Thus, a string of holdups spanning Indiana to East Texas could all be covered by moving from town to town in North-Central Texas, without the time and cost of building or redressing studio sets. In fact, 1960s urban decline suited Depression-era period pieces. A "somewhat crumbling neighborhood in Dallas" resembled Joplin, Mississippi, in the 1930s.[83]

OTTO PREMINGER AND THE LIMITS OF LOCATION SHOOTING

In many ways, Otto Preminger followed the typical trajectory for location shooting in the postwar era. Working at Fox, he rarely shot on distant locations during the 1940s or early 1950s. One exception, *The Thirteenth Letter* (1951), required extensive negotiation with Zanuck for approval to shoot exterior scenes in Quebec, with the proviso that Preminger stay under the original budget.[84] This changed with Fox's aggressive promotion of CinemaScope, which elevated the budget for *River of No Return* (1954), allowing Preminger to shoot in scenic locations in the Canadian Rockies. Becoming an independent producer in 1954, Preminger shot more frequently on location, but only in Europe for *Saint Joan* (1957) and *Bonjour Tristesse* (1958); his domestic productions, such as *Carmen Jones* (1954), *The Man with the Golden Arm* (1955), and *Porgy and Bess* (1959), remained anchored on Hollywood back lots and a handful of California locations. Yet like other directors returning from Europe in the late 1950s, Preminger sought a way to extend domestic location shooting without the unpredictable tradeoff between financial incentives and production inefficiencies abroad.

Anatomy of a Murder (1959), shot entirely in small towns on Michigan's Upper Peninsula, set a high-water mark for domestic location shooting. While saving money on set building, Preminger and his crew still had to find a number of clever technical, logistical, and promotional strategies in order to keep the film on schedule and under budget. He adopted similar techniques working in Washington, DC, for *Advise and Consent* (1962) and in New England for *The Cardinal* (1963). Preminger's films largely replicated studio aesthetics on actual locations; thus, the behind-the-scenes challenges proved more striking than the actual impact of real locations onscreen. While proving the economic viability of location shooting by the early 1960s, Preminger failed to prove that it added much production value beyond the era's typical hybrid approach of combining limited location shooting of exteriors with soundstage interiors.

Despite the commercial success of *River of No Return*, it proved how easily remote location shooting could disrupt studio efficiency. First there was the physical danger of working outside studio environments. Marilyn Monroe twisted an ankle, delaying shooting, while several stuntmen working on the titular river were lucky to escape major injuries.[85] Another complication was matching studio reproductions of the rafting scenes, unsafe for stars to shoot on location, with rear projection setups in the studios. Zanuck exacerbated the issue of matching location and studio footage by demanding new scenes to clarify the

Figure 3.1. The primary location for *Anatomy of a Murder* (United Artists, 1959) is a courtroom, which had high ceilings that could more easily accommodate lights and other equipment.

story. Jean Negulesco directed these reshoots as Preminger moved on to his next project.[86] Realistically photographed, distant scenery added production value to the film, but it also introduced an image of the story world that would be almost impossible to recapture once the first unit returned to the studio. Fitting Fox's CinemaScope strategy, the scenic landscape shots of the Canadian Rockies outshone an unambitious western story, rather than making a vital contribution to the narrative.[87]

For an independent producer such as Preminger, *Anatomy of a Murder* provided clear advantages on location over *River of No Return*. Despite the film's long running time, the vast majority of it took place in a single setting, a courtroom, a location with high ceilings and wide floor space to accommodate equipment (figure 3.1). The story also lacked the action sequences that proved risky on *River*. The source novel for the film, a best-seller based on an actual trial in Michigan, allowed Preminger to promote the realism of shooting at the actual scene of the trial.[88] In fact, St. Martin's Press, publisher of the novel, also published a behind-the-scenes book about the production, *Anatomy of a Motion Picture*, which despite the requisite self-promotion, provides valuable insights into Hollywood's late-1950s approach to location shooting. Finally, shooting in black and white complemented a true crime drama but also reduced the light levels and eliminated the need to balance color temperatures.

Despite these advantages, other exigencies pushed Preminger's unconventional decision to shoot entirely on location. Working for United Artists, there was no requirement (or overhead charge) to use a physical studio lot. Through the 1960s, United Artists was the least likely major company to shoot in Holly-wood.[89] Ironically, time pressure also pushed Preminger to remain shooting in Michigan, despite the fact that location work was less efficient than back lot pro-duction. Hoping to capitalize on the novel's current best-seller status, *Anatomy* announced theatrical booking dates on the day it began production, probably an unprecedented strategy.[90] However, this allowed Preminger to sustain nearly continuous national and local press coverage, in part spurred by the novelty of the extensive location work. David Golding and his publicity unit interfaced with seventy or more news reporters during the eight-week shoot.

Rushing the film for a July 4 release required another unique strategy: editing the film and trailers on location in a three-room hotel suite. The only produc-tion task performed in Hollywood would be lab processing.[91] Editing on location helped ensure against retakes and helped produce further publicity, including a trailer that aired on *The Ed Sullivan Show* before the film was completed.[92] In yet another piece of publicity, *Variety* accurately described such extensive work on location as an "experiment," revealing how intimately the promotional and loca-tional practices for the film tied together.[93] Domestic location shooting relied on ancillary benefits, such as press attention or new production efficiencies, as a hedge against its added costs and unpredictability.

Although the most popular urban location outside of Los Angeles, New York, offered professional production facilities, less photographed locations such as Michigan's Upper Peninsula offered greater local support. The publicity for *Anatomy of a Murder* bragged of spending $500,000 in a depressed region while hiring one thousand local extras; for these efforts, Michigan named *Anatomy of a Murder* its Product of the Year.[94] Working with the book's author, Judge John Voelker, helped secure the key location, the courthouse, where the crew gained access to the entire second floor with the permission of the County Board of Supervisors. Rather than working out of trailers, they transformed the facilities into dressing rooms, wardrobe spaces, and a lunch area. The local Chamber of Commerce secured clearances for the whole town, effectively giving free rein to the filmmakers.[95] Cooperative locals also helped augment the production value of locations. Residents supplied a locomotive, a loading crane, and seventeen cars to enliven the background for a brief scene of Jimmy Stewart and Arthur O'Connell lunching by the waterfront. An authentic absence of seagulls appeared inauthentic on camera, so the crew spread thirty pounds of fish around to attract birds and complete the mise-en-scène (figure 3.2).[96]

Other scenes required more extensive manipulations of reality. As Merrill Schleier notes, building sets on location was common practice in the 1950s for major films such as *Giant* (George Stevens, 1956).[97] Preminger brought that film's art director, Boris Leven, on his early location trips, and Leven helped assure him that they could use the small town effectively like a back lot with added scenic value.[98] Leven built a new wing onto the side of a local motel in order to

Figure 3.2. Cooperative residents in Michigan's Upper Peninsula helped secure a crane (pictured), train, and seagulls that added local detail and dynamic movement to the background of this exterior location shot for *Anatomy of a Murder* (United Artists, 1959).

accommodate a tavern next door, the scene of the crime at the center of the film (figure 3.3).[99] This anecdote appears under the aptly titled section of *Anatomy of a Motion Picture*, "Adapting Reality to Film." Unlike later periods of location shooting, or movements like Italian neorealism, Hollywood sought to make real sites function like sets, rather than transform its soundstage style to better capture real locations. And despite unrestrained access to the town, there was little time in the tight production schedule to take advantage of dozens of locations. The production used only seven locations outside of the various sections of the courthouse.[100]

Despite the limited number of sites, director of photography Sam Leavitt found the location demands to be daunting. Preminger's crew could not drive nails into the plaster walls of the judge's eighty-year-old house, in which the largest room was ten by twelve feet. The jury box took over most of the courtroom, which required upward of six actors and two hundred extras; naturally Preminger, famous for long takes featuring camera movement, called for fifteen different camera moves despite the cramped quarters. A script change made on location called for a challenging through-the-windshield shot, with dialogue and without process photography or a camera car. A "Rube Goldberg" rig of lights and camera on a low-bed truck sufficed for the scene.[101] While Leavitt revealed only a handful of his techniques, the film's seven Oscar nominations, including for Best Cinematography, demonstrated how far portable equipment and black-and-white film had advanced for location shooting. Both exteriors and interiors could be effectively captured on location, although Preminger wisely avoided the additional handicap of persistent low-key lighting.

Nonetheless, aesthetic compromises had to be made to suit the location. Leavitt achieved studio-quality lighting for medium and close shots in the courtroom, placing lights in the balconies to compensate for the lack of an overhead rig. This proved impossible for wide shots, preventing a typical use of cross-lighting. Other interiors, including small rooms in Judge Voelker's actual home, forced Preminger to direct from outside the doorway when the equipment left him no room to stand inside.[102] Interior locations bedeviled cinematographers and directors accustomed to operating on large soundstages with removable walls and ceilings; meanwhile, they added far less production value, as interior sets replicated real places far more convincingly than exterior backdrops did.

Other environmental and geographical variables shaped the production. Hoping for a less wintry setting, Preminger filmed all of his interiors before moving outdoors later in the spring. This precluded the common practice of using standby interior locations during poor weather conditions. Working far from Hollywood, Preminger started shooting with his largest cast, included in the courtroom scenes, releasing additional actors as soon as possible rather than paying them to stand by on location or flying them in and out.[103] While the weather largely cooperated, sound continued to intrude on the production. Shooting at a local jail, prisoners began to flush toilets and make additional noise to interfere with the visiting filmmakers. Heavy industrial equipment, such as the local iron barges, had to occasionally be shut down for filming.[104] Once again,

Figure 3.3. Art director Boris Leven built a new addition onto a local hotel in order to create the tavern where the murder takes place, an example of filmmakers modifying real locations to fit the script of *Anatomy of a Murder* (United Artists, 1959).

local cooperation proved key in solving these problems; unlike in Los Angeles, a single Hollywood production was a remarkable event for the whole region.

As an experiment in extensive location shooting, *Anatomy of a Murder* appeared successful, finishing on time and becoming an acclaimed box-office hit. The irony, however, is how little the finished film benefited from this approach. Unlike *River of No Return*, there are no spectacular locations. While the exteriors were the sites of the actual events of the novel, based on a true story, they depict more or less a generic, American small town. Leavitt's successful work behind the scenes ensured that lighting setups, camera movements, and compositions resembled scenes shot on a soundstage. *Anatomy of a Murder* proved that in black and white, with a great deal of ingenuity, a film could be shot entirely on location on a comparable budget to a typical studio picture. Yet the question remained whether it was worth the Herculean effort if onscreen, it looked nearly identical to a set-bound production.

Preminger himself provided a fascinating definition of location realism, not as a product of pictorial realism but, rather, as a product of the actors' immersion in the actual location. By keeping the cast and crew for an extensive stay in Michigan, he argued, "We'll live through it together and that will help to make the film more 'real' than any single thing I could do."[105] He made an additional concession to his actors, shooting many of the courtroom scenes in sequence in order to sustain performances.[106] Preminger's famous long-take style probably helped compensate for this inefficiency, allowing him to cover minutes of screen time in a single shot while minimizing the need to shoot cutaways from multiple angles. Preminger sequestered the cast like members of a jury, providing greater control over their performances and promoting their identification with the real settings; in this sense, the location largely provided an indirect sense of realism through the actors, rather than directly as a visual setting.

Buoyed by the success of *Anatomy of a Murder*, Preminger employed similar location techniques for *Advise and Consent* and *The Cardinal*. *Advise and Consent* was also based on a recent best-seller with a clear promotional angle, as a salacious depiction of Washington, DC, politics with veiled references to actual figures and events. Preminger further pushed associations with current politics, casting Peter Lawford, John F. Kennedy's brother-in-law, and attempting to cast Martin Luther King Jr. as a senator.[107] These moves not only secured publicity but, in the case of Lawford, helped secure a shot at the White House. During the five-week location trip to Washington, DC, Preminger hosted weekly press banquets, again using location shooting to drive a national publicity campaign. Nonetheless, a major city and famous location proved less accommodating than rural Michigan. Unable to halt the government, Preminger had a replica of the Senate building constructed on the Columbia Studios lot.[108] *Advise and Consent* was a hybrid production, far more typical than the experimental, total location work on *Anatomy of a Murder*.

At a higher budget and shot in color, *The Cardinal* further illustrated inherent dilemmas for domestic location shooting. In *Variety*, the film's art director, Gerry O'Hara, boasted, "When on location you have to work within the confines of a particular situation and this adds realism because you are working with real situations."[109] This is a rather-circular logic that resembles Preminger's claims about acting; locations seemed to offer realism through offscreen conditions that remained hard to pinpoint onscreen. As for greater efficiencies working on location, O'Hara noted the expensive, time-consuming process of building sets at the studio lot. Yet working on location in Massachusetts, O'Hara built an entire church and shantytown in a local quarry at an $80,000 cost.[110] Thus, while taking advantage of certain preexisting locations, Preminger still relied on set building for other sequences. Working domestically, this came with an added cost. Preminger decried union "blackmail" when the International Alliance of Theatrical Stage Employees restricted Preminger from hiring local workers and forced him to pay standbys in Hollywood.[111] He also had to hire an additional art director from the guild in order to hire O'Hara, a British citizen with whom he worked on *Exodus* (1960).[112] Ironically, shooting on location closer to home could incur more costs than working farther abroad.

Even for Preminger, who pushed the boundaries of domestic location shooting, *Anatomy of a Murder* remained a limit case. On the one hand, it proved that working in black and white, Hollywood filmmakers had the technological and logistical capacity to shoot entirely on location by 1960. On the other hand, such productions had to be carefully circumscribed for ideal conditions that minimized location difficulties. Lisa Dombrowski has noted how *Hud* (Martin Ritt, 1963) took advantage of a seemingly unexceptional location, the barren plains of Texas, to create an effective, realistic atmosphere for the film.[113] Like *Anatomy*, *Hud* also took advantage of black-and-white film, a rural setting, and a realist story line that called for little spectacular action and no landmark locations. Yet these nondescript locations seemed tailor-made for shooting closer to Los Angeles, while more distinctive locations, such as major cities, proved far more difficult to affordably capture without studio work. With rare exception, the hybrid approach remained the most effective way to combine the pictorial advantages of location shooting with the logistical advantages of the studio environment.

Working on *The Cardinal*, O'Hara hinted at the creative potential in adapting cinematic techniques to the immediate conditions of the location. However, in Preminger's films, including later productions such as *Skidoo* (1968), this meant adapting behind the scenes in order to replicate the classical Hollywood style of cinematography developed on the soundstages. These efforts normalized location shooting but also limited its potential impact onscreen. Filmmakers such as John Frankenheimer, who incorporated unsteady, guerilla-style footage into several of his 1960s films, pointed ahead toward the larger shift in location shooting that began in the late 1960s. By the second half of the 1960s, films such as *You're a Big Boy Now, Bonnie and Clyde,* and *The Graduate* pushed this premise further, pursuing far less polished cinematography in order to exploit and accentuate the real conditions encountered on location.[114]

From the mid-1940s through the mid-1960s, Hollywood developed new tools and production strategies to accommodate location shooting into the existing system. With a greater emphasis on individual pictures following the Paramount Decision and a greater demand for scenic exteriors driven by the widescreen format, domestic location shooting, when properly controlled, offered surplus production value that was unattainable on the back lot. Pushing the boundaries of location shooting, as Preminger did, set new precedents but often proved self-defeating, as much of the location footage that was achieved at great difficulty proved indistinguishable from back lot productions. It took the major stylistic changes of the late 1960s and 1970s to alter this equation, ushering in a new semi-documentary style that was more closely aligned with direct cinema and cinema verité aesthetics. In the first two decades following World War II, existing techniques dictated Hollywood's use of locations; by the late 1960s, locations began to dictate new filmmaking techniques.

NOTES

1. "Canyon Crossroads," AFI Catalog of Feature Films, accessed November 2, 2017, www.afi.com/members/catalog/DetailView.aspx?s=&Movie=51455.

2. Walter Strenge, "Realism in Real Sets and Locations," *American Cinematographer,* October 1957, 650–51, 678–80.

3. Andrew Laszlo, "Recent Trends in Location Lighting," *American Cinematographer,* September 1968, 666–68, 696–97.

4. Julie Turnock, "The Screen on the Set: The Problem of Classical-Studio Rear Projection," *Cinema Journal* 51, no. 2 (2012): 157–62.

5. Herb Lightman, "13 Rue Madeleine," *American Cinematographer,* December 1948, 88–89, 110–11.

6. Barry Salt, *Film Style and Technology: History and Analysis,* 2nd ed. (London: Starword, 1992), 241.

7. Leigh Allen, "They Do It with Infra-Red!," *American Cinematographer,* October 1949, 360, 376–78.

8. Postflashing exposed the negative to additional light during development. See Edward Lipnick, "Creative Post-Flashing Technique for 'The Long Goodbye,'" *American Cinematographer,* March 1973, 278–81, 334–35, 328–29.

9. Hollis Moyse, "Latensification," *American Cinematographer,* December 1948, 409, 426.

10. Don Hyndman, "Steady Progress in Film Improvement," *American Cinematographer,* May 1961, 299, 316, 318.

11. Ibid.

12. "'Sunlight Dims as Hollywood's Trump'—Garfein," *Variety,* October 5, 1960, 17.

13. Salt, *Film Style and Technology,* 241–42.

14. Norwood Simmons, "The New Eastman Color Negative and Color Print Films," *American Cinematographer,* June 1962, 362–63, 385.

15. George Howard, "Design Improvements in High-Wattage Filament Lamps Respond to Studio Needs," *American Cinematographer,* April 1958, 228–29, 233–34.

16. Simmons, "New Eastman Color Negative and Color Print Films."

17. Arthur Gavin, "Location-Shooting in Paris for 'Gigi,'" *American Cinematographer*, July 1958, 424–25, 440–42.

18. Salt, *Film Style and Technology*, 244.

19. Herb Lightman, "Photographing without Arc Light," *American Cinematographer*, April 1970, 306–11, 344–45, 371.

20. Robert Surtees, "The Story of Filming 'Act of Violence,'" *American Cinematographer*, August 1948, 268, 282–84.

21. Fred Foster, "The Sun Gun Photo Light," *American Cinematographer*, May 1962, 292–93, 314–18.

22. Walter Beyer, "Travelling Matte Photography and the Blue-Screen System: Part II: Specifications for Equipment and Photography," *American Cinematographer*, January 1964, 34–44.

23. Darrin Scot, "Panavision's Progress," *American Cinematographer*, May 1960, 302, 304, 320–24.

24. "Notes on Experimental Camera Work," October 23, 1946, fol. 1858, Story—memos and correspondence, Warner Bros. Archives, Cinematic Arts Library, University of Southern California, Los Angeles, CA (hereafter Warner Bros. Archives).

25. Salt, *Film Style and Technology*, 230–31.

26. "The Academy Award–Winning Nagra Recorder," *American Cinematographer*, June 1966, 409–11, 432; Jay Beck, *Designing Sound: Audiovisual Aesthetics in 1970s American Cinema* (New Brunswick, NJ: Rutgers University Press, 2016), 30–31.

27. Herb Lightman, "Matching Location Footage with Studio Shots," *American Cinematographer*, June 1950, 216.

28. Ibid, 197.

29. Patrick Keating, *Hollywood Lighting from the Silent Era to Film Noir* (New York: Columbia University Press, 2010), 3–7.

30. Joe Henry, "The Science of Process Photography," *American Cinematographer*, January 1958, 36–37, 56.

31. Wilfrid Cline, "Mobile Camera Lab," *American Cinematographer*, December 1948, 410, 423.

32. Lightman, "13 Rue Madeleine," 110.

33. William Lafferty, "A Reappraisal of the Semi-Documentary in Hollywood, 1945–1948," *Velvet Light Trap* 20 (1983): 22–26.

34. For instance, *Dark Passage* (Delmer Daves, 1947), which starred Humphrey Bogart and shot extensively in San Francisco, took eighty days, compared to sixty days for a later Bogart picture, *Chain Lightning* (Stuart Heisler, 1950). See Mike Connolly, "Production Costs Cut 25%," *Variety*, January 4, 1950, 23.

35. "Studios Broaden Program of Filming Yarns in Real Locale," *Daily Variety*, October 24, 1946, 18; "WB Scatters Units to 4 Winds: Locationing Hits Record High," *Daily Variety*, July 3, 1947, 3.

36. "RKO Will Shoot 3 August Films on Location," *Daily Variety*, July 22, 1947, 6.

37. "Studio Is Saving Set Costs thru Locale Lensing," *Daily Variety*, June 10, 1947, 4.

38. Production Budget and Cost Sheet, June 4, 1947, fol. 34, *The Naked City*, Gil Kurland Papers, Margaret Herrick Library, Academy of Motion Picture Arts and Sciences, Beverly Hills, CA (hereafter Herrick Library).

39. "Studios Broaden," *Daily Variety*, October 24, 1946, 18.

40. Production Budget and Cost Sheet, June 4, 1947.

41. "Slice Film Costs 30%," *Daily Variety*, August 18, 1947, 1, 5.

42. Darryl Zanuck, memo, May 27, 1947, fol. 144, 20th Century-Fox, Lloyd Bacon Papers, Herrick Library.

43. Darryl Zanuck, memo, December 12, 1949, fol. 138, 20th Century-Fox, Henry King Papers, Herrick Library.

44. Sumiko Higashi, "Realism in Urban Art and *The Naked City*," in *Looking Past the Screen: Case Studies in American Film History and Method*, ed. Jon Lewis and Eric Smoodin (Durham, NC: Duke University Press, 2007), 368–69; Zanuck, memo, December 12, 1949.

45. Darryl Zanuck, memo, December 12, 1949.

46. Rebecca Prime, "Cloaked in Compromise: Jules Dassin's *Naked City*," in *"Un-American" Hollywood: Politics and Film in the Blacklist Era*, ed. Frank Krutnik, Steve Neale, Brian Neve, and Peter Stanfield (New Brunswick, NJ: Rutgers University Press, 2007), 144–45.

47. Darryl Zanuck to Henry King, June 14, 1950, Henry King Papers.

48. Daily production progress reports, October 29–November 30, 1946, fol. 1488, *Dark Passage* Production File, Warner Bros. Archives.

49. John Belton, *Widescreen Cinema* (Cambridge, MA: Harvard University Press, 1992), 14.

50. Ibid., 78–97.

51. Ibid., 94.

52. "Hollywood Bigness on the Wane: 'Runaway' Fears All Too Real," *Variety*, October 10, 1956, 3.

53. Peter Lev, *The Fifties: Transforming the Screen, 1950–1959* (Berkeley: University of California Press, 2006), 202.

54. *Vertigo* shooting schedule, September 26, 1957, fol. 13, Schedules, *Vertigo* Production File, Paramount Papers, Herrick Library.

55. Abel Green, "Show Biz: Pain-in-the-Brain," *Variety*, January 8, 1958, 50; "Sam Spiegel Attacks High Ratio of Distribution Costs to Grosses," *Variety*, August 8, 1956, 7, 12.

56. Frank Daugherty, "Shooting the Entire Picture on Location," *American Cinematographer*, August 1955, 474–75, 488.

57. Gene Arneel, "Home Is Where You Shoot: But O'Seas No Longer Cheap," *Variety*, June 15, 1960, 3, 16.

58. Ibid.

59. "All That Favors Runaway Due for Think-Through," *Variety*, January 4, 1963, 4; "D.C. Eyes Runaway Pix and TV—Again," *Variety*, August 31, 1966, 2.

60. Matthew Bernstein, *Walter Wanger, Hollywood Independent* (Berkeley: University of California Press, 1994), 352.

61. "Hollywood Bigness on the Wane," 3.

62. "Coast Kids Self: European Film Production Is Still Third Cheaper; Preminger Raps U.S. 'Standbys,'" *Variety*, January 30, 1963, 5, 24.

63. Herb Lightman, "The Naked City," *American Cinematographer*, May 1948, 152–53, 178–79.

64. Herb Lightman, "Cinematographer with a 'Split Personality,'" *American Cinematographer*, February 1968, 104–7, 132–34, 138–39, 142–44.

65. Herb Lightman, "Hazardous Assignment in an Asphalt Jungle," *American Cinematographer*, July 1961, 408–9, 435–37.

66. Ellsworth Fredricks, "Seven Days in May," *American Cinematographer*, October 1963, 586–87, 609–11.

67. Vincent Farrar, "Tough Assignment," *American Cinematographer*, February 1950, 48, 62–63.

68. Arthur Gavin, "'The Defiant Ones'—Ultimate in Mood Photography," *American Cinematographer*, August 1958, 484–85, 500, 502.

69. Herb Lightman, "Voyage on a Soundstage," *American Cinematographer*, January 1965, 28–29, 68.

70. Arthur Gavin, "Not an Interior in the Picture!," *American Cinematographer*, March 1959, 166–67, 191–92.

71. Herb Lightman, "The Photography of *The Professionals*," *American Cinematographer*, February 1967, 98–101, 114, 116–17.

72. Lisa Dombrowski, "Postwar Hollywood, 1945–1967," in *Cinematography*, ed. Patrick Keating (New Brunswick, NJ: Rutgers University Press, 2014), 63.

73. In a confidential memo, Darryl Zanuck, who helped pioneer the semidocumentary, encouraged directors to work economically and abandon downbeat themes. See Darryl Zanuck to Henry King, June 14, 1950, Henry King Papers.

74. Will Straw, "Urban Confidential: The Lurid City of the 1950s," in *The Cinematic City*, ed. David Clarke (London: Verso, 1997), 110–28.

75. Arthur Gavin, "Filming 'The F.B.I. Story,'" *American Cinematographer*, May 1959, 285–87, 305–7.

76. "Script Starting Point to Save," *Variety*, February 15, 1956, 10; "Stones, Married Producers, Beat Overhead, Never Build a Set," *Variety*, May 21, 1958, 5, 20.

77. Strenge, "Realism in Real Sets and Locations," 650–51, 678–80.

78. Vaughn Shaner, "New Double-X Pan Twice as Fast as Plus-X," *American Cinematographer*, August 1960, 484–85, 493–94.

79. Bob Allen, "Shooting Under Cover with Available Light," *American Cinematographer*, August 1963, 466–67, 483–84.

80. Lightman, "Hazardous Assignment," 436.

81. Scott Higgins, *Harnessing the Technicolor Rainbow: Color Design in the 1930s* (Austin: University of Texas Press, 2009), 217.

82. Laszlo, "Recent Trends in Location Lighting," 666–68, 696–97.

83. Morton Beebe and J. Bruce Hayes, "Tinseltown on the Bay," *San Francisco Sunday Examiner and Chronicle*, August 22, 1971, 10–12, "Locations-CA, San Francisco," Clippings file, Herrick Library.

84. Foster Hirsch, *Otto Preminger: The Man Who Would Be King* (New York: Knopf, 2011), 172.

85. Brian Brennan, *Romancing the Rockies* (Markham, ON: Fifth House, 2005), 177–78.

86. Chris Fujiwara, *The World and Its Double: The Life and Work of Otto Preminger* (New York: Faber and Faber, 2008), 156–58; Hirsch, *Otto Preminger*, 205–7.

87. Brennan, *Romancing the Rockies*, 179.

88. Fujiwara, *World and Its Double*, 235–36.

89. Tino Balio, *United Artists: The Company That Changed the Film Industry* (Madison: University of Wisconsin Press, 1987), 89–91; "Whole World as UA's Background," *Variety*, June 24, 1959, 12.

90. Robert Landry, "Bureau of Missing Business," *Variety*, March 25, 1959, 19.

91. "Detroit Preems 'Anatomy': Preminger Edited Film on Location as Shot," *Variety*, May 13, 1959, 15; Landry, "Bureau of Missing Business."

92. Richard Griffith, *Anatomy of a Motion Picture* (New York: St. Martin's, 1959), 111–12, 116.

93. "Tout Value of Filming Off Lot," *Variety*, May 20, 1959, 1, 78.

94. Ibid.

95. Griffith, *Anatomy of a Motion Picture*, 45, 82.

96. Sam Leavitt, "Filming 'Anatomy of a Murder' in the Story's Actual Locale," *American Cinematographer*, July 1959, 416–17, 443.

97. Merrill Schleier, "Postwar Hollywood, 1947–1967," in *Art Direction and Production Design*, ed. Lucy Fischer (New Brunswick, NJ: Rutgers University Press, 2015), 86.

98. Griffith, *Anatomy of a Motion Picture*, 25.

99. Ibid., 87–89.

100. Ibid., 85.

101. Leavitt, "Filming 'Anatomy of a Murder.'"

102. Ibid.

103. Griffith, *Anatomy of a Motion Picture*, 30.

104. Ibid., 87.

105. Ibid., 25–26.

106. Ibid., 60–62.

107. Hirsch, *Otto Preminger*, 351; "Amusements Dubious on Negro Solon Bit," *Variety*, October 25, 1961, 20.

108. Hirsch, *Otto Preminger*, 352–53.

109. Gerry O'Hara, "British Asst. Director, Touts Value of Shooting outside Studio," *Variety*, February 27, 1963, 17.

110. "Otto Preminger Chooses," *BoxOffice*, January 21, 1963, NE-2.

111. "Coast Kids Self," 5, 24.

112. O'Hara, "British Asst. Director," 17.

113. Dombrowski, "Postwar Hollywood, 1945–1967," 68–69.

114. Laszlo, "Recent Trends in Location Lighting," 666–68, 696–97; Herb Lightman, "Raw Cinematic Realism in the Photography of 'Bonnie and Clyde,'" *American Cinematographer*, April 1967, 254–57; Lightman, "Cinematographer with a 'Split Personality.'"

CHAPTER 4

POSTWAR HOLLYWOOD, 1945–1967, PART 2

FOREIGN LOCATION SHOOTING

Daniel Steinhart

In the late 1940s, the magazine *American Cinematographer* began regular coverage of Hollywood's international productions by reporting on the experience of Hollywood cinematographers who shot films on location around the world. Up through the 1960s, dozens of articles appeared, examining productions such as *Berlin Express* (1948), shot in France and Germany; *Kangaroo* (1952), shot in Australia; *Sayonara* (1957), shot in Japan; *Exodus* (1960), shot in Israel; and *Major Dundee* (1965), shot in Mexico. Across all of these production profiles, a familiar formula emerges: while on location, Hollywood crews overcame an array of logistical and technical challenges using know-how and craft solutions that had sustained the U.S. film industry's production operations for years. "Foreign location shooting tests the mettle of any cameraman," commented the veteran cinematographer Charles G. Clarke, who specialized in location work.[1] As all of these articles were promoting Hollywood's ingenuity, *American Cinematographer*'s coverage of international film shoots also signaled how in the postwar era, Hollywood increasingly looked around the world for production opportunities due to a mix of economic and aesthetic reasons.

Curiously, throughout *American Cinematographer*'s reporting on postwar foreign location shooting, little attention was paid to the effect of this phenomenon on Hollywood labor. In 1949, the International Alliance of Theatrical Stage Employees (IATSE) and the American Federation of Labor (AFL) called this trend "runaway" production in response to the loss of employment that went along with the exportation of film projects abroad.[2] Appropriately enough, IATSE's own monthly publication, *International Photographer*, did address the issue of runaway production, but not until the early 1960s.[3] Despite the objections from film unions, Hollywood still managed to turn runaway production into a reliable, if financially risky, strategy to navigate the industry changes of the postwar era. This tactic also resulted in films that were more international in scope, bringing new sights to U.S. audiences while appealing to important foreign markets.

Runaway productions were by and large stylistically similar to films made back in Hollywood studios. While certain genres such as semidocumentary war films, adventure movies, and historical epics became more prominent, these films adhered to the stylistic conventions that had shaped Hollywood pictures for decades. However, location shooting became more salient in these movies. Now, instead of recreating Paris or a Congo rainforest in a studio or on a back lot, production units went to the real place, eroding the old industry maxim, "A tree is a tree, a rock is a rock: shoot it in Griffith Park!"[4] The industry analyst Dorothy B. Jones elaborated on this point in 1957, writing, "There used to be a saying in Hollywood that any place or any thing under the sun could be recreated on the back lot. Producers had reasoned: Why go to tremendous expense and become embroiled in the many difficulties inherent in taking a production unit abroad if it can be shot just as well or better on the back lot?"[5] By the postwar era, the circumstances of production had changed. The economic incentives were in place to impel Hollywood to shoot films all around the world. From the late 1940s to the mid-1960s, Hollywood filmmakers harnessed foreign location shooting to build a more international production industry that heralded some features of contemporary global Hollywood.[6]

The Rise of "Runaway" Productions

Hollywood studios had been making films abroad for decades, but only a few years after World War II, film companies undertook international production with a new intensity. The reasons for this move overseas were based on a convergence of economic and aesthetic factors that emerged during this period.[7] One of the most important financial reasons for shooting abroad was accessing frozen foreign earnings. Because of European countries' fragile postwar economies, they wanted to limit the outflow of U.S. dollars. These nations decided to hold the earnings that Hollywood studios made on the distribution of their own films in Europe in order to force these companies to invest in the local economies. This financial threat became a major concern for Hollywood companies, which could not afford a decline in foreign profits at a time when domestic box-office profits were falling due to dwindling audience numbers. Subsequently, a series of bilateral agreements between the United States and western European countries helped set the parameters for international postwar film relations. These agreements eased some of Europe's protectionist measures, set the conditions for the partial remittance of foreign earnings, and established the terms for accessing frozen funds.

Hollywood studios enacted a series of schemes to use the blocked monies that could not be extracted abroad, including investing in nonfilmic activities such as buying overseas real estate and investing in the shipbuilding business.[8] Film companies also engaged in film-related investments, such as purchasing foreign story properties and acquiring foreign films for distribution in the United States.[9] However, it was the investment of frozen funds in the production of Hollywood's foreign-shot films that stimulated the growth of runaway production. The frozen-fund plan was accompanied by supplemental economic incentives to work abroad, including access to foreign subsidies and cheaper below-the-line crew members. In addition, tax incentives for above-the-line personnel encouraged actors and directors to make films overseas. Abroad, they could exploit the eighteen-month tax loophole, which allowed Hollywood talent to avoid paying taxes on the money they earned while living overseas for seventeen out of eighteen months. Before the U.S. Congress repealed this tax scheme in 1953, individuals such as the director John Huston, the producer Sam Spiegel, and the actors Claudette Colbert and Gary Cooper were able to utilize the benefit by working on films in foreign countries.[10] While the financial benefits of filming overseas were debated all through the postwar era, the economic incentives were strong enough to stimulate robust international location work during this period.

By far, the most significant aesthetic reason for making films overseas was the attraction of authentic foreign locations. Many producers justified filming overseas by falling back on the idea that foreign locales could bring authenticity to films. Combined with new widescreen and color technologies, real foreign spaces offered filmmakers a way to draw in audiences with new sights, especially in the face of television, whose formal characteristics initially lacked the scope and semblance of realism that film could deliver. The promotion of international productions emphasized this notion of authenticity, along with the spectacle of mounting a major production abroad. Posters for Howard Hawks's *Land of the Pharaohs* (1955) highlighted, "Spectacularly filmed in Egypt with a cast of 11,500 by the largest location crew ever sent abroad from Hollywood!" Advertisements, trailers, and promotional featurettes all hyped authentic foreign locations to bring added value to films.[11] However, these aesthetic motives often concealed the actual economic rationales behind runaway productions and complicated the debates about the outsourcing of production work to foreign industries.

The growth of runaway production was met with resistance from Hollywood labor unions. In 1948, as MGM and 20th Century-Fox were formulating an ambitious plan to embark on production in Europe with the use of frozen funds, the Hollywood AFL Film Council began to protest the move overseas.[12] Unions applied the label of "runaway" production to this trend to underscore how employment opportunities were disappearing.[13] Throughout the 1950s,

Hollywood unions continued to fight runaway productions, specifically targeting the lure of foreign film subsidies, such as Great Britain's Eady Levy, and tax incentives, such as the eighteen-month tax clause.[14] This opposition sometimes veered into outright red-baiting. Certain union members, such as IATSE and AFL Film Council president Roy Brewer, accused Hollywood companies that shot films abroad of hiring communists from the Hollywood blacklist and working with foreign communist unions.[15] By the early 1960s, as unions intensified their fight, an unlikely alliance between unions and studio management emerged with the Hollywood Joint Labor-Management Committee on Foreign Film Production. Unions wanted to curb the outflow of production abroad, while producers hoped to reduce the labor costs that were driving productions overseas. The two forces worked together to lobby the government to enact a series of measures to promote domestic production, until disagreements within the committee led to its dissolution in the mid-1960s.[16]

During these disputes, Hollywood producers countered union protests by invoking conceptions of realism to justify the need to shoot films abroad. In an issue of the *Journal of the Screen Producers Guild* devoted to overseas production, Darryl F. Zanuck authored an article that deployed the authenticity argument. The former Fox production head turned independent producer wrote, "The only excuse in my opinion for anyone to make a picture abroad is because it cannot be properly produced anywhere else except on the locale dictated by the story. . . . What do I gain by making another six thousand mile expedition and going into territory where I have to bring everything from stars to grips? I gain only quality and realism and if I am successful, I bring to audiences a sense of honesty and show them something they have never seen before." He concluded, "The locale must be the only barometer for production abroad."[17] In practice, unions actually made allowances for films that went overseas for authentic locations. The Hollywood AFL Film Council advocated combating runaway productions except when a film required foreign locations.[18] Eventually, AFL Film Council leader Roy Brewer qualified this stance. In a letter published by the *Hollywood Reporter* in 1953, Brewer acknowledged that certain stories demanded foreign locales. However, he also indicated that many films could represent foreign settings by shooting in Hollywood studios with rear-screen projection that displayed footage shot abroad.[19] In these disputes, unions attempted to differentiate between films that were made overseas for legitimate justifications (e.g., the need for authentic locations) and those produced on illegitimate grounds (e.g., the need for cheap labor). However, Hollywood producers could hide their economic motives by using the defense of authenticity. Thus, what constituted a runaway production was frequently debatable.

One crucial sticking point was when a foreign location became a stand-in for a setting in the United States. A handful of postwar films that were set in the United States but shot in a foreign country drew the heaviest criticism, as these productions laid bare the purely economic objectives of working overseas. When setting and location did not match, unions unleashed strong disapproval. W. R. Frank's production of *Sitting Bull* (1954), a biopic about the titular Sioux Native American chief, was set in South Dakota but shot in Mexico. The film received swift criticism from the Hollywood AFL Film Council.[20] Similarly, *Daniel Boone, Trail Blazer* (1956), a U.S.-Mexico coproduction released by Republic Pictures, was set in the U.S. South but filmed in Mexico, a situation that again raised an outcry from the Film Council.[21]

Over time, though, the attacks against runaway production developed as a criticism of the general phenomenon of film jobs disappearing from Los Angeles and moving to regions both in the United States and abroad. Despite union protest, the decentralization of production, which international runaway films contributed to, forever altered Hollywood, leading to lower employment even as television production helped stabilize the falling job numbers.[22] For those companies and filmmakers that shot films on foreign locations, runaway production reshaped production practices in ways that brought about a more adaptable method of making movies.

THE PRODUCTION PRACTICES OF FOREIGN LOCATION SHOOTING

Once Hollywood companies decided to make movies overseas, filmmakers had to set up productions in locations that were for the most part unexplored by Hollywood units. Abroad, Hollywood personnel had to figure out how to organize and execute films without the help of Los Angeles–area studios and support services that had long provided the infrastructure for filmmaking. Rather than trying to adhere to procedures developed in the studio system or completely conforming to the circumstance of foreign locations, Hollywood units cut a middle path. They created a more adaptable mode of production that retained certain studio craft practices while adjusting to the conditions of foreign locations and the cultures of foreign film industries. This move toward greater production versatility helped studios turn overseas filmmaking into a viable—albeit economically uncertain—strategy to negotiate the changing industrial landscape of the postwar era.[23]

One of the primary challenges of foreign location shooting was the need for a base to organize a film shoot. Many studios looked to their network of foreign offices, which typically housed distribution operations and a small staff to scout story properties. Paramount, for example, relied heavily on its offices in London, Rome, and Paris to initiate the preparatory groundwork before a location unit traveled from Hollywood to shooting sites in Europe. These foreign offices could conduct initial location surveys and search for local crews. Often a staff member from the local region doubled as a studio liaison, helping Hollywood companies grapple with languages, politics, and bureaucratic protocols. In Paramount's

Paris office, the Frenchman Édouard de Segonzac arranged the preproduction of French location work on *Little Boy Lost* (1953), *To Catch a Thief* (1955), and *Funny Face* (1957), as well as the location filming in Morocco for *The Man Who Knew Too Much* (1956). In addition to these offices, a handful of production service companies that catered to Hollywood location shoots opened up in cities such as Rome, which hosted a heavy concentration of runaway productions.[24] These companies prefigured the film commissions that spread globally in the 1970s and 1980s.

Even as Hollywood units increasingly worked on foreign locales, they still had to depend on studios that could supply soundstages and a headquarters to mount location shooting in nearby regions. The studios in the metropolitan areas of London, Rome, and Paris all offered production spaces and offices. The Hollywood majors with ties to foreign studios were in a strong position to quickly launch foreign productions that used frozen funds in the late 1940s. MGM owned a modern British studio in Borehamwood, while Warner Bros. had Teddington Studios, although it carried out most of its British productions at the studios of the Associated British Picture Corporation (ABPC), which Warner Bros. partly owned. In Rome, Cinecittà was the most important studio for Hollywood's Italian productions. Largely in disrepair by the end of the war, the great Italian studio had functioned as a munitions depot and a refugee camp.[25] MGM used frozen lire to help rebuild the studio, so that it could shoot its epic production of *Quo Vadis* (1951) there. Cinecittà went on to serve as the production base for many Hollywood films shot in Italy and beyond, including *Roman Holiday* (1953), *Barefoot Contessa* (1954), *Helen of Troy* (1956), *War and Peace* (1956), *Boy on a Dolphin* (1957), *A Farewell to Arms* (1957), *The Nun's Story* (1959), *Ben-Hur* (1959), and *Cleopatra* (1963). Paris had numerous soundstages, but after the war, many studios were understaffed, undersupplied, and beset by soaring production costs.[26] Hollywood units usually opted to shoot on location in France and capture studio interiors in other countries or Hollywood.

Beyond the production centers of London, Rome, and Paris, Hollywood companies utilized film infrastructure in Spain, where the producer Samuel Bronston built a studio outside Madrid for a series of epic films that took advantage of cheap labor, wide-open landscapes, and backing from Spain's Franco regime.[27] Mexico also afforded Hollywood units with locations and soundstages in Mexico City's various studios, some of which U.S. film companies had strong investments in since the mid-1940s.[28] While the Hollywood film industry had been defined by a clustering pattern of studios and service companies in the Los Angeles area, runaway productions were drawn to these new areas of agglomeration that could handle big-budget Hollywood production.[29] These clusters formed organizational nerve centers that furnished location units with equipment and crews as they ventured around the world.

With the move overseas came a greater reliance on location production managers who could navigate the protocols and customs of working on foreign locales. Trained in the studio system, these production managers brought expertise and a commitment to learning the intricacies of getting a production off the ground. The exact designation of who acted as production managers abroad was somewhat loose, with assistant directors, producers, and business managers filling the role. Eventually, a new class of location production managers who specialized in international work emerged. Individuals such as C. O. "Doc" Erickson, William Kaplan, Robert Snody, and Henry Henigson administered film shoots in Europe, South America, Africa, and Australia. Henigson, a business manager in charge of MGM's European productions, had a reputation as a strict, budget-minded administrator. His most pivotal work occurred in Italy, where he coordinated the productions of *Quo Vadis*, *Roman Holiday*, and *Ben-Hur*. In the process, he helped promote Hollywood craft practices within the culture of Italian production. Even as location production managers such as Henigson accrued more international experience, Hollywood companies also became familiar with foreign personnel too. Eventually foreign production managers became key organizers for Hollywood shoots as well. From one film to another, some Hollywood companies rehired a group of French workers, including Michel Rittener, Julian Derode, and Christian Ferry. These production specialists were effective intermediaries linking Hollywood crew members to their foreign counterparts.

The need for Hollywood filmmakers to work in a more versatile manner on location was exemplified in Hollywood crews' assimilation of foreign methods and the studio production ideas that they concurrently brought with them. In order to work on foreign locations, Hollywood units had to adjust to the working hours and labor demands of foreign unions, especially in hiring a certain percentage of non-Hollywood crew members. The need to conform to foreign unions was counterbalanced by applying Hollywood production routines. Studios could promote industry practices by supervising their location units, but the geographical distance between the foreign shooting site and home studio complicated the situation. Certainly, a studio's control of the moment-to-moment decisions of a far-away unit was reduced. Independent productions also had a fair amount of freedom overseas even if they were still beholden to studios because of financial ties. Nevertheless, Hollywood studios attempted to promote production protocols from afar as location units tried to put these directives into action. One approach was for studio executives and production heads to visit location units. With the growth of commercial airline travel in the 1950s, studio personnel could fly to locations around the globe to check up on their foreign units. In 1949, Darryl F. Zanuck, who was then head of production at Fox, used his studio's private plane to visit the sets of *Night and the City* (1950) in London, *Under My Skin* (1950) in Paris, *The Big Lift* (1950) in Berlin, and *The Black Rose*

(1950) in Morocco.[30] A further means of supervision was for studios to look to on-location proxies, who could represent the studios' interests and ensure that they were kept up-to-date on shooting progress. Exacting managers such as Henry Henigson ensured that foreign productions followed Hollywood protocols. The act of communication via letter and cable was an additional way that studio managers in Hollywood could track their location units. On the production of *Roman Holiday*, regular letters and cable dispatches allowed Paramount a degree of administrative control of spending, hiring, and filming, all of which Henigson and producer-director William Wyler had to justify to the studio.[31]

Finally, the viewing of dailies from footage shot overseas by Hollywood executives allowed studios to examine the precise creative decisions that took place on location. With the support of Technicolor labs in London and later in Rome and Paris, reliable film processing could supply rushes for both the foreign units and the studios back in Hollywood. These studios could then shape the look of the film, especially with regard to the proper application of widescreen. Even without the guidance of studios, though, Hollywood filmmakers rarely broke from the stylistic regimes of their domestic industries. Many of these filmmakers had operated in the studio system for years, absorbing the creative solutions of big-budget moviemaking that now proved workable in new locations. The commitment to these conventions helped influence the aesthetics of location shooting.

THE AESTHETICS OF FOREIGN LOCATION SHOOTING

Hollywood filmmakers had to contend with countless creative decisions that went into capturing a foreign location. Even while working with foreign crews in new environments, these filmmakers did not produce neorealist films or movies influenced by emerging new waves and verité documentaries. They continued to produce Hollywood-style films with a greater accent on the role of locations within a film's visual design. Unlike most postwar realist movements, Hollywood's runaway productions were mostly big-budget films that took advantage of lower overseas costs in order to realize higher production values. Moreover, these films rarely represented the social realities of foreign lands and cultures that contemporaneous film movements abroad were committed to. Even if Hollywood film producers appealed to realism by capturing and promoting authentic foreign locales, this brand of realism was determined by the stylistic practices that filmmakers took overseas from their experience of working in studios.

The development of Hollywood's foreign location shooting from the late 1940s to the mid-1960s did not follow a clear progression away from studio work toward ever-increasing realism. Some of the boldest uses of real-world locales occurred in the late 1940s in Germany, where Fox and MGM relied on heavy location work to exploit the spectacle of postwar destruction. Partly spurred by the semidocumentary cycle in Hollywood, films such as *The Search* (1948), *The*

Big Lift, and *Decision before Dawn* (1951) derived much of their realistic quality from extensive location shooting among the ruins of war. These films also benefited from technical developments such as portable lighting units and the latensification process, which increased the speed of film to facilitate shooting location interiors and night scenes.[32] Alternatively, some foreign-set films from the 1960s combined location and studio work even as new widescreen developments had been heightening a semblance of spectacle and realism. Even though Martin Ritt's *Paris Blues* (1961) was hailed for its New Wave naturalism, it blended real Parisian sites with scenes filmed on soundstages.[33] Many international productions throughout the postwar era were in fact shot on foreign locales and in studios, where rear projection remained a dependable technique to represent a far-away setting and allow filmmakers to control sound, image, and performance.

Whether a film was shot entirely on location or it was shot in both studios and authentic locales, Hollywood filmmakers upheld the stylistic conventions of the studio system. One mechanism for maintaining Hollywood style was to bring location shooting in line with reigning conventions of composition. Vital for location shooting was the notion that an image should convey depth. Faced with open spaces and an abundance of natural lighting, Hollywood filmmakers could select a locale and frame it to achieve a sense of deep space. Filmmakers exploited architectural elements that formed recessional lines and vanishing points to encourage viewers to appreciate depth whether in an exterior or interior locale.[34] Additionally, filmmakers could combine pieces of a setting and actor placement to layer foreground, middle ground, and background to generate a series of overlapping depth cues that could produce spatial deepness.[35] In *Plunder of the Sun* (1953), director John Farrow combines many of these options. In one scene that integrates locations from the Zapotec ruins of Monte Albán and Mitla in Oaxaca, Mexico, Farrow uses bright sunlight and open space to render an expanse in deep focus. As an insurance adjuster and an archeologist hatch a plot to uncover hidden treasure, architecture creates both multiple planes and a recessional line for a synthesis of eye-catching visuals (figure 4.1).

The creative choice to bring viewers' attention to the depth of backgrounds went against another prevailing convention of shot arrangement: that the spectacle of a location background should not distract from the main action.[36] Via composition, focus, and editing, filmmakers had to render essential moments of movement and dialogue so that locations receded to nondistracting background elements. At times, a film might cut from an establishing shot that highlighted a striking environment to a closer shot of a character in that location, thereby eliminating the potentially distracting background. At other times, a film could cut from a location shot to a studio shot, where production design and rear projection represented the setting. This shift from location to studio allowed for a greater command of composition and more control over sound. MGM's *Kim* (1951) reflects the location-to-studio option by cutting from establishing shots of

Figure 4.1. A shot in Oaxaca with multiple planes and a recessional slant between the actors in *Plunder of the Sun* (Warner Bros., 1953).

acting doubles captured on location in India and Pakistan to close shots of the real actors in a studio, where rear projection depicts the background. The use of doubles also reveals the economics of combining studio and location work, since the studio did not have to pay to send some of the film's stars abroad.[37]

When Hollywood developed new widescreen systems in the early 1950s, studios routinely paired widescreen with authentic foreign locations. This association endured through the 1950s and into the 1960s as newer widescreen formats were introduced. Foreign locales appeared in the inaugural Cinerama production, *This Is Cinerama* (1952), which highlighted sites such as the Scala Theater in Milan and Edinburgh Castle in Scotland. This film was followed up with more global views in other Cinerama productions, including *Cinerama Holiday* (1955) and *The Seven Wonders of the World* (1956), which were essentially travelogues. The spectacle of foreign locations rendered in widescreen carried over into the fictional realm. This impulse found expression in promotional campaigns, which frequently matched foreign locations with widescreen in the imagery and rhetoric of advertisements and trailers. A trailer for Fox's *House of Bamboo* (1955) flaunts the CinemaScope filming in Tokyo and Yokohama. The voice-over narration boasts, "Sensational in locale, as the magic cameras of CinemaScope go to Japan for the first time to capture thrills never filmed before!" These kinds of rhetorical flourishes called attention to how international productions could exploit widescreen to present "exotic" views in a manner that television could not yet approximate.[38]

During this period, studios aimed to differentiate their products while standardizing a Hollywood style that united widescreen framing with location shooting. These studios had to work out how to render foreign locations in these new widescreen formats and observe the conventions of composition. Initially, the switch to widescreen's more horizontal film frame took many staging and compositional possibilities off the menu. CinemaScope's image distortion and anamorphic lenses, which were less sensitive to light, resulted in many limitations on moving actors through space and composing in depth.[39] However, by moving outdoors into open spaces with ample natural light, filmmakers could return to former practices that allowed them to stage scenes in depth and sharp focus. As an *American Cinematographer* article insisted, "CinemaScope is ideally suited to spectacle films in which most of the action can be played against huge outdoor panoramic vistas."[40] Along with highlighting the spectacle of foreign locales, widescreen location films helped bring back recessional compositions and depth staging. Filmmakers also sought out locations that could highlight the depth and width of the new screen format. In the Technirama production of *El Cid* (1961), the cornering of a Moorish king takes place atop Spain's Peñíscola fortress rampart. The walkway's recessive thrust connects a sword-wielding Spanish fighter in the left foreground, the trapped king in the center of the frame, and his rebelling subjects in the distance (figure 4.2). Like many films of the era, the use of foreign locations to enhance the features of these new formats reflected the discourse around widescreen, which treated the technology as a participatory medium that aimed for increased three-dimensionality.[41]

By the mid-1960s, Hollywood's foreign location films reached a kind of stylistic plateau. Foreign units had mastered location work with regard to both organizing production overseas and pulling off the aesthetics of location shooting,

Figure 4.2. A widescreen shot in Peñíscola with the recessional line of a rampart walkway connecting various points of interest in *El Cid* (Allied Artists, 1961).

even incorporating new widescreen technologies into this practice. At the same time, filmmakers proceeded to match foreign locations with studio work, running counter to the trend of near-total location shooting found in European new waves and new cinemas. The interplay of a studio's fabrication and a location's authenticity bespeaks the sheer stylistic variety that existed in postwar Hollywood production. One film that reflected this balance of location shooting and studio work was the international production of *The Nun's Story*. The Warner Bros. film demonstrates the trials of working in multiple countries and the organizational decisions the studio made to coordinate and supervise the production. This case study also exhibits the creative choices that the foreign unit made to attain the realism and expressivity that could come from working on location.

THE PRODUCTION AND LOCATION WORK OF *THE NUN'S STORY*

In the late 1950s, Warner Bros. undertook *The Nun's Story*, a prestigious production based on the titular novel by Kathryn Hulme. The film follows Sister Luke (Audrey Hepburn) from Belgium to the Congo as she struggles between her prodigious nursing talents and her devotion to the humbling rules of her congregation. Once in the Congo, she endures spiritual struggles and a bout of tuberculosis. After returning to Belgium during the outbreak of World War II, she decides to leave the order and return to civilian life. Reflecting this mix of international settings, the production was a global venture, shot in Cinecittà studios and on location in Belgium and its then colony the Belgian Congo. During the planning of the film, director Fred Zinnemann wrote to Hepburn to share some of the hurdles of the undertaking. "From a production point of view," he explains, "this is one of the most difficult pictures I have ever been connected with. In my opinion, the only way to eliminate confusion and resulting delays and excessive costs is to prepare the production as systematically and carefully as if it were a military operation."[42] Zinnemann's invocation of the military reflects a metaphor that has been a common trope of international location shooting. In staging this major production away from the infrastructure of Hollywood, the director conceived of filmmaking as a military-style mobilization of equipment, cast and crew across far-flung locales. For Zinnemann and his company, the aesthetic struggle was how to creatively explore location shooting under the strain of what was being viewed as a filmmaking offensive.

Preplanning for the film got under way in the spring of 1957 with periodic production meetings and location surveys across the United States, Europe, and the Belgian Congo. The production commenced in late January 1958 in the Congo and lasted until early March, before moving to Rome for studio work from March to June. This lengthy studio interlude was followed by a second location shooting phase in Belgium for the rest of June.[43] The filming order was somewhat unusual since most international productions tended to shoot all of their location work before moving into studios. This typical shooting schedule helped art directors match studio-built interiors to the already-filmed authentic exteriors. The sequence was also insurance for the location unit so that anything not accomplished in the real world could be done on studio sets. On *The Nun's Story*, however, weather considerations largely controlled the filming plan. Based on climate charts generated for Belgium and the Congo, the schedule dictated that location work would be done in the better conditions of February and March in the Congo and May and June in Belgium.[44] Studio work in Rome was therefore a kind of respite from bad weather.

As with most runaway productions, making *The Nun's Story* overseas was based on a mix of financial and aesthetic considerations. The settings suggested by Hulme's novel determined the decision to shoot in Belgium and the Congo. The choice to film in Roman studios was for the most part shaped by the ability to apply frozen earnings to the production. In order to gain permission to deblock lire, Warner Bros. had to submit a script draft to Italian authorities. Upon approval, the production withdrew monies from a cinematographic account into which the frozen funds were transferred.[45] This money was applied to the salaries of Italian personnel, transportation costs to the various locations, and the purchase of equipment and production materials.[46] While Warner Bros. could use notions of authenticity to justify shooting in Belgium and the Congo, the financial advantages of working in Roman studios as opposed to Hollywood studios exposed the economic motives for filming a major motion picture abroad.

As Hollywood's foreign units moved into new shooting areas, location scouting helped filmmakers identify picturesque scenery and infrastructure to sustain a large-scale production. This reconnaissance was typically completed before the core unit from Hollywood arrived. For *The Nun's Story*, multiple location surveys were done across Europe and the Congo to perform story research. Zinnemann along with screenwriter Robert Anderson and Warner's British production executive Gerald Blattner visited Brussels, Paris, Lourdes, Rome, and the Congo to scout locations and visit convents in order to research the life of nuns. While visiting various convents in Europe, the location party was unsuccessful at witnessing sacred rituals to determine how to film them. "We usually saw nothing but architecture instead of their daily life," complained Zinnemann.[47] In Flanders and Italy, the lack of cooperation from churches was particularly strong owing to the film's story, which culminated in Sister Luke leaving the church. Zinnemann and producer Henry Blanke conducted more location surveys in Europe and the Congo, while production manager Julien Derode performed his own reconnaissance in Belgium to secure shooting permissions and accommodations for the cast and crew.[48] Ultimately in Belgium, the production shot in Brussels, Bruges, and Antwerp while housing the cast and crew in Ostend.

Traveling farther afield into untapped shooting locations proved more complex for Hollywood's survey teams since the relationship to local contacts had not

been developed yet. For the Congo section of *The Nun's Story*, Warner Bros. had
to rely on the ties between Belgium and its colony to access locations and acquire
permission to film there. In Belgium, Zinnemann and various production personnel worked with the Ministry of Colonial Affairs and the influential Belgian
Mining Syndicate to facilitate shooting in the Congo.[49] Warner Bros. also took
advantage of its connections at the State Department to obtain help from the U.S.
ambassador in Brussels and the consul general in the capital of Léopoldville to
gain local cooperation in the colony.[50] In the end, the location unit filmed in the
city of Stanleyville, which also served as a production base for treks to the Congo
River, the village of Wagenia, and the leper colony of Yalisombo, whose actual
patients appeared in the film. Belgium's colonial rule was short-lived, however.
Soon after filming in the Belgian Congo, a rebellion erupted that led to the country's independence from Belgium in 1960, when the former colony was renamed
the Republic of the Congo.[51]

To support the film's location work, Warner Bros. looked to its global network of studios and foreign offices. In Rome, Cinecittà was the primary space for
shooting studio interiors. However, because the production of *Ben-Hur* occupied
many of the soundstages at Cinecittà, *The Nun's Story* production used studio
space at the nearby Centro Sperimentale di Cinematografia, Italy's national film
school. Cinecittà also functioned as the production base to orchestrate the location excursions to Belgium and the Congo, which had the picturesque locales
dictated by the story but not the moviemaking infrastructure to support extensive studio work. This mix of European studios and location shooting in African
colonies followed a pattern established by earlier films. For *The African Queen*
(1952), John Huston filmed in the Congo and Uganda and shot interiors at the
Isleworth and Shepperton Studios in Great Britain. For *Mogambo* (1953), John
Ford worked in Tanzania, French West Africa, and Equatorial Africa and at
MGM's British studios.

Additional organizational backing for location work came from Britain's
ABPC Studios, where many of Warner's overseas productions were set in
motion. ABPC's chief of production, Gerry Blattner, helped with scheduling
The Nun's Story, securing crew and equipment, and arranging transportation.[52]
Warner Bros. leaned on its network of distribution offices in Brussels, Paris, and
Rome for assistance with location scouting and making contacts with various
religious groups. At the studio's Paris office, staff member Henri Descombes con-
sulted with Blattner on the complications of hiring French crew members, many
of whom were part of the communist-controlled CGT union. These negotiations came at a time when the Hollywood AFL labor group attacked Fox and
MGM for employing procommunist technicians in France, so Warner Bros.
had to tread carefully.[53] In this new era of international production, studios
looked to their global system of studios and offices to understand the politics of
foreign filmmaking.

Away from the infrastructure of Hollywood, Warner Bros. faced the problem of how to gather equipment needed to prop up the scale of *The Nun's Story*. As with many overseas location productions, Warner Bros. collected camera, sound, electrical, and grip equipment from various global sources. Along with production materials available at Cinecittà, equipment was exported from Warner Bros. in Burbank, ABPC Studios in Great Britain, rental houses in Paris, and a Mole-Richardson shop in Rome.[54] The U.S.-owned Mole-Richardson firm had a production plant in London and outlets across Europe, which could all supply Hollywood's runaway productions with equipment they were accustomed to. In order to transport all these materials to the shooting locations, Warner Bros. employed a series of shipping agents to oversee imports and exports in the United States, Belgium, Italy, and the Congo.[55] Even as jet travel was ushering in a new age of mobility in the late 1950s, a complex equipment-heavy operation such as the *Nun's Story* production needed to depend on transoceanic transportation and shipping that was modernizing in the postwar era.[56]

Another obstacle of working away from the Hollywood studios was finding skilled crew members. An indispensable source for finding foreign labor was consulting with other Hollywood filmmakers who had shot overseas. The director King Vidor, who had made *War and Peace* in Italy, shared with *The Nun's Story* production a list of Italian workers.[57] Similarly, the director Robert Wise drew from his experience of filming *Helen of Troy* abroad to recommend personnel from Great Britain and Italy, noting their skills and multilingual abilities. He also suggested the value of bringing Hollywood workers who were "adaptable." Prior to the production of *The Nun's Story*, Wise wrote to producer Henry Blanke, "It is terribly important that any of the people you bring from the studio be carefully screened so that you get people who will not only do a first-rate job for you, but will have personalities that will help create an atmosphere of good will on the sets abroad."[58]

The production organizers were especially interested in individuals with location experience. For example, Warner Bros. hired the Britain-based continuity supervisor Elaine Schreyeck, who had worked on a range of Hollywood's international pictures, including *Saadia* (1954) in Morocco, *The Living Idol* (1957) in Mexico City, and *The Quiet American* (1958) in Saigon and Rome.[59] The final crew list was made up of individuals from Italy, France, Great Britain, Belgium, and the Congo.[60] Many of the film's department heads came from Hollywood to ensure that this international crew followed Hollywood methods. Cinematographer Franz Planer, chief grip Weldon Gilbert, and property master John More were able to bring the ranks of their departments in line with Hollywood techniques. For the foreign workers, the opportunity to work on the film provided employment opportunities and valuable training for large-scale productions. Sergio Leone, one of the film's assistant directors, went on to make his own international coproduction epics.

Key to organizing the shoots across three different countries was the preliminary work of the "advanceman." Dispatched from Hollywood, general production manager Chuck Hansen prepared each location before the first unit arrived. Once shooting commenced, he moved on to the next location. Picking up where Hansen left off, a string of additional production managers and assistant directors subsequently supervised each shoot.[61] In Italy, production manager Orazio Tassara handled the studio work. In the Congo and Belgium, Julien Derode, who could communicate in French with the locals in both countries, served as the location production manager. This relay system of production management helped promote efficiency and uninterrupted work in response to the difficulty of coordinating across multiple locations.

With this versatile operation in place, Fred Zinnemann and his department heads had the organizational basis to create the film's high-production values in a variety of locales. Shooting on location was a fundamental aesthetic practice for the director, who had previously worked in war-torn Germany in *The Search* and Italy in *Teresa* (1951). "The location is an actor, a dramatically active ingredient in itself," declared the director.[62] Zinnemann claimed that working on location was not only a stylistic choice but a matter of creative freedom too. "I have to go where the story is," explained the director. "If you take *The Nun's Story*, for example, you *have* to go into the Belgian Congo to make it. I don't find any real disadvantage to being on location. Sometimes it's a very good thing, as in the case of *The Nun's Story*. It's very good away from the studio control. We were far into the jungle, and it was good because we were on our own."[63]

Mirroring Zinnemann's attitude toward location shooting, a number of scholars have resorted to ideas of freedom to put forward a persuasive reason why Hollywood filmmakers wanted to shoot overseas in the postwar era.[64] Despite the distance between the studio and its foreign location unit, Warner Bros. nevertheless employed a number of ways to supervise its productions abroad. The studio used its British production chief, Gerry Blattner, as a proxy by relying on him to monitor the film from ABPC Studios and with visits to the set in Rome. From Burbank, Warner Bros. production executive Steve Trilling encouraged Blattner to keep Zinnemann "in line so the picture is made at the lowest price possible."[65] Producer Henry Blanke was required to send regular progress reports to Blattner, who subsequently passed on the developments from these reports to Burbank. Because the studio was having trouble recouping the costs on large-scale productions, Trilling implored Blanke to keep spending down while still striving for the quality that Zinnemann was known for.[66]

Warner Bros. also observed the shooting results by viewing dailies, which were processed at Technicolor London. Two copies of the rushes were made. One copy was first viewed by Blattner in London and then sent to Burbank, where Trilling and studio head Jack Warner could assess the look of the film. A second copy was delivered to Zinnemann wherever he was shooting.[67] At the outset of

Figure 4.3. A shot along a canal in Bruges captures a muted palette and recessional sweep into the distance in *The Nun's Story* (Warner Bros., 1959).

the shoot, the studio was concerned with the slow filming progress due to prob-lems in the Congo, including production setbacks, heavy rains, and illness that befell actors Audrey Hepburn and Peggy Ashcroft. Even when the unit returned to Rome to shoot studio interiors, Warner Bros. executives pressed Zinnemann on filming fewer takes and less coverage. Trilling even suggested that Zinnemann should cut out scenes in order to shorten the length of what was becoming a long film. The director countered that since there was a five-day delay in receiving the dailies, they needed to protect themselves by shooting a lot of footage. Still, Zinnemann promised to work quickly and reduce spending. He even eliminated some scenes from the shooting script and filmed certain sequences with multiple cameras to make more progress.[68] Even though the foreign unit could escape the watchful eyes of Warner Bros. executives, the studio still managed to assert some control, especially when it came to financial issues.

Negotiations between the studio and filmmakers carried over to the look of the film. Zinnemann originally wanted to shoot the Belgium scenes in black and white and the Congo scenes in color "so that the austerity of Europe would contrast with the bursting tropical fertility of the African scenes."[69] However, Warner Bros. executives opposed the idea. As a compromise, Zinnemann and cinematographer Franz Planer shot the Belgium scenes in muted colors and the Congo scenes in richer colors. While on location in Belgium, the crew tried to film exteriors on overcast days to enhance the scenes' sober mood.[70] Zinnemann also used urban design and architecture to produce a striking sense of depth along the canals in the Flemish city of Bruges (figure 4.3). At Cinecittà, an almost monochromatic look is established with the aid of set design, makeup, and the

Figure 4.4. A shot in the Congo contrasts with the Belgian locations through warmer tones and slices of background nature in *The Nun's Story* (Warner Bros., 1959).

nun's black-and-white habits, which all conveyed the asceticism of convent life. This approach was juxtaposed with the pictorialism of the Congo locations, where the nuns' white garments stand out from the warmer tones and the rich greens of nature (figure 4.4). Franz Planer was partly able to achieve this look by harnessing the natural light and physical properties of the Congo landscape. He explained, "I expected a harsh strong light. But instead, the recurring rainstorms gave the atmosphere a certain 'veil'—a kind of natural diffusion. The hot ground steams after a rain and tiny particles of water hang suspended in the air for many hours afterwards, so that even in the strongest sunlight there is a soft effect."[71] By capitalizing on the unique features of Belgium and the Congo, Planer and Zinnemann turned the locations into bold expressive designs.

This contrast of place is not without its dubious qualities. The concepts that the African locales represent "tropical fertility" and a land that provokes Sister Luke's inner life reflect a troubling colonialist imagery that was common in Hollywood films shot throughout Africa. Films such as *King Solomon's Mines* (1950) and *Mogambo* use African locations and their people as both settings and pictorial elements that tend to exoticize African cultures. As Ella Shohat and Robert Stam claim, "the Third World becomes the stuff of dreamy adventure" in these narratives of colonialism and imperialism.[72] This colonialist attitude is commonly reflected in contemporaneous articles about foreign location work in publications such as *American Cinematographer*. For some productions, this view defined the relationship between adventurous Hollywood department heads and "native" casts and crews that needed training.[73] For *The Nun's Story*, this perspective shaped the aesthetic discourse, perpetuating the connection between the Congo and exoticized qualities. A writer for *American Cinematographer* notes, "In dazzling contrast to the convent sequences are the scenes shot in the Belgian Congo. The verdant lushness of the foliage itself, the foaming turbulence of jungle rivers, the colorful trappings of the natives—all combine to produce an almost kaleidoscopic effect. In psychological contrast to the earlier sequences one is made strikingly aware that here is life—primitive, violent, surging with color."[74] While the film's location shooting reveals how filmmakers can transform real-world locales into arresting visuals, it also shows how actual people and places can be relegated to problematic symbols and elements of décor, a tactic that masked many of the social realities in the Congo.

The making of *The Nun's Story* brings to light how a Hollywood studio undertook a global production with substantial location work in order to produce a film that could stand out in an unpredictable movie business. In executing this production, Warner Bros. took advantage of a range of beneficial conditions, from using frozen funds and an international network of studios and offices to exploiting Belgium's colonial rule over the Congo. The film moreover demonstrates that locations can be narrativized by developing a dynamic, if questionable, pattern of contrasts between interior and exterior, Belgium and the Congo, and austerity and vibrancy.

CONCLUSION

Hollywood's postwar runaway productions persisted into the mid-1960s with mixed results. On the one hand, Hollywood filmmakers continued to shoot movies overseas, having mastered the logistical and aesthetic challenges of working on location. On the other hand, Hollywood companies altered their strategy for international productions in response to changes in production trends. By the early 1960s, a handful of high-profile overbudget films, such as *Mutiny on the Bounty* (1962) and *Cleopatra*, exposed that many of the financial risks of foreign location shooting could spin out of control, especially at a time when overseas production costs were rising.[75] At the same time, Hollywood studios rediscovered the benefits of shooting big-budget epics in the United States. Sections of *Spartacus* (1960) and the entirety of *The Greatest Story Ever Told* (1965) proved that major productions could be made domestically with the support of Hollywood unions.[76] Starting in the mid-1960s, the takeover of studios by conglomerates such as Gulf+Western, Transamerica, and Kinney led to cost-cutting measures that included a reduction in costly foreign location shoots. Perhaps the most significant shift in the industry's foreign policy was that Hollywood studios were financing and distributing what were legally deemed foreign films, which were part of the flourishing new waves emerging out of France, Italy, and Great Britain.[77] Arguably, Hollywood's early postwar investment in the foreign film infrastructure, its employment of foreign crews, and it exportation of equipment and production practices helped stabilize the industries in Europe. As some industry analysts predicted, these contributions inadvertently created thriving rivals.[78]

From the late 1940s to the mid-1960s, Hollywood's postwar runaway productions pointed to how foreign location shooting could become an important aesthetic element to differentiate Hollywood cinema from the competition of television. Filmmakers also learned to work overseas in a more adaptive manner while using location shooting for decorative and expressive purposes. Whatever aesthetic innovations were realized, though, they were had at the expense of the employment of U.S. film labor. Through the ongoing decentralization of filmmaking and the loss of jobs, international location work in the postwar era helped to alter the landscape of Hollywood for years to come.

NOTES

1. Clifford Harrington, "Hollywood's Globetrotting Cameraman," *American Cinematographer*, January 1958, 34.

2. An early mention of the term "runaway" production can be found in "IA Backs AFL Film Council on 'Runaway' Foreign Production," *Hollywood Reporter*, February 18, 1949, 4.

3. Al St. Hilaire, "To Runaway or Not," *International Photographer*, January 1962, 17; "Hollywood's Production Runaway," *International Photographer*, December 1963, 12, 16.

4. Richard Dyer MacCann, "Hollywood Faces the World," in *The Movies in Our Midst: Documents in the Cultural History of Film in the United States*, ed. Gerald Mast (Chicago: University of Chicago Press, 1982), 667.

5. Dorothy B. Jones, "Hollywood's International Relations," *Quarterly of Film Radio and Television* 11, no. 4 (1957): 370.

6. This chapter draws on research from Daniel Steinhart, *Runaway Hollywood: Internationalizing Postwar Production and Location Shooting* (Oakland: University of California Press, forthcoming). Analysis of contemporary global Hollywood can be found in Greg Elmer and Mike Gasher, eds., *Contracting Out Hollywood: Runaway Productions and Foreign Location Shooting* (Lanham, MD: Rowman and Littlefield, 2005); Ben Goldsmith and Tom O'Regan, *The Film Studio: Film Production in the Global Economy* (Lanham, MD: Rowman and Littlefield, 2005); Toby Miller, Nitin Govil, John McMurria, Richard Maxwell, and Ting Wang, *Global Hollywood 2* (London: BFI, 2005); Janet Wasko and Mary Erickson, eds., *Cross-Border Cultural Production: Economic Runaway or Globalization?* (Amherst, NY: Cambria, 2008); Courtney Brannon Donoghue, *Localising Hollywood* (London: BFI, 2017).

7. Many of these reasons have been examined in Thomas Guback, *The International Film Industry: Western Europe and America since 1945* (Bloomington: Indiana University Press, 1969); Peter Lev, *The Fifties: Transforming the Screen, 1950–1959* (Berkeley: University of California Press, 2003); and Robert R. Shandley, *Runaway Romances: Hollywood's Postwar Tour of Europe* (Philadelphia: Temple University Press, 2009).

8. Ben Pearse, "How the Movies Get Their Money Out of Europe," *Saturday Evening Post*, November 27, 1954, 43; Guback, *International Film Industry*, 120–22.

9. "20th Buys Story with Iced Coin," *Daily Variety*, April 27, 1949, 1; "Metro Buys Thriller with Iced Money," *Daily Variety*, May 25, 1949, 1; "Lesser Learns 'Tarzans' Can Be Lensed More Profitably Here than in Africa," *Daily Variety*, June 18, 1951, 4.

10. "Only Huston and Spiegel, of All Filmsters Who Tried, Get 18-Mo. Tax-Free Ride," *Daily Variety*, July 24, 1953, 1, 12; Eric Hoyt, "Hollywood and the Income Tax, 1929–1955," *Film History* 22 no. 1 (2010): 15–16.

11. Daniel Steinhart, "'Paris . . . as You've Never Seen It Before!!!': The Promotion of Hollywood Foreign Productions in the Postwar Era," *InMedia* 3 (2013), http://inmedia .revues.org/633.

12. "Metro Will Shoot Five Pix on Far Away Locations," *Daily Variety*, June 21, 1948, 9; "Zanuck Talks of Big Prod'n Abroad," *Daily Variety*, August 30, 1948, 12; "California Solons Fite Quota," *Daily Variety*, March 31, 1949, 5.

13. "'Runaway' Boycott before AFL Council," *Hollywood Reporter*, September 26, 1949, 3; "AFL Report on Pix Abroad Is Delayed," *Daily Variety*, September 27, 1949, 2.

14. In 1957, the Hollywood AFL Film Council commissioned the economic historian Irving Bernstein to develop a report on the state of the film industry, including the effects of runaway production. Irving Bernstein, *Hollywood at the Crossroads* (Hollywood, CA: AF of L Film Council, 1957).

15. "Roy Brewer Explains IA's 'Runaway' Pix Complaint," *Hollywood Reporter*, February 2, 1953, 8; "Hollywood Unionists See 'Red' in All-Out Rage over Runaway Subsidy," *Variety*, October 24, 1962, 26; Rebecca Prime, *Hollywood Exiles in Europe: The Blacklist and Cold War Film Culture* (New Brunswick, NJ: Rutgers University Press, 2014).

16. Murray Schumach, "Hollywood Seeks to Spur U.S. Films," *New York Times*, February 5, 1962, 21; Murray Schumach, "Hollywood Asks for Federal Help," *New York Times*, April 24, 1962, 31; Camille K. Yale, "Runaway Film Production: A Critical History of Hollywood's Out-sourcing Discourse" (PhD diss., University of Illinois at Urbana-Champaign, 2010), 102–3.

17. Darryl F. Zanuck, "Shoot It Where You Find It," *Journal of the Screen Producers Guild*, December 1960, 5, 31.

18. "'Runaway' Boycott before AFL Council," *Hollywood Reporter*, September 26, 1949, 3.

19. "Roy Brewer Explains IA's 'Runaway' Pix Complaint," *Hollywood Reporter*, February 2, 1953, 8.

20. "'Sitting Bull' Filming in Mexico Is Protested," *Hollywood Reporter*, February 17, 1954, 3; "IATSE Local Stirs Up Sioux to Protest Shooting of 'Sitting Bull' in Mexico," *Daily Variety*, February 23, 1954, 1, 3; "Bob Goldstein May Save Scalp of 'Sitting Bull,'" *Daily Variety*, February 23, 1954, 1, 3.

21. "Ask AFL-CIO Boycott of 'Dan Boone,'" *Daily Variety*, March 29, 1956, 1, 2.

22. Bernstein, *Hollywood at the Crossroads*, 30–36.

23. Daniel Steinhart, "A Flexible Mode of Production: Internationalizing Hollywood Filmmaking in Postwar Europe," in *Behind the Screen: Inside European Production Cultures*, ed. Petr Szczepanik and Patrick Vonderau (New York: Palgrave, 2013), 135–51.

24. "Production Service Firm Formed in Rome," *Daily Variety*, March 6, 1962, 4.

25. Noa Steimatsky, "The Cinecittà Refugee Camp (1944–1950)," *October* 128 (Spring 2009): 23–55; David Forgacs and Stephen Gundle, *Mass Culture and Italian Society from Fascism to the Cold War* (Bloomington: Indiana University Press, 2007), 131.

26. "French Costs Kill H'wd but Own Industry Booms," *Hollywood Reporter*, May 9, 1949, 3. For an overview of French studios, see "Les Studios française" supplement in *La Technique Cinématographique*, April 1953, 99–113.

27. Neal Moses Rosendorf, "'Hollywood in Madrid': American Film Producers and the Franco Regime, 1950–1970," *Historical Journal of Film, Radio and Television* 27 no. 1 (2007): 77–109.

28. Edwin Schallert, "Filming at Peak South of Border," *Los Angeles Times*, October 2, 1955, E1; Paul P. Kennedy, "Like Beans, Mexican Movies Jump," *New York Times*, October 18, 1964, X7.

29. Allen J. Scott, *On Hollywood: The Place, the Industry* (Princeton, NJ: Princeton University Press, 2005).

30. "Zanuck Abroading to Visit 20th Units," *Daily Variety*, June 13, 1949, 2; "20th Frozen Coin for 5 Pix Abroad," *Daily Variety*, June 27, 1949, 1, 9.

31. Various correspondence, *Roman Holiday* (Paramount), William Wyler Papers, Margaret Herrick Library, Academy of Motion Picture Arts and Sciences, Beverly Hills, CA

(hereafter Herrick Library); various correspondence, *Roman Holiday* (Correspondence 1952–1953), Paramount Pictures Production Records, Herrick Library.

32. Hollis W. Moyse, "Latensification," *American Cinematographer*, December 1948, 409, 426–27; Phil Tannura, "The Practical Use of Latensification," *American Cinematographer*, February 1951, 54, 68–70; Lisa Dombrowski, "Postwar Hollywood, 1947–1967," in *Cinematography*, ed. Patrick Keating (New Brunswick, NJ: Rutgers University Press, 2014), 66–68.

33. *Paris Blues* review, *Daily Variety*, September 26, 1961, 3.

34. Joseph V. Mascelli, "How and When to Frame a Scene," *American Cinematographer*, March 1958, 174; Charles Loring, "Pictorial Composition—Key Element in Cinematography," *American Cinematographer*, August 1962, 489.

35. John Alton, *Painting with Light* (Berkeley: University of California Press, 1995), 123, 125–26.

36. Howard T. Souther, "Composition in Motion Pictures," *American Cinematographer*, March 1947, 84–86, 112; Charles Loring, "Techniques for Filming Exteriors," *American Cinematographer*, January 1953, 39, 42–45.

37. The cinematographer Burnett Guffey discusses this method on *Me and the Colonel* (1958) in Arthur E. Gavin, "Rural Route for Realism," *American Cinematographer*, September 1958, 576.

38. Steinhart, "'Paris . . . as You've Never Seen It Before!!!"

39. David Bordwell, "CinemaScope: The Modern Miracle You See without Glasses," in *Poetics of Cinema* (New York: Routledge, 2008), 281–325.

40. "CinemaScope—What It Is; How It Works," *American Cinematographer*, March 1953, 134.

41. Bordwell, "CinemaScope," 286–87; John Belton, *Widescreen Cinema* (Cambridge, MA: Harvard University Press, 1992).

42. Fred Zinnemann to Audrey Hepburn, July 29, 1957, *The Nun's Story* (Correspondence 1957), Fred Zinnemann Papers, Herrick Library.

43. Various reports, January–June 1958, *Nun's Story* (Production Progress Reports), Warner Bros. Archives, Cinematic Arts Library, University of Southern California, Los Angeles, CA (hereafter Warner Bros. Archives).

44. "Various climatic data for Brussels (Belgium)," n.d., *The Nun's Story* (Location Belgium), Warner Bros. Archives; G. L. Blattner to Henry Blanke and Fred Zinnemann, August 22, 1957, *The Nun's Story* (Steve Trilling File), Warner Bros. Archives.

45. G. L. Blattner to Steve Trilling, June 15, 1957, *The Nun's Story* (Steve Trilling File), Warner Bros. Archives.

46. Umberto Orlandi to M. Greenberg, November 13, 1957, ibid.

47. Fred Zinnemann to Steve Trilling and Henry Blanke, June 17, 1957, ibid.

48. Julien Derode, "Report Belgian Survey," December 13–18, 1957, *The Nun's Story* (Location, Belgium), Warner Bros. Archives.

49. Henry Blanke to Steve Trilling, April 19, 1957, *The Nun's Story* (Steve Trilling File), Warner Bros. Archives.

50. Henry Blanke to Fred Zinnemann, May 16, 1957, ibid.

51. Any mention of political turmoil is absent in the correspondence from *The Nun's Story* file at the Warner Bros. Archives and the Fred Zinnemann Papers at the Herrick Library.

52. G. L. Blattner to Steve Trilling, June 15, 1957, *The Nun's Story* (Steve Trilling file), Warner Bros. Archives.

53. Henri Descombes to Gerry Blattner, August 30, 1957, ibid.

54. "Points raised at meeting held on Monday, 28th October, 1957" and "Points discussed at meeting held on 2nd November, 1957," *The Nun's Story* (Location, Belgium), Production Notes, n.d., *The Nun's Story* (Publicity), Warner Bros. Archive.

55. "General Procedure for Shipment of Equipment and Materials," October 31, 1957, *The Nun's Story* (Correspondence, Manifests, Shipping Lists Relative to Overseas Shipping), Warner Bros. Archive.

56. Vanessa R. Schwartz, "Dimanche à Orly: The Jet-Age Airport and the Spectacle of

Technology between Sky and Earth," *French Politics, Culture & Society* 32 no. 3 (2014): 24–44; Robert Gardiner, ed., *The Shipping Revolution: The Modern Merchant Ship* (Annapolis, MD: Naval Institute Press, 1992), 42–62, 105–6; William J. Bernstein, *A Splendid Exchange: How Trade Shaped the World* (New York: Atlantic Monthly Press, 2008), 361.

57. Henry Blanke to Fred Zinnemann, July 30, 1957, *The Nun's Story* (Production), Fred Zinnemann Papers, Herrick Library.

58. Robert Wise to Henry Blanke, August 28, 1957, *The Nun's Story* (Production Notebook), Fred Zinnemann Papers, Herrick Library.

59. G .L. Blattner to Henry Blanke, September 11, 1957, *The Nun's Story* (Steve Trilling File), Warner Bros. Archives.

60. "Complete Unit List," June 18, 1958, *The Nun's Story* (Correspondence, Manifests, Shipping Lists Relative to Overseas Shipping), Warner Bros. Archives.

61. Henry Blanke to G. L. Blattner, August 28, 1957, *The Nun's Story* (Steve Trilling File), Warner Bros. Archives.

62. Fred Zinnemann, *A Life in the Movies: An Autobiography* (New York: Scribner, 1992), 90.

63. "Revelations," *Films and Filming* 10, no. 12 (1964), reprinted in *Fred Zinnemann Interviews*, ed. Gabriel Miller (Jackson: University of Mississippi, 2005), 7; original emphasis.

64. Aida A. Hozic, *Hollyworld: Space, Power, and Fantasy in the American Economy* (Ithaca, NY: Cornell University Press, 2001), 93, 97. Goldsmith and O'Regan, *Film Studio*, 11.

65. Steve Trilling to G. L. Blattner, April 29, 1957, *The Nun's Story* (Steve Trilling File), Warner Bros. Archives.

66. Steve Trilling to Henry Blanke, January 8, 1958, ibid.

67. Various correspondence, January–March 1958, ibid.

68. Various correspondence, March-April 1958, *The Nun's Story* (J. L. Warner File), Warner Bros. Archives.

69. Brian Neve, "A Past Master of His Craft: An Interview with Fred Zinnemann," *Cineaste* 23 no. 1 (1997), reprinted in *Fred Zinnemann Interviews*, 153.

70. Herb A. Lightman, "Shooting Black and White in Color," *American Cinematographer*, August 1959, 486–87, 499–500.

71. Ibid., 500.

72. Ella Shohat and Robert Stam, *Unthinking Eurocentrism: Multiculturalism and the Media*, 2nd ed. (New York: Routledge, 2014), 124.

73. Robert Surtees, "Location Filming in Africa for 'King Solomon's Mines,'" *American Cinematographer*, April 1950, 122–23, 136; Frederick Foster, "Assignment in India," *American Cinematographer*, June 1952, 252, 260; Hilda Black, "Filming 'Return to Paradise' in Samoa," *American Cinematographer*, April 1953, 156–57, 188–89, 191.

74. Lightman, "Shooting Black and White in Color," 499.

75. Murray Schumach, "Paramount Gives Hollywood Hope," *New York Times*, September 25, 1962, 32.

76. "AFL-CIO Helps Sell 'Spartacus' Tix as Part of Its 'Runaway' Campaign," *Daily Variety*, January 18, 1961, 3; "SEG's 'Greatest' Victory in 'Runaway' Fight," *Daily Variety*, May 16, 1962, 1, 7.

77. Tino Balio, *The Foreign Film Renaissance on American Screens, 1946–1973* (Madison: University of Wisconsin Press, 2010); Guback, *International Film Industry*, 171, 176–78.

78. "New Rival in Europe Is Seen," *Daily Variety*, September 13, 1949, 8; "Golden Says Prod Abroad Suicidal," *Hollywood Reporter*, September 13, 1949, 1, 5.

CHAPTER 5

THE AUTEUR RENAISSANCE, 1968–1979

Lawrence Webb

"Going to real locations for movies has grown so popular," wrote Charles Champlin in the *Los Angeles Times* in October 1971, "that the idea of shooting a feature film on a sound stage in Hollywood or elsewhere has come to be as rare and reactionary as wearing sleeve garters or spats."[1] As Champlin's comments suggest, location shooting had become an integral part of Hollywood filmmaking by the early 1970s. The move away from studio production, under way since World War II, was now accelerating at a new pace, a trend that was widely discussed in the trade press, film magazines, and mainstream newspapers. From one perspective, it was a development that mapped readily onto a widening cultural and generational rift in American society. In this sense, Champlin's suggestion that studio filming had become not just unfashionable but even "reactionary" gestures at a wider turn against the aesthetics and politics of the studio system. The qualities that could be assigned to location shooting—authenticity, realism, immediacy, contemporaneity, social awareness, imperfection—might now be seen as polar opposites of the slick artifice and illusionism of studio production. For the young, pop-culture-literate audience that Hollywood was seeking to recapture, as for a new generation of filmmakers who were breaking into the industry, location shooting embodied the values of an emergent "new" Hollywood and signaled a departure from the passé traditions of the "old" one. Yet Champlin's remarks were, of course, overstated for journalistic effect: studio production declined but never entirely vanished, and the shift toward location shooting was not simply a cultural trend but also a product of industrial change, technological innovation, and a profound shake-up in Hollywood's working practices and aesthetic values.

While Champlin and other critics emphasized shifting audience expectations and cultural patterns, the trade press focused more squarely on industrial priorities. *Variety* highlighted the importance of location shooting at the turn of the 1970s as the symbol of a new industrial paradigm, sketching out "a new concept of Hollywood in the jet age." As the trade paper put it, Hollywood was no longer "a studio-rooted 1930s factory town for making make-believe, but a base of operations from which compact mobile film crews deploy about the country and the world making films about the real world."[2] This vision of location shooting as central to the organizational logic of a modernized, restructured, and highly flexible film industry was also shared by unions, especially outside Los Angeles. In an opening address to the Conference of Motion Picture and Television Unions in 1973, New York guild representative Robert Hyle celebrated a "new era of mobility" in contrast to a "period dominated by fixed studios and the backlot." Technological advances, Hyle contended, had made it possible to shoot on location "under conditions which would have been costly, difficult and almost impossible before." Such changes were also symptomatic of a new type of storytelling and a different approach to production design. As Hyle put it, "The romantic and elaborately fashioned sets of the past usually do not fit into the new pattern. Today's stories call for in many cases the so-called documentary feeling, the urban background, the streets and houses of cities and black communities. Symbolically speaking, the backlot of Hollywood has given way to the backstreets of the cities."[3] Both of these accounts connect a heightened realist sensibility with a new industrial paradigm based on mobility and flexibility. Location shooting provided the key to both, enabling a renewed cinematic engagement with contemporary America and a means to disaggregate production from the fixed site of the studio to the "real world" beyond it.

Taken together, these various commentaries draw attention to the significance of location shooting to the advent of a "New Hollywood" in the late 1960s and 1970s, whether viewed in relation to economics, politics, or aesthetics. However, though location shooting is often mentioned in summaries of the New Hollywood's stylistic break with the classical cinema, it is rarely elaborated on in any detail.[4] This chapter unpacks the complex and overlapping factors that pushed filmmaking away from the studio and traces some of the key trends in location techniques and aesthetics. As this chapter demonstrates, location shooting had already been established as a viable practice during the postwar period, but it took on a new importance in the economic and cultural turmoil of Hollywood at the end of the sixties. The decade that followed became a testing ground for location-based filmmaking, a practice that became central to New Hollywood's emerging political economy and visual style.

THE END OF THE STUDIO ERA

As chapters 3 and 4 in this volume make clear, location shooting had become well established both domestically and overseas since World War II. But to what extent had it become standardized as a Hollywood production technique? And what governed the decision to shoot on a set or a location in the late 1960s? Behind-the-scenes materials from the period suggest that for a studio project, shooting on soundstages or the back lot was still a viable and cost-effective option and in many cases remained the default position, especially for interiors. For a major production, the choice between location and studio was made at the level of individual scenes and could be subject to fraught negotiation among the director, executives, and production heads.

John Gregory Dunne's account of working practices at 20th Century Fox in his behind-the-scenes exposé *The Studio* provides valuable insights into this decision-making process during the making of *The Boston Strangler* (Richard Fleischer, 1968).[5] As Dunne recounts, Fox's standard practice was to distribute copies of the shooting script to studio department managers, who would then calculate below-the-line costs. Following these estimates, key decisions about filming—including the crucial choice between location and studio—were made collectively at the final budget meeting, in this case headed by director Richard Fleischer, producer Robert Fryer, and Fox's assistant head of studio production, Louis "Doc" Merman. Together with production staff and department heads, the three men worked through the breakdown of the film's ninety sequences and 256 scenes. Dunne's play-by-play account of this discussion reveals a dynamic process of negotiation and compromise among multiple creative and managerial voices. Throughout the meeting, the choice between location and studio work is assessed in relation to several competing and interrelated criteria, which cluster around cost, authenticity, and logistics.

Even for *The Boston Strangler*, a project with such readily apparent place specificity, it was not necessarily a given that a majority of scenes would be shot in Boston. The assistant production head's preference for sets suggests that studio work was still the default option at Fox for particular types of scenes, especially for interiors, as long as it reduced below-the-line costs and did not detract from the perceived quality or prestige value of the production. In Dunne's account, Merman frequently suggests building new sets or reusing standing sets available on the Fox lot—for example, offering a set from the television series *Felony Squad* (ABC, 1966–69) as a double for the Boston police headquarters. In contrast, Fleischer tends to push for location shooting when possible and to resist Merman's interventions for reasons of narrative plausibility and authenticity. Defending the use of a real gay bar in Boston, he argues that locations provide an ineffable sense of local color and authentic texture, creating "a better feeling, a better sense of place" for the audience.[6] At the same time, Fleischer also concedes that generic spaces for relatively short sequences could just as easily be mocked up on the back lot—for example, dressing up Fox's "French Street" to double as a Boston alley. And while it would be relatively easy to characterize these exchanges as a struggle between the studio's financial rationalization and the director's artistic prerogatives, both participants' comments show an awareness of the competing claims and relative benefits of studio and location.

This push and pull between authenticity and financial imperatives is also complicated by issues of logistics and technical control. Fleischer prioritizes realism, though he also expresses a competing desire for control over the shoot—especially the ability to stage complex shots and intricate camera movements, which at this point were much easier to achieve in the predictable environment of the studio. As he explains, "If we have an interior where there's a lot of people, which means a lot of staging and a lot of camera movements, we'll do it here. You can get more control on a stage. Otherwise, if there's just a small group of people, I'd rather use the real thing on location."[7] While the director focuses on the micro level of the shot, the studio production heads are alive to logistical complexities at the macro scale, which inevitably affected the bottom line. For example, the Fox production managers and Fleischer discuss a scene to be filmed at Providence Airport, which they eventually decide to relocate to Santa Monica Airport. This switch came with drawbacks, from the difficulty in obtaining historically accurate aircraft to continuity problems with weather, but staying local enabled the cast and crew to return immediately to film the next scene in Hollywood without accumulating extra expenses. From the studio's perspective, then, the authenticity of a location was a relative, rather than an absolute, value, and in the final instance, high overheads and salary costs could easily tip the balance toward a substitute location or a studio stand-in. Each of these individual decisions recorded by Dunne shows a careful calibration of costs and benefits and a production model in which location shooting was a significant but not yet dominant practice.

Working outside the studio had clear advantages: it offered distinctive and spectacular backdrops, had become a marker of quality and authenticity, and was increasingly expected by audiences. Yet, as Dunne's book shows, these values had to be balanced against the pragmatic realities of studio management. Location work was frequently more expensive, harder to control, and logistically complex, and it carried risks and contingencies that were hard for studios to rationalize. But *The Studio* captured Fox, and the studio system more generally, on the brink of historic change, and while the basic factors governing the choice between studio and location remained relatively constant, the assumptions driving the decision-making were soon overturned by shifts in studio economics, technology, audience preferences, and aesthetic conventions.

New Hollywood: Industry, Economics, Institutions

Though *The Boston Strangler* was a modest success, the other major films under production at Fox during Dunne's visit—*Doctor Dolittle* (Richard Fleischer, 1967) and *Star!* (Robert Wise, 1968)—were disastrous flops. In late 1969, *Variety* reported an "economic crisis" in Hollywood, with three consecutive quarterly losses at Fox totaling just under $22 million, largely attributed to the spectacular failure of these expensive road-show releases. This was not simply the mismanagement of a single studio: Fox, MGM, Paramount, and Warner Bros. faced combined losses totaling $110 million in late 1969, and the total shortfall for the majors between 1969 and 1971 has been estimated at $600 million.[8] The studios were forced to recalibrate their relationship with the audience and to reassess the profitability of particular types of material. One of Darryl Zanuck's first moves at Fox was to write off an extensive backlog of story properties that were now considered unsuitable for the contemporary market. As *Variety* put it, "management has bluepenciled certain items in an active awareness of the current switch back to modest negative costs and younger audience appeal. All companies display nervousness on what will sell today, or a year and a half from now."[9] These two priorities—lower costs and an emphasis on the youth market—both favored smaller projects shot on location over elaborate studio productions. Although *Doctor Dolittle* had been partly shot on location in the United Kingdom, among the other notable box-office flops of the 1968–69 season were lavish, studio-based musicals such as *Star!* and *Hello, Dolly!* (Gene Kelly, 1969). In contrast, the groundbreaking hits of the same period, *The Graduate* (Mike Nichols, 1967), *Bonnie and Clyde* (Arthur Penn, 1967), and *Midnight Cowboy* (John Schlesinger, 1969), were emphatically location-shot films made for significantly lower budgets.[10] Likewise, the unexpected success of *Easy Rider* (Dennis Hopper, 1969) demonstrated that a film shot largely on exterior locations for less than half a million dollars could pay handsome dividends at the box office.

From a long-term perspective, the expansion of location shooting was driven by existing trends, including the shift to the package-unit system, the rising importance of independent firms, high studio overheads, and the divestiture and redevelopment of studio real estate. Though these patterns had emerged after the breakup of the vertically integrated studio oligopoly, they were brought fully into focus by the financial pressures of the 1969–71 crash, which set off a new round of industrial restructuring. During the downturn, the studios capped budgets, reduced production slates, cut staff, slashed overheads, and liquidated assets. This had the immediate effect of prioritizing smaller-scale projects that were increasingly likely to shoot outside the studio. It also precipitated a sharp turn toward package deals rather than in-house production. According to *Variety*, the combined annual output of the major studios declined steeply, almost halving from 200 films in 1968 to 108 in 1971. At the same time, independent features surged, growing from 32 in 1968 to 148 in 1971, which represented an increase from 13.8 percent to 57.8 percent of the total U.S. production slate in only three years.[11] What these figures indicate is not an explosion in genuinely independent filmmaking, however, but a strategic recalibration of the majors away from in-house production to financing and distribution deals. Executives began to reimagine the studio less as a manufacturing concern and more as a hub of finance, distribution, and marketing. United Artists, which had never owned studio space, presented itself as a model. As Richard Zanuck predicted, "All the studios will go the way of United Artists. You may soon find one or two occupying a single office on the Sunset Strip."[12] Though Fox and the other majors did not fully divest themselves of their studios, this nevertheless suggested a new streamlined conception of the "studio" not as a physical space of production but rather as a command-and-control center from which filmmaking might be outsourced.

This emerging shift in the mode of production had been captured a few years earlier by Charles Champlin. As he explained, using another sartorial metaphor, "The studios themselves are leaner and quicker on their feet. With the rise of independent production, their function has changed and they oversee, in rough terms, not an assembly line for ready-mades but a kind of co-operative of custom tailors."[13] The trend accelerated in the early 1970s. In search of innovative content and a means to assimilate the cultural dynamism of the period, studios began to establish agreements with small firms, often led by emerging directorial talent—for example, Columbia with Bob Rafelson's BBS, Warner Bros. with Coppola's American Zoetrope, and MGM with Robert Altman's Lion's Gate. At the level of budgeting and planning, these small companies prioritized locations for both artistic and economic reasons. For an independently produced film, even with guaranteed distribution from a major company, location shooting was likely to be the cheaper option. The alternative, renting studio space for extended periods, could be prohibitively expensive. The sky-high prices of rentals—Dunne records up to $6,000 a day for MGM's "New York Street," for example—meant that prolonged studio work was essentially out of bounds for smaller companies. And for the majors, the declining volume of film production meant that if studio space was not filled with television work, it risked obsolescence: soundstages and back lots were downsized, redeveloped, and in the case of MGM, sold wholesale.

For the geographers Michael Storper and Susan Christopherson, this reorganization of Hollywood production (if not its distribution network) was a case study for the development of post-Fordist "flexible specialization."[14] Refashioning the business as a group of major financier-distributors collaborating with an ecology of small firms incentivized filmmaking beyond Southern California, where cheaper and less regulated workforces might be found. Shooting beyond the thirty-mile studio zone allowed production companies to cut costs by employing nonunion labor. In the straitened circumstances of the early 1970s, when an emerging global recession was compounding Hollywood's local crisis, such an ability to trim costs could be decisive in making a project financially viable. For *The Candidate* (Michael Ritchie, 1972), shot entirely on location in the vicinity of San Francisco, producer Walter Coblenz estimated that using guild extras—who might easily cost twice as much as nonunion actors—could account for almost 20 percent of the total budget of $1.5 million.[15] For a picture with eighty locations and extensive crowd scenes requiring some seven hundred extras, reaching a compromise with the Screen Actors Guild was key to keeping the production afloat. Coblenz explained, "We've got 100 to 125 actors in this film and a crew and staff of 40. If this picture was done in Hollywood, it would cost $3.5 million and the script would end up on the shelf."[16] As AFL-CIO president Don Haggerty complained, the incentives of location shooting outside Hollywood included "avoidance of studio overhead, avoidance of state corporate taxes on production, free or cheap city and state licensing, the ability to dodge payment on fringe benefits, cheaper extras, and loose or non-existent union regulations that allow production savings."[17]

As these comments suggest, the expansion of domestic location shooting was met with resistance from Los Angeles craft unions, which viewed the trend as an extension of the overseas runaway production problem they had been combating since the 1940s. In New York and other developing production centers, however, the steady flow of work from Hollywood was warmly received. Hollywood's increasing tendency to shoot on location beyond Southern California had not gone unnoticed by state and municipal governments, which rapidly formalized their efforts to attract film production, accelerating the outward flow of productions from the West Coast to far-flung destinations across the United States and Canada. From the mid-1960s, this expansion of the geographical range of location shooting in the United States was driven by the competitive activities of a new institution: the film office or film bureau. New York City led the way in 1966, when Mayor John Lindsay established the Mayor's Office of Motion Pictures and Television.[18] Working against the prevailing view of New York as unwelcoming to film crews, the film office offered a streamlined, "one-stop shop" for shooting permits, a full-time film commissioner with direct access to the mayor, and even a dedicated police unit to work with location crews. This move toward municipal deregulation and proactive support for Hollywood shoots was also matched by a new openness regarding censorship, which opened the door for grittier, less flattering portraits of the city (for example, representations of the subway, which had previously been carefully monitored).

The innovation of Mayor Lindsay's film office was soon replicated in cities and states across the United States and Canada. By the time of the first convention of film commissioners, or "Cineposium," in 1976, some thirty city or state film offices had been established, fueling what the New York Times referred to as "an ever spreading though undeclared war for location shooting."[19] An individual hit movie could be enough to spur local government into action. In Georgia, for example, Governor Jimmy Carter formed a new Motion Picture and Television Advisory Committee following the success of Deliverance (John Boorman, 1972), which spent around half of its $2 million budget in the state. The region's rural landscape played a starring role in the film and featured prominently in Warner Bros.' publicity materials, including a behind-the-scenes featurette. Undeterred by the film's less-than-flattering image of the locals, sightseers had flocked to the area around the Chattooga River. Such synergies between movies and place marketing were undoubtedly attractive to state governments, which began to understand the "hard" economic rewards as well as the "soft" branding effects of Hollywood production. The screenwriter Warren Skaaren, then director of the Texas Film Commission, explained, "Movie-making is an industry that creates jobs, attracts money and tourists, and provides generally favorable exposure that just can't be bought."[20] The standard film office promotional drive, according to the *New York Times*, included "brochures, production guides, letters, good-will telephone calls from the governor, visits from special representatives, and, occasionally, even a touch of Barnum Ballyhoo."[21]

Aside from the business of attracting production, film offices also frequently assisted with the location-scouting process. *American Cinematographer* noted that the Texas Film Commission had "documented the topography, architecture, and general physical characteristics of hundreds of locations all over the state," maintaining a visual library with around five thousand stills and eighteen hours of color film.[22] Film commissions often shaped the scouting and decision-making process and, in turn, helped form the filmmakers' approach to the local environment. For example, during preproduction for Alan J. Pakula's *The Parallax View* (1974), the Seattle Film Office suggested shooting at the Space Needle, which became the stage for an iconic assassination sequence. In the same scouting visit, Pakula also discovered the totem pole that was used in an early establishing shot of the Space Needle and the marching band that appears in the climactic sequences of the film.[23]

New Hollywood: Aesthetics and Techniques

These industrial and institutional shifts made location shooting increasingly desirable as a production model. But the economic and the cultural are not so easily disaggregated in Hollywood, where the difficulty of manufacturing products that capture the imagination of audiences inevitably brings questions of aesthetics and taste back into the equation. If rapid cultural change and the unpredictable viewing habits of sixteen- to twenty-five-year-olds had led the studios into dire financial straits at the end of the sixties, one remedy was to find new creative voices that might reestablish a connection with that demographic. The emerging "auteurs" of the New Hollywood had disparate backgrounds, but one common factor that linked them was their lack of familiarity with the Hollywood studio as a production environment. In most cases, they had gained formative experience in different filmmaking contexts where location shooting was common, whether in film schools (Martin Scorsese, Francis Ford Coppola, George Lucas), documentary film (John Boorman, John Schlesinger, Haskell Wexler), European cinema (Roman Polanski, Milos Forman), or television (William Friedkin, Robert Altman).[24] This was also the case for some of the era's most influential

cinematographers, among them László Kovács and Vilmos Zsigmond, both of
whom had trained in Budapest and famously shot documentary footage of the
Hungarian Revolution on the streets of the city.

For these filmmakers, working on location was second nature, and the techniques and technologies that often accompanied location work—handheld camera, available light, zoom lenses—were habitual choices. The aesthetic shift is
palpable in early films by New Hollywood directors, such as *You're a Big Boy
Now* (Francis Ford Coppola, 1966) and *Who's That Knocking at My Door* (Martin Scorsese, 1967), each of which made extensive use of New York locations.
Both directors had attended university film programs (Coppola, UCLA; Scorsese, NYU), where low-budget, seat-of-the-pants filmmaking was an essential
component of their training. They were also aficionados of European cinema,
and their early pictures drew inspiration from across the Atlantic. For Coppola
and Scorsese, as for many other directors of their generation, the inclination
toward location shooting was an index of the pervasive influence of the French
New Wave and other "new cinemas" in American film culture during the sixties.
As Geoffrey Nowell-Smith has argued, location shooting was central to postwar European cinema, and its use was as often driven by ethics and politics as
by necessity. For Rossellini and De Sica, Antonioni and Godard, all of whom
deployed location shooting in different ways, leaving the studio behind was not
just a production choice but a worldview or a philosophy, a vital component of
cinema's engagement with material and social reality.[25] The U.S. directors were
less prone to intellectualize their practice, but in the late sixties, location shooting clearly met a pressing need for a more culturally relevant and socially aware
cinema—in the words of *Time* magazine, filmmaking that displayed "a heady
new freedom from formula, convention and censorship."[26]

Location shooting was a significant enabling factor behind this break with
tradition. At a practical level, working away from the studio made it easier for
filmmakers to depart from Hollywood's entrenched conventions and craft practices. From this perspective, the location shoot could be seen as a crucible of
technical innovation and aesthetic change, where moving from the predictable
and controllable environment of the soundstage to the contingency of the location demanded ad hoc decision-making and creative problem-solving. As Jay
Beck has argued with respect to sound recording, small location crews often
broke down established hierarchies and blurred boundaries between crafts, particularly in nonunion settings.[27] Independent companies such as BBS, American
Zoetrope, and Lion's Gate were at the forefront of these developments. Though
relations between the various creative talents involved were often complex, and
sometimes conflictual, the location shoot at its best offered a new kind of collab-
orative process with the potential to overturn outmoded working practices and
open up artistic horizons. At the same time, however, it is important to recognize
the extent to which successful location shooting, especially for a project with

mainstream distribution, necessarily involved controlling the filmmaking environment, minimizing contingencies, and mitigating risks. Hollywood filmmakers in this period worked on both sides of this equation, creating new methods and techniques while simultaneously assimilating location work into established standards of professionalism and quality.

The notion that the location shoot might offer a qualitatively different filming experience was demonstrated by late 1960s films such as *Medium Cool* (Haskell Wexler, 1969). Filmed in Chicago during the tumultuous events of August 1968, *Medium Cool* showed how a location could become an active part of the filmmaking process rather than just a static backdrop to be matched to a preexisting idea. As Wexler later explained,

> On a location film you have your concepts in mind and you look for locations that fit those concepts. You're looking for, let's say, a huge parking lot. That's a perfect place. Then you go along and you come to an empty parking lot that has beautiful yellow lines, a beautiful pattern, and you get up on top of Dodger Stadium and look down, and you say, "It would be great to do this thing with no cars, just use the patterns of the lines and have the figures small on your screen." So then you change your concept; you change this particular thing that you're going to photograph.[28]

As Wexler suggests, the visual qualities of a particular location might alter the filmmakers' approach, generating new concepts and cinematic strategies. But locations are social as well as visual environments, and the possibilities and constraints they afford can generate narrative as well as aesthetic effects. *Medium Cool* famously pushed this working method to another level. Using a script that was flexible enough to incorporate the inevitable protests around the Democratic National Convention, however they might develop, Wexler allowed the unfolding action in the city's streets and public spaces to become a living, breathing part of the film. In the climactic sequences of *Medium Cool*, the characters wander through unstaged, violent clashes between protestors and police, bringing together fiction and nonfiction, Hollywood and cinema verité. Although the film's radical mixing of modes was rarely (if ever) matched, this working method nevertheless enacted a symbolic shift away from the primacy of the shooting script toward an acceptance of the contingencies of the filmmaking environment, with regard to both mise-en-scène and narrative action. For other filmmakers, the contingency of the location became a way to reenergize genre filmmaking. While shooting *The French Connection* (1971), William Friedkin transposed documentary techniques into a generic framework to create a sense of stripped-down immediacy for his New York pursuit sequences. Using a technique that he later called "induced documentary," Friedkin would rehearse the actors without the camera crew present. When the scene was ready to be filmed, he instructed cinematographer Owen Roizman and his team to "find the action" as if covering a live event on television news.[29] The zooms, whip pans, and reframing of the action generate a sense of imperfection and liveness that belies the carefully choreographed movements of the actors in the scene.

These new techniques were underwritten by technological innovation, which was a crucial, though not always primary, driver of change during the period. Whereas in previous decades, location shooting had often been seen to restrict the possibilities available to filmmakers, a series of technological advances during the 1960s and 1970s made it easier to stage complex action and maintain high production values outside the studio. New technologies pushed down costs and made it less logistically complex to film on location. Working with fewer people and smaller, lighter equipment, location crews became more mobile and agile. The flexibility of location work was transformed by a series of technological innovations, from lightweight cameras to the Cinemobile equipment van, which are discussed in further detail below. Advances in film stock and lighting equipment made it easier to achieve professional results in "available light" or low-light settings. Faster (more light-sensitive) film stock played a key role. In particular, Eastman Color Negative 5254, introduced in 1968, made it viable to film exteriors in color with available light, an important advance given that color stock had become standardized for mainstream releases by the late 1960s.[30] The potential of fast stocks was also realized by the simultaneous development of high-speed lenses and new portable xenon and metal halide arc lights.[31]

Such changes in working practices and filming technologies helped establish what Carlo Rotella has called a "location aesthetic" in New Hollywood cinematography.[32] Though the history of film style is necessarily influenced by multiple, overlapping factors, the emerging naturalistic style of cinematography in the late 1960s was demonstrably shaped by the experience of working outside the studio and the need to establish up-to-date conventions of realism. Drawing on varied influences from European film, documentary, underground cinema, and television, New Hollywood filmmakers adopted a series of techniques that crystallized into a period style. This style was catalyzed in the first instance by the exigencies of working outside the studio, and though it was not subsequently limited to location work, it remained closely associated with it. The key hallmarks of this style include handheld camera, available light, telephoto and zoom lens work, and photographic imperfections such as lens flare. Beyond cinematography, it might also be signified by a looser approach to blocking and staging—for example, allowing people and traffic to momentarily obstruct the camera.[33] Not all of these were exclusively location techniques, and not all were present in every case; but the prevalence of nonstudio work in the 1960s and 1970s nevertheless enabled these elements to become codified as a particular location look for the period. This style, above all associated with the grainy quality of footage shot with available light, became a key marker of difference between the New

Hollywood and the studio system, with its emphasis on interior sets, three-point lighting, and the aura of technical perfection.

In early New Hollywood films, this location aesthetic was seen to offer a new kind of realism that challenged classical conventions. Given the importance of "realism" as a key term in craft discourse throughout Hollywood history, its deployment in the 1960s might suggest continuity rather than a break with studio traditions. Yet, as contemporary discussions of *Bonnie and Clyde* show, the documentary-style naturalism offered by location cinematography could be seen as a challenge to traditional production values and ideas of quality. An extensive profile in *American Cinematographer* emphasized the film's "raw cinematic realism," which it framed as a departure from Hollywood conventions. The article emphasizes the authenticity of the filming process, drawing attention to the use of the actual small-town Texas locations visited by the real-life outlaws, and its variation from cinematographic standards more generally. As veteran director of photography Burnett Guffey noted of Penn and Beatty, "They were out to get stark realism on celluloid. Nothing was to be beautiful. Everything was to be, you might say, *harsh*—and that's the way it was through the whole picture."[34] This look was achieved by removing fill lighting and the kind of soft, diffused lighting conventionally used to glamorize actors, and through a subdued approach to color in production design. The overall effect was to avoid the image being slick or pretty; for Herb Lightman, the result had "a raw quality that might be called 'documentary.'"[35]

As these descriptions of *Bonnie and Clyde* as "rough" and "raw" suggest, the accentuated docurealism of the period was not always achieved through a greater fidelity of the image. Drawing on the influence of documentary, the roughness and grainy quality of the image alongside "imperfections" such as lens flare became key markers of cinematographic authenticity. In the first instance, this was a by-product of working in low-light settings on location. Cinematographers such as Gordon Willis, Vilmos Zsigmond, and Owen Roizman developed techniques to compensate for lower amounts of light, which produced a distinctive grainy aesthetic. Two strategies were widely used to counteract underexposure. First, cinematographers experimented with overdeveloping or "pushing" the film stock in processing, which tends to flatten contrast and expose grain in the image. Used heavily by Roizman on *The French Connection*, this technique created the "dismal, dreary look" that underscored the unprettified vision of the city streets.[36] Another common technique, pioneered by Zsigmond and others, was to "flash" the film stock by exposing it to a controlled amount of light in a printer before shooting. For films such as *McCabe and Mrs. Miller* (Robert Altman, 1971) and *The Long Goodbye* (Robert Altman, 1973), this created a "washed out," hazy feel to the image. Both of these techniques were driven by low-light locations in the first instance, though the available light look quickly became conventionalized and sought after as a distinctive aesthetic in itself. As Owen Roizman explained about *The French Connection*, "That's the effect I worked for throughout the picture, that feeling of available light—but it wasn't. I can tell you the times I used available light and it wasn't very often. I didn't light any exterior day scene—that was all available light." While filming in the Westbury Hotel, the crew rigged lights to achieve what Roizman calls an "available light look."[37] As this suggests, the *look* of available light had rapidly become as important as the reality. This intangible but undeniable contemporary feel of the location aesthetic made it the baseline style for many filmmakers.

Another key marker of location-based realism was the lens flare, or the technique of allowing light to hit the lens at such an angle as to create artifacts (rings, circles, lines, or areas of haze) on the surface of the image. Flares were previously regarded by Hollywood cinematographers as a mistake but became increasingly acceptable, even fashionable, after their repeated use in late-sixties films such as *Easy Rider*. By drawing attention to the physical properties of the lens and therefore the presence of the camera itself, lens flares break with the transparency of classical realism. In contrast, the location aesthetic subtly draws attention to the process of filming as a means of authentication. Like the shakiness of handheld camera, lens flare reminded audiences of documentary or newsreel footage, making its photographic "imperfection" a desirable marker of documentary veracity rather than Hollywood artifice. In *Easy Rider*, for example, sunlight flaring in the lens fit perfectly with *Easy Rider*'s ethos of cultural critique. In the New Orleans sequence in particular, it also evoked drug-altered perception and symbolized the meeting of avant-garde style with the mainstream. However, along with available light, the lens flare soon became codified and conventionalized as an industry practice, and by the mid-1970s, it had been assimilated into Hollywood's stylistic vocabulary. In *The Sugarland Express* (Steven Spielberg, 1974), a more mainstream instance of the road movie, a huge lens flare follows the climactic shoot-out and the death of the male protagonist. The director of photography, Vilmos Zsigmond, defended the technique in *American Cinematographer*, positioning its artistic validity in *The Sugarland Express* against the tendency to use it as an empty stylistic flourish. "You cannot simply show your techniques and your lens flares for no reason," said Zsigmond. "I'm sure that today there are fifty cameramen who can get excellent lens flares, but that's not enough. I do think that sometimes you can use a lens flare in a way that has meaning."[38] As Zsigmond suggests, the technique had both psychological and narrative motivation in *The Sugarland Express*, but his comments nevertheless underline how the stylistic novelty, even radical charge, of its deployment in *Easy Rider* had quickly dissipated.

Whereas the classical studio style generally prioritized medium-length lenses, New Hollywood filmmakers frequently turned to extreme lens lengths for location work. At one end of the scale, location interiors were often cramped and inflexible, requiring wide-angle lenses to create a plausible sense of space. Conversely, the need to cover action at a distance for exterior shots, often in crowded and unpredictable urban settings, gave telephoto and zoom lenses a new utility. In *Midnight Cowboy*, for example, director of photography Adam Holender repeatedly used a telephoto lens to frame Joe Buck (Jon Voight) and Ratso Rizzo (Dustin Hoffman) within the bustling environment of Manhattan streets. In this case, the telephoto lens not only enabled the camera operator to work at a safe distance from the action and without drawing attention from passersby but also created the distinctive compression of depth planes that allows the protagonists to be singled out from the crowd, directing the attention of the viewer toward the subject of the shot. Similarly, extreme zoom lenses were crucial to the bravura opening sequence of *The Conversation* (Francis Ford Coppola, 1974), in which the bird's-eye view of the couple's conversation in San Francisco's Union Square provides a visual analogue to the audio-surveillance operation of Harry Caul (Gene Hackman). Shooting the scenes from the surrounding rooftops, the crew was able to incorporate the daily activities of the square into a carefully staged sequence.

REALISM: SPACE AND PLACE

New York City's recently streamlined permitting process also made it feasible to shoot in an extensive range of locations across different parts of the city and to move crews between them with relative ease. Hollywood crews had filmed in the Bronx, Brooklyn, and Queens only sporadically in the 1940s and 1950s, but the new crime films accentuated the outer boroughs and reveled in the mise-en-scène of the marginal and the run-down.[39] *The French Connection* was a case in point, using eighty-six separate locations across the city, taking in Manhattan (upscale environs including Madison Avenue, Park Avenue, and Central Park, alongside grimier locations in Little Italy and the Lower East Side), Brooklyn (including sections of Bedford-Stuyvesant, Bensonhurst, and Coney Island), the Bronx (Hunt's Point), Queens (Maspeth), and the desolate industrial landscapes of Wards and Randalls Islands. The film's signature car chase was also notoriously shot without permits under the L-train along Eighty-Sixth Street in Brooklyn. For the sheer range of New York locations, *The French Connection* was unmatched by any movie since the 1948 crime film *The Naked City* (Jules Dassin, 1948) (figure 5.1).

Whereas *The Naked City*'s impossible but enticing claim to capture "the city as it is" positioned the film as a break with studio convention, seventies movies were routinely staked on this kind of geographical authenticity and the appearance—if not always the reality—of a one-to-one relationship between narrative setting and filming location. Nevertheless, while urban location shooting had already become commonplace by 1971, the striking authenticity and urban "grit"

Figure 5.1. William Friedkin and crew on location in New York for *The French Connection* (20th Century Fox, 1971)

of *The French Connection* likewise became central to its consumable identity. The press release emphasized the readily quotable statistic of "86 locations," repeated by Pauline Kael in her *New Yorker* review, while the trailer foregrounded the nail-biting car chase through the city streets. As Kael remarked, *The French Connection* and films like it had "captured the soul of this city in a way that goes beyond simple notions of realism. The panhandler in the movie looks just like the one who jostles you as you leave the movie theatre; the police sirens in the movie are screaming outside; the hookers and junkies in the freak show on the screen are indistinguishable from the ones in the freak show on the streets."[40] Richard Zanuck concurred, proudly recalling in a later television interview, "It was tough,

it was gritty, it was grainy, it was realistic. . . . The other pictures looked like movies; this looked like the real thing."[41]

Just two years after Fox had hit the rocks with *Hello Dolly!* and *Star!*, then, the
grimy New York locations and rough-and-ready aesthetics of *The French Connection* had moved the studio into a new paradigm. For the film's producers,
this sense of place-based authenticity outweighed the not-insubstantial logistical problems of the shoot. "Filming in New York in the winter presents unique
problems to the filmmaker," noted Phil D'Antoni. "Juggling schedules and locations, cooperating with various city authorities, moving hundreds of people
and heavy equipment all over town, often in snow and sleet, but it was worth
it. We achieved a 'feel' of the streets impossible to duplicate on a Hollywood
studio lot."[42] However, if New Hollywood movies were frequently more closely
attuned to the realities of their narrative settings, their presentation onscreen
was no less a fictional contract, as filmmakers still necessarily pieced together
fragmented parts of the city in ways that were not entirely faithful to its actual
layout. This kind of "creative geography" is visible, for example, in an early scene
in *The French Connection* in which Popeye Doyle and Cloudy Russo pursue a
suspect through alleyways and across abandoned lots. Here, Friedkin cuts locations in Brooklyn and Harlem into one seamless chase sequence. A native New
Yorker might just have been able to spot the transition, but it worked for the vast
majority of the global audience, as Friedkin was well aware. When a local resident wrote to Friedkin to complain about the implausibility of a car chase down
Eighty-Sixth Street, Friedkin replied, "If I was making the film just for Bensonhurst, I would, perhaps, have erred on the side of accuracy, but the film was made
for a worldwide audience, most of which has never even heard of Bensonhurst."[43]

AUTEURISM AND PLACE

As the example of *The French Connection* suggests, location shooting became
bound up with the discursive and commercial functions of auteurism. For New
Hollywood directors such as Friedkin, working on location became a mark of
their auteur status, signifying a range of values such as authenticity, artistic integ-
rity, and creative control. This could operate in a variety of ways. For directors
such as Martin Scorsese, Woody Allen, and John Waters, authorship became
integrally attached to the particularity of place. Repeated settings, such as Allen's
New York, firmly linked the textual to the biographical and became central to
the films' reception as auteur products. In this respect, a region, a city, or even a
specific neighborhood—such as Scorsese's Little Italy—could become a leitmotif,
a theme with personal and emotional investment that recurs across the director's oeuvre and frames its circulation and reception. More pragmatically, place
association might also function as a kind of industrial or cultural positioning—
for example, Waters's link with the second-tier city of Baltimore bolstered his

"off-center," outsider status, while Coppola's base in San Francisco helped establish his aura of creative independence and maverick entrepreneurialism.[44]

For other New Hollywood auteurs, the place specificity offered by location shooting was less important than the working methods and model of authorship it enabled. In the case of Robert Altman, the process of location shooting itself became aligned with an idiosyncratic, personalized artistic practice, especially the "free-wheeling," quasi-countercultural atmosphere of his shoots. Despite Altman's repeated claims that his films were created collectively, the eccentric working processes and off-Hollywood vibe associated with an Altman production became a key component of his authorial signature. For Altman, as for many independently minded directors at the time, location shooting held both strategic and creative value. In the first instance, shooting far afield from Los Angeles maintained distance, both physical and psychological, from the studios and their corporate management culture. Operating outside the studio complex also gave Altman relative freedom with his working practices, allowing him to operate a looser, improvisational method that became his trademark. Though his breakthrough hit *M*A*S*H* (1970) was primarily lensed on the Fox lot, subsequent Altman films were characterized by their location shoots—working, for example, in Houston (*Brewster McCloud*, 1970), British Columbia (*McCabe and Mrs. Miller*, 1971), Los Angeles (*The Long Goodbye*, 1973), Mississippi (*Thieves Like Us*, 1974), Reno (*California Split*, 1974), and Nashville (*Nashville*, 1975).

New Hollywood: Mobility and Flexibility

The varied sites of Altman's films in the 1970s highlight the increased geographical mobility of location work during the decade. As these examples suggest, the inherent flexibility of Hollywood's new business model relied on increased mobility at the level of the film shoot, allowing filmmakers to choose between competing locations across the United States, Canada, and beyond. This structure was catalyzed by a number of technological innovations that increased the mobility and flexibility of location shooting, including Arriflex and Panaflex cameras, the Steadicam camera mount, and the Cinemobile equipment van. In turn, these operational changes helped facilitate genres and cycles of films that display the critical importance not just of authentic place but also kinetic and complex movement through it. Across films of the period, the mobility and flexibility of the location shoot enabled and intensified a dynamic relation to space and place.

The heightened mobility of the location shoot was a defining feature of the road movie, often viewed as the emblematic genre of the late 1960s and early 1970s. The motif of the journey was by no means new to American culture, but it found renewed importance in films such as *Bonnie and Clyde, Easy Rider, The Rain People* (Francis Ford Coppola, 1969), *Two-Lane Blacktop* (Monte Hellman,

1971), *Vanishing Point* (Richard C. Sarafian, 1971), *Badlands* (Terence Malick, 1973), *Scarecrow* (Jerry Schatzberg, 1973), *The Last Detail* (Hal Ashby, 1973), and *Thunderbolt and Lightfoot* (Michael Cimino, 1974). For early examples of the cycle, such as *Easy Rider* and *The Rain People*, the protagonists' voyages of self-discovery across rural and small-town America paralleled the films' mode of production. Taking a small crew on an improvisatory journey without a fully developed shooting script, both of these productions allowed the contingencies of the road to push the narrative in different directions. As Coppola recalled, the traveling location shoot offered a new model for developing a film on the fly: "We traveled for four months through eighteen states, filming as we went. . . . We did not set out with a finished screenplay in hand but continued filling it out as shooting progressed. When I spied a setting that appealed to me along the way, we would stop, and I would work out a scene for the actors to play."[45] Similarly, Dennis Hopper and Peter Fonda recalled "tearing up the script" before setting out on the road.[46] This method was a departure from contemporary location standards, even for the late 1960s. While the Texas shoot for *Bonnie and Clyde* was relatively unusual in its range, *American Cinematographer* still described the production convoy as a heavy military operation resembling "the logistics of a Napoleonic army on the move—twenty vehicles including a dozen trucks for props, wardrobe, special effects, camera, sound equipment and, finally, an entourage of seventy, which included actors and technical staff."[47] In contrast, *Easy Rider* and *The Rain People* flaunted their stripped-down and lightweight production apparatus as a break with studio convention.

While *Easy Rider* and *The Rain People* were trailblazers, the availability of lighter cameras made location crews increasingly flexible across the board. Handheld camerawork, already popular in New Hollywood film, was significantly improved by Arri's Arriflex 35 BL (1972), which Barry Salt describes as "the first production camera to fully realize the concept of being completely balanced when handheld on the cameraman's shoulder,"[48] and later by Panavision's Panaflex (1973). These lightweight cameras made it easier to film inside moving vehicles, which helped propel the already-existing subgenre of the car-chase movie to further success at the box office. This trend arguably started a few years earlier with the spectacular use of San Francisco in *Bullitt* (Peter Yates, 1968), which kick-started a cycle of car-chase films, including *The French Connection*, *The Seven-Ups* (Philip D'Antoni, 1973), *The Sugarland Express*, *Smokey and the Bandit* (Hal Needham, 1977), and *The Driver* (Walter Hill, 1978).[49] Though there were clear areas of overlap with the road movie, these films tended to emphasize the visceral thrills of the chase, rather than the cultural critique often embedded in the cross-country journey. Of these films, *The Sugarland Express* is notable as both Spielberg's debut as feature director, following a formative period in television production for Universal, and the production debut of an important new camera, the Panaflex 35 mm. As an in-depth profile in *American Cinematographer*

Figure 5.2. An interior car shot filmed with the Panaflex camera in *The Sugarland Express* (Zanuck-Brown / Universal Pictures, 1974)

explained, Panavision carefully selected the Zanuck-Brown/Universal production as a test case for the equipment. As the company saw it, the feature "posed some unique photographic problems and would give the Panaflex an 'acid test' kind of shakedown."[50] Among these challenges were the extensive interior car sequences, which required the camera operator to work with minimal space and limited lighting and to achieve movements, such as 360-degree pans, that would be near impossible with a bulkier camera (figure 5.2). Zanuck described Panaflex as "super-efficient, super-quiet, super-small and super-light"; Spielberg concurred, adding that it would "revolutionize the business."[51] Its revolutionary quality lay not only in its size and maneuverability but also in its quietness, which allowed the camera to get extremely close to the microphone without compromising the sound recording. For Zsigmond, the flexibility and unobtrusiveness of Panaflex offered a new kind of realism through stylistic transparency—as he put it, "What we're going for is reality. . . . We would like the audience to feel that they're with us every single minute—inside of the car, outside of the car, everyplace—and we would really like not to be noticed at all. We're trying to make it look as though there're no cameras and no lighting involved at all."[52]

As with earlier films such as *The Rain People*, the crew was relatively small and the equipment lightweight. According to the unit manager, they were "doing a picture in a non-studio way, with a small, handpicked crew moving like greased lightning."[53] The production took in over fifty locations over a forty-eight-day schedule, including San Antonio, Houston, Austin, and a range of small towns and rural spots. This stripped-down working method, along with the new camera, enabled what Spielberg and cinematographer Vilmos Zsigmond described as a "documentary approach."[54] The pair viewed documentaries to find "creative solutions" to the problems of location shooting and resolved to shoot as much as possible with available light and direct sound. Spielberg and Zsigmond also insisted that process shots were strictly off-limits, which demonstrates the extent to which codes of realism had evolved around location shooting.[55] Alongside other successful car-chase films of the 1970s, *The Sugarland Express* established the standard for complex location photography in moving vehicles, while bridging between the introspection of the late-1960s road movie and the family-oriented entertainment of the postclassical action film.

Though lighter cameras such as Panaflex brought new possibilities for hand-held work, the results could be shaky and unstable—acceptable enough for an independent production, perhaps, but still potentially a concern for major studio releases. These problems were effectively solved by the introduction of Garrett Brown's camera-stabilization device Steadicam, first marketed in 1975, which quietly revolutionized traveling shots by making it possible for a single camera operator to achieve smooth, complex motion without laying track. By insulating the camera from the jerky movement of the operator's body, it allowed fluid and almost uncannily balanced motion as well as intricate camera movements such as 360-degree pans.[56] According to its promotional material, Steadicam offered "total freedom of movement while recording extremely steady and jitter-free handheld moving shots of dolly-quality smoothness."[57] The impact of Steadicam was easily visible in *Rocky* (John G. Avildsen, 1976) and *Marathon Man* (John Schlesinger, 1976), both of which realized the device's potential for fluid movement through urban space. In *Rocky*, the smooth yet embodied motion of the camera through the streets of Philadelphia suited both the film's social realist tendencies and the euphoric rush of its self-improvement story line. On the shoot of *Marathon Man*, Steadicam enabled smooth, unbroken tracking shots around Central Park and allowed the crew to weave their way unobtrusively through the crowded sidewalks of Manhattan's Diamond District. In both cases, Steadicam did not enable a new technique—handheld camera in urban locations—so much as help to standardize and professionalize it. By eliminating the bumpiness of handheld camerawork and smoothing its rougher edges, Steadicam helped bring it into line with traditional conceptions of Hollywood realism, and by enabling complex and elaborate movement through screen space, it helped establish a new kind of intensified visual style.[58]

While Panaflex and Steadicam enabled flexibility at the level of individual shots and setups, the increased geographical mobility of Hollywood crews was facilitated by Cinemobile, an equipment truck that won its inventor, Fouad Said, a Scientific and Technical Award from AMPAS in 1970. Said graduated from USC as a cinematographer in 1957 and first developed Cinemobile for use on the television series *I Spy* (NBC, 1965–68), a groundbreaking production that made international travel and exotic locations its trademark.[59] Although Cinemobile units incorporated cutting-edge filmmaking equipment, their primary contribution was logistical rather than purely technological. What Said's company offered was the opportunity to rent bespoke vehicles designed to transport location shooting equipment: a lightweight generator and the latest high-tech filming gear, from cameras and lights to electrical cables and tracks. *Variety* pinpointed its contribution, noting, "Those old hands who claim all this is nothing new, that studios have been loading up trucks and moving on locations since the invention of the camera, are missing the point. The compact mobile systems are creating a new location technology and system of production."[60] Cinemobile was routinely glossed in the press as a portable studio—the *Los Angeles Times* dubbed it a "motion picture studio on wheels," for example[61]—but this formulation misses the target, as the vans were, of course, not studios per se, and the equipment they carried was specifically tailored for locations rather than soundstages (as Said himself explained, "studio and location shooting are two completely 'different animals'").[62] Rather than providing a "mobile studio," Cinemobile units offered the technical resources to turn any location *into* a studio or, to put it more precisely, into an environment where studio-standard production could take place. By maximizing efficiency and portability, Cinemobile helped create a more cost-effective infrastructure for location shooting, effectively narrowing the gap between studio and location and, by extension, the split between independent and mainstream filmmaking practices.

In February 1971, *Variety* drew a direct contrast between Cinemobile and the Hollywood studio as symbols of emerging and declining production models. With 20th Century Fox on a complete production hiatus and soundstages at other studios frequently as "silent and still as tombs," *Variety* intuited it "a sign of the changing movie making technology that a dozen units of expanding Cinemobile Studios Systems [were] in operation at the same time, several paradoxically on Los Angeles locations."[63] The integration of Cinemobile into the industry had been relatively rapid, and as *Variety* suggested, its success had not coincidentally occurred during the crisis of 1969–71, when cutting budgets and slashing overheads were the order of the day. After Cinemobile's extensive use on television serials in the late 1960s, its first application on a feature film was *Take the Money and Run* (Woody Allen, 1969), shot on location in San Francisco. The film's associate producer, Jack Grossberg, estimated that Cinemobile had saved the production twenty shooting days and reduced the crew by fifteen to twenty people a day, saving around $400,000 in total.[64] Such economic incentives drove the exponential expansion of the company over the period of the industry downturn: while only three productions made use of Cinemobile in 1968, the number had grown to 102 features by 1971.[65] For productions that required extensive outdoor work across multiple sites, Cinemobile units quickly became indispensable. Endorsing the Cinemobile in *American Cinematographer*, William Fraker claimed that the vehicles made it possible to film forty to forty-five setups and make up to six major location moves per day, gaining up to two hours of extra productivity. For road movies such as *Vanishing Point* (Richard C. Sarafian, 1971), shot across the landscape of the U.S. Southwest, or

Figure. 5.3. Cross-promotional advertising for Cinemobile
and *The Godfather* (Paramount, 1972).

westerns such as *Jeremiah Johnson* (Sydney Pollack, 1972), filmed in nearly one
hundred locations across Utah, Cinemobile enabled multiple setups in one day
while maintaining professional standards in often-difficult natural terrain.[66]
Shooting on the move across multiple sites had become both technically viable
and economically sustainable—in essence, the independent spirit of projects
such as *Easy Rider* had been mainstreamed.

The extensive cross-promotional advertising for Cinemobile and *The Godfather* (Francis Ford Coppola, 1972) (figure 5.3) suggests that Cinemobile was
already becoming well integrated into major studio productions by the early
1970s.[67] As with many innovations produced by small firms, some of the studios tried to develop rival equipment; in this case, Paramount, Columbia, and
Universal all developed their own versions, with varying degrees of success.[68]
But this process of imitation and assimilation attests both to the specific contribution of the Cinemobile as an apparatus and to the value of location shooting

to the business at large. Though Cinemobile arguably accelerated trends that were already in motion, and its technical achievements could be replicated by other companies, its impact as an industry service was nevertheless far-reaching. By enabling multiple setups in a day and making a greater range of equipment readily available on the go, Cinemobile created a more efficient, cost-effective, and robust infrastructure for location shooting. As the financial balance tipped away from the studio and high-quality, professional work became possible with smaller crews, location shooting became normalized as an industry practice.

CHALLENGES, CONFLICTS, AND LOCATION DISASTERS

The geographical distribution of location shooting across the United States also brought filmmakers into contact with regions, urban areas, and minority populations that had been marginalized during the studio era. This brought a new visibility to specific local neighborhoods and ethnic groups, particularly African Americans, but it was also a source of conflict in urban areas such as Harlem. As the so-called blaxploitation cycle made clear, the studios were fast catching up with the opportunity offered by the hitherto-neglected black audience, which constituted an increasingly significant market share, especially in urban centers. But Hollywood crews were still overwhelmingly white, and the fault lines between filmmakers and locals mirrored the racial divisions that were insistently present at a national level; as David Lamb wrote in the *Los Angeles Times*, producers were "frustrated and discouraged at trying to solve the same problems on a small scale that the nation has had difficulty with on a large scale." Reporting from the set of *Come Back, Charleston Blue* (Mark Warren, 1972), Lamb noted that "filming a major movie on location in Harlem, which Hollywood has long ignored, like other black ghettos, is all small steps, taken one at a time. It involves demands boiled into concessions, misunderstandings painfully transformed into trust, a plethora of problems and rewards never experienced by producers who shoot only on the sets of Studio City or the streets of Burbank."[69] Location shoots could become a site of tension or even outright conflict. Don Siegel recalled how the shoot of *Madigan* (1968) had run into problems in Harlem, when Richard Widmark's car was "dangerously rocked" by a group of teenagers and the prop supervisor was mugged. Shooting was relocated to the familiar territory of downtown Los Angeles and a matte shot used to replace the Civic Center with an image of a New York skyscraper. Such a retreat was hardly acceptable, though, for later films that thrived on gritty local detail. For shoots in African American neighborhoods, especially those perceived to be ghettos, community relations became a routine part of production planning, leading the Congress of Racial Equality (CORE) and other organizations to play an active role in brokering negotiations between film companies and local communities. For example, after a request from CORE, the producers of *Across 110th Street* (Barry Shear, 1972) participated in an apprentice program to help smooth relations between the film crew and the community in Harlem.[70]

Such conflicts on location could create negative publicity for the studios. But the use of specific locations and even the process of location filming, along with its challenges and setbacks, could equally become part of a film's marketable identity and promotional strategy. This was especially the case for projects such as *Jaws* (Steven Spielberg, 1975) and *The Deer Hunter* (Michael Cimino, 1978) that employed extensive location work in unforgiving natural environments. By the mid-1970s, the industry was increasingly incorporating the backstory of a film's production into its promotional materials, whether in magazine features, trailers, behind-the-scenes shorts, or tie-in books. This sated audience desires for "insider" information while allowing the studios to manage their reputation through carefully performed self-disclosure. *Jaws* was a case in point. Two "making-of" books by Carl Gottlieb and Edith Blake, released in the same year as the film, were frank about the various crises that had beset the production, which could easily be read about in the press in any case.[71] These books, alongside other promotional materials for the film, show how the location shoot became a focal point for industrial self-reflection at precisely the point when it became most problematic.

Blake's and Gottlieb's accounts both frame the filming of *Jaws* on Martha's Vineyard as a narrative of obstacles overcome by authorial ingenuity and Hollywood professionalism. Spielberg insisted on shooting at sea, despite the difficulties that inevitably entailed. He later recalled, "I was hell bent on shooting on the open seas, and if they insisted I shoot it in the tank, I was absolutely going to quit the movie. . . . The '70s was a time when the environment was crucial to the storytelling."[72] As Spielberg suggests, *Jaws* was caught between the realist aesthetics of the first wave of New Hollywood, which required shooting at sea rather than in a studio tank, and the new challenges of the spectacular, technology-driven spectacle of the second wave—in this case, creating a plausible mechanical shark that would provide visceral thrills for the audience. Alongside the extensive physical effects work required for the shark, the production also used recent developments in camera equipment to overcome the challenges of filming in the water. For the film's signature shark's-view shots, Spielberg's team made heavy use of the "waterbox," a device developed by Panavision for *Deliverance* that allowed the camera to be submerged in water so the lens could sit just above the surface.

After a series of setbacks, including a sinking boat and a camera lost at sea, the shoot on Martha's Vineyard eventually went 104 days over schedule, with costs spiraling to nearly $12 million, around three times the original budget. But the various paratexts circulating before and after the film's release typically managed to recuperate the problems of the location shoot into a positive narrative. The two books, as well as profiles in magazines such as *American Cinematographer*, reveal many of the inherent challenges of location shooting but manage to reinscribe them within a counternarrative about auteurist vision, consummate professionalism, and the ingenuity of Hollywood craftspeople. The film's status as a blockbuster "event film" is therefore justified by the exceptional narrative behind its creation. According to this framing, the film is shot on location at all costs, a product of the director's single-minded quest for authenticity, but the problems this generates must be faced by the collective endeavors of the cast and crew. Challenges are overcome and disasters averted, and while the location shoot takes the project to the brink, no obstacle is insurmountable for the team of Hollywood professionals. While this script was repeatedly found in official or semiofficial paratexts, it was also common in more autonomous reporting in outlets such as *American Cinematographer*. In a profile of *The Deer Hunter*, for example, Scott Henderson reported that the crew had "cracked up physically and psychologically" while they were "seared on location by the blistering heat of the hottest American summer in 20 years, chilled to the bone in the frigid cloud of the Cascade Mountains, sweltering in the poisonous snake-ridden jungles of Thailand, [and] turned blue in the freezing waters of the River Kwai." Yet, in Henderson's words, the final product was "flawless in its technical quality" and showed no outward signs of such stresses and strains, a testament to the filmmakers' "dedication, determination and sheer uncompromising perfectionism."[73] Here, the press coverage highlights the spectacular qualities of the location shoot and affirms its status as an arena for (male) professionalism and endurance in the name of artistic endeavor.

Alongside this promotional framing, the critical and commercial success of films such as *Jaws* and *The Deer Hunter* smoothed over the difficulties of their shoots. Other productions were not so fortunate, and the most famous cases of budget overrun in the late 1970s were closely associated with high-profile auteurs losing control over challenging locations and going ruinously over schedule. This was the case with *Days of Heaven* (1978), for which Terence Malick and cinematographer Néstor Almendros notoriously insisted on shooting during the "magic hour" before sunset, though the undeniable artistry of the end result helped to justify the means. For other productions, the cost-reward equation tipped in the other direction, and the disaster that Spielberg had narrowly averted with *Jaws* materialized first with the critical and commercial failure of *Sorcerer* (William Friedkin, 1977) and more famously with the troubled shoots and runaway budgets of *Apocalypse Now* (Francis Ford Coppola, 1979) and *Heaven's Gate* (Michael Cimino, 1980). In each case, an emblematic New Hollywood director was seen to have been overwhelmed by the natural terrain and nearly defeated in his own hubristic attempts to master it. The behind-the-scenes stories of *Apocalypse Now* and *Heaven's Gate*, recorded in the documentary *Hearts of Darkness* and Steven Bach's book *Final Cut*, respectively, flipped the *Jaws* script and placed the auteur at the center of a costly location disaster. *Apocalypse Now* could be partially redeemed by its critical success, especially at the Academy Awards, as well as its substantial box-office returns, but it was hard to dispel the negative associations it had created between auteurist autonomy and complex location shoots. *Heaven's Gate*, on the other hand, lost nearly $44 million and was widely credited with sinking United Artists.[74] The decline of the so-called auteur renaissance was undoubtedly a more complex phenomenon and, for many observers, had already set in by 1976–77, but these two films nevertheless became influential symbols of wider shifts in the industry. The famously troubled shoots had multiple impacts on the business, but one effect was to link extensive location shooting with directorial profligacy, spiraling costs, and ultimately, box-office failure.

THE END OF THE 1970S: A RETURN TO THE STUDIO

In the context of *Apocalypse Now* and *Heaven's Gate*, a strategic recalibration of studio and location work seemed necessary to reestablish managerial control and budgetary restraint. At the same time, an emerging trend was pushing filmmaking back to the studio for different reasons. As the industry stabilized and then boomed in the late 1970s, the most successful blockbuster hits were science fiction films—most famously, *Star Wars* (George Lucas, 1977) and *Close Encounters of the Third Kind* (Steven Spielberg, 1977)—that relied heavily on visual effects, especially optical printing, models, and computer-controlled traveling mattes. As the successes of *The Godfather*, *The Exorcist*, *Jaws*, and *Rocky* made clear, the seventies blockbuster was by no means a predominantly studio-based affair, but the rise of the science fiction A film tipped the realism of the seventies toward the more artificial and stylized tendencies that were to typify the decade that followed.

According to the cinematographer Conrad Hall, the location-based realism of the New Hollywood was already on the wane by 1975: "For a long time, in films, we went through a phase of non-reality. Then all that changed. We've now just completed a phase of ultra-reality. We've had it and I think it's turning back onto itself. There now seems to be more of a balance of location and studio filming, with the major decision being how best you can control what you're trying to do to get what you want. So achieving realness is not necessarily the most ideal aspect."[75] As Hall suggests, while the turn against the perceived "non-reality" of studio production had been wide ranging, the documentary-inflected aesthetics of the late sixties and early seventies could relatively easily be displaced by other priorities or alternative conceptions of what "realness" might mean. Location shooting had been intimately linked to discourses of realism and authenticity in the seventies, but those qualities are, of course, mutable and historically specific. By the end of the decade, the intensive development of special effects techniques meant that location shooting was no longer the only method of achieving images that filmmakers and audiences would recognize as "realistic." As Julie Turnock has shown, companies such as Industrial Light & Magic developed special visual effects in dialogue with New Hollywood conventions of photorealism, not in opposition to them.[76] Whereas studio-era films had frequently strived to make locations look like studios, the converse was now true, in that the soundstage and optical effects work of the late 1970s and early 1980s was designed to blend seamlessly with the location aesthetic. Location shooting was not so much displaced, then, but rather reintegrated into a transformed, high-tech filmmaking process with new priorities and production values.

Close Encounters of the Third Kind exemplifies this recalibration of the Hollywood production model in its multilayered integration of location shooting, elaborate sets, and innovative visual effects. As the production designer Joe Alves noted, the film was defined by its "vast scale" and "tremendous scope."[77] In the first instance, this sense of scale is supplied by the iconic power of the natural landscape, especially the Devil's Tower in Wyoming, which was initially captured by location shooting but later reproduced using models and matte paintings. At the same time, *Close Encounters* also broke new ground by integrating science fiction spectacle with the plausible, everyday mise-en-scène of suburban life. Much of the film's first hour was shot on location in California, Wyoming, and Alabama, with a few brief scenes in India. This material was augmented with matte paintings, models, animation, and front-projection techniques to depict the characters' initial "encounters" with extraterrestrial technology. Spielberg's film also heralded the return of large-scale process shots: the spectacular scenes of the starry sky at night—impossible to capture conventionally on 35 mm—were achieved using what was then the largest front-projection screen ever built. With the spatial authenticity and realist tone of the picture having been established through location shooting, the film's climactic thirty-five-minute alien-contact sequence takes place entirely on two vast sets built in disused hangars outside Mobile, constituting perhaps the largest studio sets then constructed.[78] As this suggests, a high-budget project could use locations to create a baseline style of realism but might integrate this material with extensive sets and visual effects work. Nevertheless, despite this partial return to the soundstage, the dispersed geographical coordinates of *Close Encounters* suggested that this did not necessarily mean a return to the physical space of the Los Angeles studios. Similarly, for *Star Wars*, location shooting in Tunisia and Guatemala was augmented with extensive studio work at Elstree Studios in London and visual effects processes realized by Industrial Light & Magic in Van Nuys, California.

As Jon Lewis and Julie Turnock have both argued, the priorities of auteurs such as Spielberg and Lucas subtly shifted from production to postproduction: mastery over post, especially visual effects, displaced mastery over the location.[79] In the struggle for creative control, authorship could now be asserted at the level of the frame, which allowed the director to regain ownership over the finished product and its "final cut." As a result, the improvisatory and contingent location-based methods of directors such as Altman and Friedkin became difficult to combine with extensive visual effects work, which required shots to be precisely preplanned, choreographed, and storyboarded. This was the case for a certain tendency in mainstream filmmaking, at least, though in the 1980s and beyond, the connections between authorship, place, and regional identity became even more pronounced for indie filmmakers.

CONCLUSION

During the late 1960s and 1970s, the technology, infrastructure, and working practices for Hollywood location shooting were firmly established, as was its central role in facilitating the flexible production strategies of the post-studio-system corporation. At an artistic level, location shooting was crucial to the films of the New Hollywood, whether one considers filmmaking techniques, visual style, or the complex interplay that developed between diegetic worlds and "real" place. Location practices also became bound up with the ideology of auteurism in multiple, overlapping ways. But by the end of the 1970s, studio work, which had remained a component part of the production process, took on renewed importance for spectacular blockbuster pictures that prioritized high production values and frequently relied on the creation of fantasy environments through visual effects. To an extent, Hollywood returned to the hybrid approach of the past, joining location footage together with studio and visual effects work. Yet the hypermobility and flexibility of New Hollywood has remained a constant in the Global, Conglomerate, or Digital Hollywood that superseded it, even if place specificity has often been supplanted by the economic logic of global runaway production and the principle of interchangeability (visible, for example, in the "license plating" trend for Vancouver and Toronto to stand in for any number of U.S. cities). Just as location shooting remains central to the political economy of Hollywood, the techniques it catalyzed in the filmmaking of the 1960s and 1970s—dynamic mobile cameras, the aesthetic of "available light," lens flare, and the use of zoom lenses—formed the bedrock of the visual style of Hollywood cinema in the late twentieth and early twenty-first centuries.

NOTES

1. Charles Champlin, "A Return to Studio Shooting?," *Los Angeles Times*, October 15, 1971, G1.

2. "Bus Studios: Boom in Gloom," *Variety*, April 1, 1970, 20.

3. Robert Hyle, "Movies in the Age of Mobility," *Back Stage*, March 23, 1973, 7.

4. One exception is David Cook's history of American cinema in the 1970s, though location shooting is still discussed relatively briefly. Cook, *Lost Illusions: American Cinema in the Shadow of Watergate and Vietnam, 1970–1979* (Berkeley: University of California Press, 2000).

5. John Gregory Dunne, *The Studio* (London: W. H. Allen, 1970).

6. Ibid., 123.

7. Ibid., 123–24.

8. Cook, *Lost Illusions*, 3.

9. "Fox Adjusts to Letdown Films," *Variety*, November 26, 1969, 3.

10. Compare, for example, the budgets of *Star!* ($14m), *Doctor Dolittle* ($17m) and *Hello, Dolly!* ($25m) with *Easy Rider* ($360,000), *Bonnie and Clyde* ($2.5m), *The Graduate* ($3m), and *Midnight Cowboy* ($3.2m).

11. "U.S. Film Starts, '71 over '70, Runaways Down from 60 to 42: Independents Fill Gap of Majors," *Variety*, January 12, 1972, 4.

12. Joyce Haber, "Zanuck Sees More Low-Budget Films," *Los Angeles Times*, October 9, 1969, G21.

13. Charles Champlin, "Booming Filmland's Big Turnaround," *Los Angeles Times*, November 7, 1965, B1.

14. Michael Storper and Susan Christopherson, "Flexible Specialization and Regional Industrial Agglomerations: The Case of the US Motion Picture Industry," *Annals of the Association of American Geographers* 77, no. 1 (1987): 104–17.

15. Bruce Bahrenburg, *Filming the Candidate* (New York: Warner Paperback Library, 1972), 82.

16. Ibid., 80.

17. Earl C. Gottschalk, "Goodbye Hollywood: More Movie Makers Do Filming in Sticks for Realism, Savings," *Wall Street Journal*, July 25, 1972, 1.

18. For a more in-depth discussion, see Lawrence Webb, *The Cinema of Urban Crisis: Seventies Film and the Reinvention of the City* (Amsterdam: Amsterdam University Press, 2014), 75–80. The office was renamed the Mayor's Office of Film, Theatre and Broadcasting in 1982.

19. Phyllis Funke, "How You Gonna Keep 'Em Down in Hollywood Once You've Seen the Sticks?," *New York Times*, September 22, 1974, 135.

20. Leonard F. Coleman, "Filmmaking in the Lone Star State," *American Cinematographer*, October 1973, 1283.

21. Funke, "How You Gonna Keep 'Em Down," 135.

22. Coleman, "Filmmaking in the Lone Star State," 1283.

23. Funke, "How You Gonna Keep 'Em Down," 135.

24. A high proportion of television production in this period was studio based, but Friedkin worked on TV documentaries, while Altman directed episodes of location-produced shows such as *Route 66*.

25. Geoffrey Nowell-Smith, *Making Waves: New Cinemas of the 1960s* (London: Continuum, 2008), 68–79.

26. Stefan Kanfer, "The Shock of Freedom in Films," *Time*, December 8, 1967, http://content.time.com/time/magazine/article/0,9171,844256,00.html.

27. Jay Beck, *Designing Sound: Audiovisual Aesthetics in 1970s American Cinema* (New Brunswick, NJ: Rutgers University Press, 2016).

28. Howard Schwartz, "An American Film Institute Seminar with Haskell Wexler, ASC," *American Cinematographer*, June 1977, 608.

29. Director's commentary for *The French Connection*, DVD, 20th Century Fox Home Entertainment, 2003.

30. Barry Salt, *Film Style and Technology: History and Analysis* (London: Starword, 1983), 252.

31. Ibid., 271.

32. Carlo Rotella, *Good with Their Hands: Boxers, Bluesmen, and Other Characters from the Rust Belt* (Berkeley: University of California Press, 2002), 127–28.

33. Rotella refers in particular to the "traffic wipe"—the practice of allowing cars to momentarily move in front of the camera while filming on the street.

34. Herb A. Lightman, "Raw Cinematic Realism in the Photography of 'Bonnie and Clyde,'" *American Cinematographer*, April 1967, 254.

35. Ibid.

36. "Photographing *The French Connection*," *American Cinematographer*, February 1972, 161.

37. Ibid., 184.

38. "The Moving Camera," *American Cinematographer*, June 1974, 689.

39. Richard Koszarski's research demonstrates that the Bronx, Brooklyn, and Queens were important sites for studio production and independent filmmaking before World War II. See Koszarski, *Hollywood on the Hudson: Film and Television in New York from Griffith to Sarnoff* (New Brunswick, NJ: Rutgers University Press, 2008). However, the outer boroughs were only occasionally used for Hollywood location shooting in the 1940s and 1950s, in films such as *Marty* (Delbert Mann, 1955), shot in the Bronx, and *The Wrong Man* (Alfred Hitchcock, 1956), shot in Queens.

40. Pauline Kael, "The Current Cinema: Urban Gothic," *New Yorker*, October 30, 1971, 113.

41. *The Poughkeepsie Shuffle: Tracing "The French Connection,"* dir. Mark Leven (BBC, 2000).

42. "Photographing *The French Connection*," *American Cinematographer*, February 1972, 159.

43. William Friedkin to Dr. Pearl Wiesen, April 24, 1972, Friedkin Papers, Margaret Herrick Library, Academy of Motion Picture Arts and Sciences, Beverly Hills, CA.

44. See Lawrence Webb, "Remapping the Conversation: Urban Design and Industrial Reflexivity in Seventies San Francisco," *Post45*, July 2014, http://post45.research.yale.edu/2014/06/remapping-the-conversation-urban-design-and-industrial-reflexivity-in-seventies-san-francisco/.

45. Gene D. Phillips, "Francis Ford Coppola Interviewed," in *Francis Ford Coppola: Interviews*, ed. Gene D. Phillips and Rodney Hills (Jackson: University Press of Mississippi, 2004), 147.

46. *Easy Rider: Shaking the Cage*, dir. Charles Kiselyak (Columbia TriStar, 1999).

47. Lightman, "Raw Cinematic Realism," 255.

48. Salt, *Film Style and Technology*, 275.

49. See Tico Romao, "Guns and Gas: Investigating the 1970s Car Chase Film," in *Action and Adventure Cinema*, ed. Yvonne Tasker (London: Routledge, 2004), 130–52.

50. Herb A. Lightman, "The New Panaflex Camera Makes Its Production Debut," *American Cinematographer*, May 1973, 564.

51. Ibid., 598.

52. Ibid., 617.

53. Joseph McBride, *Steven Spielberg: A Biography* (London: Faber and Faber, 1997), 213.

54. Ibid.

55. Ibid.

56. See Ted Churchill, "Steadicam: An Operator's Perspective," *American Cinematographer*, April 1983, 36–39, 113–20.

57. Cinema Products Corporation advertisement for Steadicam, *Broadcasting*, March 28, 1977, 65.

58. See David Bordwell, "Intensified Continuity: Visual Style in Contemporary American Film," *Film Quarterly* 55, no. 3 (2002): 16–28.

59. Cecil Smith, "Fouad Puts Film Savvy on Wheels," *Los Angeles Times*, June 24, 1969, C13.

60. "Bus Studios: Boom in Gloom," 20.

61. Smith, "Fouad Puts Film Savvy on Wheels," C13.

62. Ahmed Fouad Said, "The Diversification of Cinemobile Systems Inc. into Feature Film Production" (master's thesis, University of Southern California, June 1973).

63. "Cinemobile Units as Studio Contrast," *Variety*, February 3, 1971, 7.

64. Said, "Diversification of Cinemobile Systems." As these figures come from Said's own master's thesis at USC, they are to be treated with a little caution, although other contemporary sources also suggest that substantial savings were achieved by using Cinemobile units.

65. Ibid.

66. Syd Cassid, "Studios Schedule 20 Productions for Camera Starts during July," *Box-Office*, June 29, 1970, 8.

67. Sidestepping the problematic labor and community relations on the troubled film shoot, Cinemobile and Paramount developed a series of advertisements in the trade press that associated Cinemobile with the branded identity of what it announced as "the year's biggest motion picture," joining the image of the Cinemobile van with elements of the film's poster design, from the distinctive typeface to the iconic puppet strings (tagline: "Behind the scenes Cinemobile pulled the strings on 'The Godfather' and 101 other films in 1971"). These advertisements demonstrate Cinemobile Systems' attempt to position itself within the very heart of the Hollywood film industry, as well as the industry's willingness to embrace it. It may also have offered Paramount a chance to present the film's location shoot as a success, countering negative publicity about union strife, clashes with Italian American pressure groups, and budget overrun that was circulating in the press at the same time.

68. Al Delugach, "Film Studio in a Van: Profit Potential Is Epic," *Los Angeles Times*, November 5 1972, I1; see also Dan Knapp, "Mobile Cinema: Will It Really Do the Job?," *Los Angeles Times*, August 2, 1970, M1, 13.

69. David Lamb, "Realities Shake Harlem Film Set," *Los Angeles Times*, April 2, 1972, B1.

70. William Wolf, "On Location in Harlem—Black and White," *Los Angeles Times*, July 9 1972, X24.

71. Edith Blake, *On Location . . . on Martha's Vineyard: The Making of the Movie "Jaws"* (New York: Ballantine, 1975); Carl Gottlieb, *The Jaws Log: Expanded Edition* (New York: Newmarket, 2001).

72. Peter Biskind, *Easy Riders, Raging Bulls: How the Sex-Drugs-and-Rock'n'Roll Generation Saved Hollywood* (London: Bloomsbury, 1998), 263.

73. Scott Henderson, "Behind the Scenes of *The Deer Hunter*," *American Cinematographer*, October 1978, 960.

74. David Cook, *Lost Illusions: American Cinema in the Shadow of Watergate and Vietnam, 1970–1979* (Berkeley: University of California Press, 2000), 62–63.

75. Conrad Hall, "Photographing *The Day of the Locust*," *American Cinematographer*, June 1975, 723.

76. Julie Turnock, *Plastic Reality: Special Effects, Technology, and the Emergence of 1970s Blockbuster Aesthetics* (New York: Columbia University Press, 2015).

77. Joe Alves, "Designing a World for UFOs, Extraterrestrials and Mere Mortals," *American Cinematographer*, January 1978, 34.

78. Ibid.

79. Turnock, *Plastic Reality*; Jon Lewis, "The Perfect Money Machine: George Lucas, Steven Spielberg and Auteurism in the New Hollywood," *Film International* 1, no. 1 (2003): 12–26.

CHAPTER 6

THE NEW HOLLYWOOD, 1980–1999

Noelle Griffis

In 1984, Georgia scored two college-football-related victories over longtime rival Alabama. Only one of those occurred on the field. Alabama, a state known for its fanatical college football culture, lost the chance to have the story of Paul "Bear" Bryant's championship seasons at the University of Alabama filmed in Tuscaloosa. Instead, the honor went to Georgia for reasons both personal and political. Bryant had given the producer Larry Spangler permission to make a film about his life with the express hope that the production would bring jobs and other economic benefits to the people of Alabama. However, Bryant died in 1983, and his family, represented by his daughter, Mae Martin Tyson, objected to the casting of Gary Busey in the title role. Following Tyson's lead, the University of Alabama, Governor George Wallace, and other state officials refused to cooperate with *The Bear* (Richard C. Sarafian, 1984), withholding memorabilia and denying permits for key locations such as the University of Alabama's football field. Georgia's film commission swiftly stepped in, promising university locations and landscapes that could easily play the role of Alabama onscreen.[1]

While serving as Georgia's governor, Jimmy Carter established the state's first film commission in 1973, recognizing the economic potential of hosting a Hollywood feature following the production of John Boorman's *Deliverance*. Film offices in other states throughout the South followed close behind, including one in Alabama set up by the Wallace administration in 1976. Alabama business and political leaders were eager to join the "New South" economy by promoting the state's inexpensive resources and its antiunion labor policies to attract business, including the film industry. With landscapes ranging from the Gulf of Mexico's white sand beaches to the lower Appalachian mountain range, Alabama offered similar geographic possibilities to Georgia and equally advantageous weather for filming outdoors. In the mid-1970s, Bob Rafelson set and filmed his offbeat comedy *Stay Hungry* (1976) in Birmingham, and Steven Spielberg chose Mobile as one of the primary shooting locations for *Close Encounters of the Third Kind* (1977), constructing the colossal spaceship set in abandoned World War II airship hangers at Brookley Air Force Base. The Los Angeles transplant Phil Cole left a position at MGM to head the Alabama film office, quickly establishing himself as a leader within the emergent field. By 1984—the same year that state representatives declined to assist the producers of *The Bear*—the Alabama state film commission included twelve regional offices and an annual operating budget of $250,000, allowing the state's film office to market itself aggressively with resources that matched top production outposts such as Illinois, New Jersey, Georgia, and New York.[2] Alabama even hosted the 1984 Cineposium, an annual business meeting for film commissioners, in Mobile. *Variety* noted that Alabama might be forging a new path for the industry after Cole announced plans to raise money through bonds for studio construction.[3] However, Alabama failed to develop as a production site of any consequence, while Georgia thrived, regularly hosting major television series and feature films and eventually developing into a major regional production center.

What, then, accounts for the success of a place to develop a local production industry, and what are the long-term consequences? In 1986, Georgia's Governor Joe Frank Harris (1983–91) explained exactly why his state aggressively courted Hollywood: "The revenue from film production is found money. Film companies don't tax the infrastructure, don't use schools, don't require new roads, and don't pollute the air and water. All they leave behind is what they've spent."[4] In return, Georgia could offer cheaper locations, labor, and accommodation than New York, Los Angeles, or many overseas locations. "Shoot here for Peanuts," read an advertisement for the Georgia film commission.[5]

Yet, as histories of other Georgia productions reveal, getting on Hollywood's radar is not just a matter of offering permits in exchange for clean "found money." In addition to cooperation and local expertise, the success of the state's production industry required sustained investment from both public and private sources for infrastructure (from studio space to film labs), a professional local labor pool, and regular promotion of the state's unique landscapes and generic locations. The Georgia film commission's role in the production of *The Bear* exemplifies how government policy and cooperation had become central to location decisions by the 1980s, well before the introduction of production tax rebates. It also shows how the film and television industry benefited from the growing competition among film offices that gave producers a continuously expanding range of shooting options despite the instability of government policy and the rotating door of elected and appointed officials. Despite early enthusiasm and Cole's best efforts to do the same in Alabama, the inability, or the refusal, of

THE NEW HOLLYWOOD, 1980–1999

state authorities to continually dedicate resources to production development contributed to Alabama's retreat from the race to become Hollywood's back lot.

The Bear marked the beginning of a string of films set in Alabama but filmed in its neighboring state, including *Fried Green Tomatoes* (Jon Avnet, 1991), *My Cousin Vinny* (Jonathan Lynn, 1992), and *Forrest Gump*, Robert Zemeckis's 1994 Academy Award–winning hit about a simple man from the fictional Alabama town of Greenbow, featuring scenes shot in Georgia, North Carolina, South Carolina, Maine, Utah, and California, among others, but none in Alabama.[6] Ben Goldsmith and Tom O'Regan have identified the shift from creatively necessitated to economically driven runaways as part of the "transformation of the logic of location production" from the 1950s and 1960s, when location shooting had been employed primarily "to service the project needs of international blockbusters."[7] City, state, and national film bureaus began to rapidly develop to serve the needs of both the creatively and economically driven runaway. As Lawrence Webb has noted, by the late 1960s, "Hollywood location shooting, dramatically increased by studio sell-offs and new production practices, presented itself as an ideal clean industry—and not coincidentally, one that came pre-packaged with glamour as well as with powerful branding opportunities."[8]

Locations developed as a full-fledged international ancillary enterprise involving government agencies, location scouts, and production liaisons in the 1980s and 1990s, loosely bookended by the 1983 incorporation of the Association of Film Commissions International (AFCI) and the production tax credits first introduced by the Canadian government in 1997.[9] This chapter addresses the professionalization of location management and the development of regional production centers in response to the growth of global conglomerate Hollywood, or the New Hollywood (1980–99), and the parallel rise of a regionally situated, American independent cinema. In what follows, I trace some of the primary ways that hitching government interests to those of film and television production has altered the cinematic landscape in spatial, economic, and aesthetic terms. First, I turn to the "film bureau phenomenon" and the growth of "Hollywood's back lot" in the United States during the 1980s, identifying the range of ways cities and states marketed themselves to lure creative and economic runaways, with an emphasis on the rapidly growing production industries in the U.S. South.[10] The competition between southern "right-to-work" states across the Sun Belt region and into North Carolina and Virginia reveals a complex web of factors—from weather and landscape to infrastructural support and sociopolitical climate—that contributed to the success of some emerging production hubs and the failure of others. Moreover, while good weather and the novelty of the contemporary U.S. South onscreen may have initially brought more commercial production to southern states in the 1970s, "Hollywood's southern strategy" was in fact part of a much larger shift toward globally dispersed production and thus provides a generative case study for assessing the effects of industrial changes on location shooting during the 1980s and 1990s.[11]

The second half of the chapter turns to the technical and aesthetic changes that resulted from or contributed to the accelerated decentralization of production and the cultural significance of the shift from the creative to the economic runaway. While a major Hollywood production can bring international attention to a little-known locale, it can also negate local distinctions when one place doubles as another or is rendered unrecognizable through cinematography and special effects. The rise of the global blockbuster during this period contributed to this erasure of local specificity, while simultaneously providing financing for lower-budget productions that foregrounded locative authenticity. With support from independent distributors and studio specialty divisions (e.g., New Line, Orion, Sony Pictures Classics, Miramax), independent filmmakers began garnering widespread attention for character-driven narratives that were often made, by necessity, in their own neighborhoods and adopted hometowns. By presenting their distinct visions of both urban life and rural Americana, filmmakers such as Jim Jarmusch and Spike Lee in New York, Penelope Spheeris in Los Angeles, Kevin Smith in New Jersey, Gus Van Sant in the Pacific Northwest, and Richard Linklater in Texas tied their auteurism to place and, in doing so, discovered an audience for offbeat stories that continued the tradition of using location shooting as a means of exploring the cultural experience of place.

HOLLYWOOD'S BACK LOT

Beginning in the 1980s, Georgia, Texas, North Carolina, and Florida each made concerted efforts to profit from Hollywood's growing reliance on location production to compete with Los Angeles, New York, and increasingly Vancouver and Toronto for a share of the domestic production market. The progress and setbacks of these new southern markets illustrate the practical and political challenges that can complicate the development of a production center and differentiate a "fly in, fly out" production site from a full-service regional production hub. When major cities such as New York and San Francisco began catering to the film industry in the 1960s, city leaders promoted location filmmaking as the only way to authentically render the cities' iconic landmarks and cityscapes onscreen: a New York setting demanded real New York locations, they claimed. Alternately, sustained production growth in regional production centers outside of major U.S. cities depended more on geographic diversity that allowed places such as Toronto, Florida, or Illinois to double or stand in for a multitude of settings. For example, Chris Lukinbeal credits the production boom in North Carolina and Florida to their landscape variety and the availability of "generic" locations (e.g., prisons, schoolyards, parking lots, lakes and rivers) for filming.[12] The Blue

Figure 6.1. A Suburb of Tampa, Florida, dressed for *Edward Scissorhands* (20th Century Fox, 1990).

Ridge Mountains of North Carolina and Virginia could play the Catskills in *Dirty Dancing* (Emile Ardolino, 1987); Lakeview/Tampa, Florida, provided "a kind of generic, plain-wrap suburb" loosely based on the Burbank, California, of Tim Burton's childhood for *Edward Scissorhands* (1990).[13] In reference to a 1980 ad for the Alabama Film Office that promised mountains, sea sides, cities, and rural communities, the *American Film* writer Julian Smith remarked that the ad "pretty much sums up the appeals most states make: official cooperation and a variety of scenery. *We're different—but we're like everywhere else*"[14] (figure 6.1).

   In the 1980s, urban planners and geographers began to take note of the dispersal of Hollywood production across North America. While American-financed films shot outside the United States increased from approximately 35 to 60 percent in the 1960s, that number dropped to 46 percent by the mid-1980s. During the same period, domestic production outside California increased by 30 percent.[15] The economic geographers Michael Storper and Susan Christopherson hypothesized that Hollywood—the place and the mode of production—might be losing its status as the undisputed center of the U.S. film industry due to the studio system's "vertical disintegration" and the "flexible specialization" of the workforce, which allowed producers to work cheaper, faster, and outside the confines of the studio (or Los Angeles, specifically) as needed.[16] Their prediction of Hollywood's decentralization, as their later work has acknowledged, never fully materialized. Preproduction planning and postproduction still located Los Angeles as the industrial nexus, and the studios and surrounding areas have continued to produce the greatest amount of content in North America. The film scholar Gary

Edgerton more accurately recognized the rise in domestic runaways as a "cost effective decision by Hollywood to venture beyond its own immediate environs, and employ the other forty-nine states as an extended backlot."[17]

Edgerton dubbed the growing influence of film commissions in the U.S. film industry the "film bureau phenomenon" and described the shift as follows:

> At least in a geographic sense, the business of motion picture production in America is now becoming nationalized as film commission input from many major cities and all the states across the U.S. is a significant catalyst in ensuring this growing tendency towards on-location shooting. Likewise, movie bureaus themselves have become a force to be acknowledged in the industry as a whole. . . . Clearly, the amount of reward that is possible in attracting a major motion picture or television production on-location has encouraged each and every state to institutionalize an extreme form of civic boosterism in the hope of a richly rewarding potential return.[18]

The AFCI formed in 1975 to serve as the central organizing body for the new film commissioners, who were otherwise forging a new tax-supported service industry through trial and error. The association held its first official event, Cineposium, the following year.[19] Cineposium remains the annual AFCI conference and is currently billed as an educational event featuring "seminars designed to teach film commissioners about the management and processes unique to the film commission business."[20] Industry leaders including MPAA president Jack Valenti, studio executives, and entertainment lawyers began attending Cineposium meetings in its early years, weighing in on topics such as "the economy of motion picture production in the 80s" and "the impact of cable TV and video production."[21] The more experienced commissioners led roundtables on how government liaisons could help productions navigate local and federal parks policies, union requirements, and immigration laws. How to market a city, state, territory, or nation to the industry became a regular theme of conference talks. Although North American bureaus competed with one another, the establishment of AFCI ensured a degree of uniformity and professionalization and ultimately benefited them as they faced greater competition from more developed and better funded national film commissions in Europe and Australia. Moreover, as AFCI president Joe O'Kane noted in 1986, "Nobody gets an entire movie."[22] For example, the location manager Mike Meehan reportedly traveled over twenty thousand miles in search of the ideal Rust Belt settings for *Gung Ho*, Ron Howard's 1986 comedy about the U.S. auto industry in the age of globalization. Howard ultimately selected locations in Ohio and Pennsylvania after both state film commissions aggressively courted the film's producers. Therefore, in addition to becoming an expert on the locations, policies, labor laws, and business climate of their home territory, film commissioners had to build strong relationships with bureaus in neighboring states (and provinces) and have a grasp of the national and international scene.

The primary functions of a government-run film office are to assist with a variety of city and state services (e.g., access to water and electricity, street closures, police assistance), to negotiate rates with area businesses for supplies and accommodation, to act as a liaison between the industry and local labor, and to lobby for policy designed to grow an emergent production economy. But as competition grew throughout the 1980s and 1990s, so did the services offered by more developed commissions as they wooed producers with everything from lavish hotel suites to helicopter location tours.[23] Providing exceptional assistance also became a way to publicize location offices. Georgia delivered fifteen hundred national guardsmen to the set of *Invasion U.S.A.* (Joseph Zito, 1985), the Middlesex County commissioners (in Massachusetts) gave the American Playhouse television series *Concealed Enemies* (1984) access to their county courthouse for six months, Kentucky approved a producer's request to flood a valley, and Minnesota allowed a production to cover a significant stretch of paved roads with dirt.[24] The executive director of the Minnesota Motion Picture and TV Board, E. Buffie Stone, explained, "We never say no to a producer or director."[25] In some cases, commissioners would make a name for themselves through their reputation for going to extreme lengths to help secure productions. The Philadelphia commissioner R. C. Staab became nationally renowned for convincing businesses around Philadelphia to allow for extravagant and disruptive film shoots (e.g., a hang-gliding scene in the middle of Wanamaker's department store for the 1987 film *Mannequin*) and taking the initiative to reach out to leading directors, including Joel and Ethan Coen, to offer location ideas for their forthcoming scripts.[26] Alternately, withholding support quickly garnered negative attention, as illustrated by the *New York Times*' coverage of *The Bear*. Similarly, when Richard Maulsby of the Washington, DC, Office of Motion Picture / TV Development refused to provide assistance to Columbia Pictures' Robert Kennedy biopic after the production booked hotels in Virginia, the *Washington Post* ran the headline, "District Snubs Film Crew for Staying in Roslyn: District Withdrawing Film Crew's Welcome."[27] While the hotel decision clearly negated the economic justification for the district to provide tax-funded services, the news coverage added to the perception that filming in the nation's capital was not worth the hassle.

In addition to skilled personnel, cities and states that attracted the most business had significant marketing and publicity budgets dedicated to hosting industry parties for studio executives in Los Angeles and New York and to the production and distribution of print materials. Location commissions ran ads in the trades (such as *Variety* and *Back Stage*) and designed manuals to illustrate "the uniqueness and variability of the home terrain and the accessibility of support services."[28] For example, the Nevada film commission ran an advertisement in 1984 promising producers no "red tape," twenty-four-hour assistance, "spectacular" locations, and low costs—all standard language and practices for state-commission publicity materials. More compellingly, the ad featured an image of eight mustangs in full stride above the tagline, "Tell Their Story." In a market flooded with film bureau ads featuring state logos on film reels, each promising diverse landscapes, cooperation, and no "red tape," Nevada made the state's thirty thousand wild mustangs—"one of the last remnants of the real West"—its unique selling proposition (figure 6.2).[29]

State commissions also began to publicize their practical and technical expertise. Presaging the contemporary era of tax-based incentives, the Arkansas Office of Motion Picture Development offered a 5 percent rebate to any production that spent $1 million in state during a one-year period in 1983 and cut the rate for eligibility by half the following year in order to encourage more independent production.[30] During the same period, New Mexico reported going from last to sixth place nationally in production revenue after its new governor, Toney Anaya, a self-described "film buff," increased the film office's budget for promotional needs and eliminated permit requirements in most of the state's locations. Moreover, New Mexico touted the availability of its technical offerings, which included "two Tulip cranes, Panavision cameras, and two new sound stages."[31] Texas, as one might expect, went bigger. The Dallas Communication Complex at Las Colinas allowed filmmakers to complete all stages of production and postproduction in state.[32]

By 1979, every state already claimed to have a commission, though these ranged from a dedicated full-service department to a single appointee who counted film liaison as one of his or her many duties. Three years later, the president of the AFCI and director of the New York City film office, Nancy Littlefield, estimated that over one hundred commissions had formed in the United States, its territories, and Canada.[33] California, having led the industry in production since the early studio era, became the last state to appoint a statewide commissioner in 1985.[34] The Golden State's late entry was evidence of how cooperative government policy had become inextricably linked to location production over the past decade. But even with California's improved efforts, there remained several reasons for a commercial production to head elsewhere: Los Angeles had a notoriously difficult and expensive permit situation, West Coast International Alliance of Theatrical Stage Employees (IATSE) rules made overtime more expensive than almost anywhere else (outside of New York), and Screen Actor's Guild (SAG) restrictions made shooting a crowd scene prohibitively expensive for the majority of productions.[35] Strict union oversight also kept workers locked into their specified roles, whereas crews could be more flexible in laxer jurisdictions, thereby speeding up the production process (e.g., a driver might help move props or wrap a wire in his or her downtime). While Los Angeles maintained the lion's share of feature production, it began losing television and production

Figure 6.2. 1980s trade advertisements for Nevada's and Missouri's film commissions.

work to cheaper markets, where content demands for new video and later digital platforms necessitated flexible specialization.

In the mid-1980s, Storper and Christopherson developed a four-tiered model to describe the different types of production centers that had developed over the past decade as a result of dispersed production in North America.[36] Cities, states, and provinces that merely provided service assistance to filmmakers and production companies were designated "occasional" production sites, whereas a place that invested in infrastructure—typically through public-private partnership— could develop into a "second order production center."[37] Second-order centers maintained commission budgets that approached or exceeded $250,000 and reported millions (if not hundreds of millions) in annual expenditures from the production industry. Storper and Christopherson designated production industries that benefited from their proximity to the primary production centers of Los Angeles and New York (e.g., Toronto, Vancouver, and Philadelphia) "edge centers."[38] However, as production industries developed over the next two decades, especially with the rapid growth of Toronto and Vancouver, the distinctions between primary, second-order, and edge centers began to dissolve.

By the time of Storper and Christopherson's study, North Carolina had emerged as a prime example of a second-order center, due in large part to the private investment in studio infrastructure by Dino De Laurentiis, who relocated his production operation to Wilmington, North Carolina, while filming *Firestarter* (Mark L. Lester, 1984). The state commission formed in 1980, and by 1983, the film office had been credited with helping to bring in over $248 million in expenditures from the industry—a remarkable sum considering that the commission had been instituted without state funding.[39] Production expenditure estimates include everything from direct pay to local workers to money spent on gas and office supplies, but the exact amount spent by a production remains notoriously difficult to verify. Moreover, it is in the interest of both commissioners and industry personnel to inflate these numbers to assure lawmakers that film-office budgets and other incentives are worth the costs. When Wilmington's studio construction broke ground in 1986, it anticipated a wave of facility development in locations across the United States, including New York, San Francisco, Dallas, and Florida.[40]

Throughout the 1980s, rapid growth in the cable television and home video markets increased the demand for independently produced, lower-budget fare.[41] These smaller projects were ideally suited for taking advantage of cost-saving locations and could potentially sustain a labor force in between the occasional presence of a big-budget feature or major television series. Moreover, as "negative pickups"—or independently produced films financed and distributed by studios—accounted for nearly half of major studio releases, there was, theoretically, ample opportunity to simultaneously profit from the mainstream industry while cultivating a local production economy. At the same time, the amount spent on the average studio feature release (the negative cost) dramatically increased, from $9.4 million in 1980 to $26.7 million in 1990.[42] Therefore, with greater competition on the low end from cable, video, and independent productions and ever-expanding expectations for each successive blockbuster release, budget and control remained deciding factors for choosing when and where to go on location. While studio-produced features continued to shoot primarily in and around Los Angeles, New York, and London, staying close to the largest soundstages, independent productions more frequently worked outside of these major cities.[43]

While second-order production centers still operated in relation to Hollywood, plans for developing regional production industries independent of the dominant commercial industry began to gain traction. Noting that postproduction facilities were also under development in several regional outposts, AFCI president Joe O'Kane proclaimed, "What's happening now is a push for full-fledged regional production centers." With enough local financing for local production, these centers could, in theory, declare themselves truly independent. O'Kane called regional production growth "good news for everyone except the entrenched Hollywood businesses."[44] O'Kane's assessment was a curious statement to come from the spokesperson of an organization that formed to assist and benefit from the already-established film and television industries, but his nod to the possibility of alternative, local filmmaking pointed to the contradictory discourses regarding the role of production incentives coming from several city and state commissions. While commissions still advertised local offerings to Hollywood personnel, many were also making moves to develop more "homegrown" features, made by and for people in their respective state or region.[45] During this time, Georgia, Illinois, and Texas were all starting to bankroll a handful of low-budget local features,[46] and investment accountants in Arkansas set up a $2 to $3 million fund to assist homegrown productions.[47] Florida, which counted itself as the third-largest production center in the United States during the years that the NBC series *Miami Vice* (1984–89) filmed in state, created a cash-prize screenwriting contest, sponsored by Governor Bob Graham, to support local independent filmmakers. However, part of the prize included a trip to Los Angeles to meet with industry insiders, suggesting that while the contest could legitimately assist resident filmmakers, it was also a publicity stunt designed to show off the state's filmmaking activities to studio executives.[48] Florida's plan was telling, as supporting the local film scene was hardly seen as oppositional to Los Angeles–based studios and producers; instead, growing an independent scene became another way to market locations to Hollywood.

Location production professionals, made up of government-appointed film commissioners, location scouts, and production managers, grew directly out of the hypermobility of film production in the New Hollywood and the necessity of adaptability to the rapidly changing media and entertainment industries.

But rather than drawing together traditional industry personnel (e.g., craft workers, producers, exhibitors), the association brought government officials, generally from departments of economic development or tourism, into the industrial fold. In *Production Cultures*, John T. Caldwell discusses the industry's proclivity for "speaking to itself about itself," through the cultivation of professional gatherings and "deep texts," which include trade discourse and industrial promotional materials.[49] Significantly, Caldwell sees the industry's reflexivity as a tool that "promotes flexibility and responsiveness in new forms of media conglomeration."[50] While Cineposium created a platform for commissioners to develop a distinctive production culture with others in the field, the Los Angeles Locations Expo—first held by AFCI in 1985 in coordination with the American Film Marketing Association—provided a venue for AFCI to present itself as a formidable force within the industry. The Expo remained an annual industry event, inviting members to promote their services for an increasingly global market to studio executives and production teams at a central location. The international growth of the AFCI presented challenges for its members, who were expected to represent constituents and bring money, jobs, and cultural visibility back home, while competing to provide a global industry with cost savings and cheap labor.

Global Blockbusters and American Independents

As the "New Hollywood" made the transition to "Global Hollywood," the Los Angeles–based industry—the global "nexus" of production, marketing, and distribution planning—had not disintegrated but, rather, extended its reach.[51] High-profile multibillion-dollar media mergers and acquisitions, from the Time Inc. acquisition of Warner Communications in 1989 to Viacom's $35.6 billion purchase of CBS in 1999, bookended the decade.[52] Time Warner's release of *Batman* (Tim Burton, 1989) broke box-office records, showcasing the potential of using "the whole machine" of a multimedia conglomerate for marketing, tie-ins, merchandising, and international promotion.[53] *Batman*'s success presaged the industry's shift from star-driven midbudget pictures to "tent-pole" event releases, often franchises "that could carry a studio's entire production slate and drive the parent company's far-flung entertainment operations as well." As Tom Schatz explains, the tent-pole strategy "was bolstered enormously by the foreign market surge during the 1990s, as media conglomeration and globalization proved to be a mutually reinforcing phenomenon."[54] In some cases, media conglomeration has had a direct effect on the development of media hubs, as demonstrated by Orlando's boom following the construction of MGM Disney studios. Throughout the 1980s and 1990s, the interplay between studio space and location shooting remained vital even as new technologies aimed to recreate the advantages of soundstages while shooting on location.

Figure 6.3. For *Indiana Jones and the Temple of Doom* (Paramount, 1984), Spielberg
supplemented soundstage production with lavish location shoots in exotic locations.

At one end of the spectrum, the production of Hollywood blockbusters produced by studio conglomerates became increasingly global, not only with regard
to financing and distribution but with the biggest franchises such as *Indiana
Jones and the Temple of Doom* (Steven Spielberg, 1984) also making use of the
transnational network of Hollywood and government-backed studios to showcase the far-reaching and exotic sets available to a multimillion-dollar spectacle.
Although Spielberg's big-budget sequel traversed Macau, Sri Lanka, London,
and San Francisco for its eighty-five-day shoot, approximately 80 percent of
the globe-trotting adventure was filmed on soundstages. The real jungles of Sri
Lanka were set against painted and miniature facades of palaces, and the effects-
heavy action film made ample use of the blue screens at Lucasfilm's Industrial
Light & Magic complex in San Rafael, California (figure 6.3). In the 1970s, both
George Lucas and Spielberg had been known as the leaders of a new generation
of filmmakers "leaving the studios behind,"[55] but as their budgets increased and
computerized visual effects became more advanced and integral to their films,
soundstages became more appealing to filmmakers at the helm of expensive
franchise pictures (especially for the few who owned their own facilities). Spielberg attributed his newfound preference for studio production to "getting older"
and his need to maintain a greater degree of control over his films: "I don't want
to wait. When it rains on me, and I want sun, or when it's sunny and I want it to
be overcast. I feel better when I can control the environment."[56] *Batman* filmed
almost entirely at Pinewood Studios in England, with supplementary interior
and exterior scenes filmed at manors (for Bruce Wayne's house) and industrial
plants (for Axis Chemical Plant) in the region. Derek Meddings (known for his
work on several Bond films, the Superman series, and Hammer Films) relied primarily on traditional effects techniques—miniatures, painted mattes, in-camera
optical effects—and a sparing use of blue screen to create Gotham City in the

studio.[57] The production of the Indiana Jones films and *Batman* pointed to a greater reliance on large-scale, fully equipped studios for big-budget genre films in the 1980s and 1990s.

Some relatively low-budget features also displayed a renewed interest in a studio aesthetic. Francis Ford Coppola shot his musical *One from the Heart* (1982) almost entirely on soundstages, a notable departure for the filmmaker following his infamously difficult and overbudget location shoot for *Apocalypse Now* (1979). *American Cinematographer* remarked on Coppola's unusual choice of recreating real Las Vegas locations for his film, including downtown corners created at scale, motels, McCarran Airport, and a model of the full Las Vegas strip in miniature: "*One from the Heart* marks the first time in recent motion picture history that actual existing locales have been re-created on Hollywood soundstages."[58] Coppola used all nine studios at his independent production company Zoetrope to construct an intentionally unrealistic aesthetic to dramatize emotion and create a sense of fantasy, in contrast to the realist settings that he favored throughout the 1970s.[59]

But for the majority of films, shot at least partially on location, advancements in camera mobility, power generators (allowing for studio-grade electrical setups on location), lighting, and film stock—in addition to the cooperation of film commissions—helped to bring studio-level efficiency on location.[60] *American Cinematographer* dedicated its March 1992 issue to location shooting, placing emphasis on the advantages and the challenges of the practice from both aesthetic and economic perspectives. Noting that cities, states, and countries were "vying for a greater share of industry production revenues and thus providing filmmakers with a wider range of shooting options," contributor Rick Baker predicted, "The option of location shooting may be changing more than just the look and feel of films made in the '90s."[61] A profile on *Fried Green Tomatoes*, set in Alabama and filmed in Georgia, illuminated the practical, logistical, and artistic concerns that made for a successful location shoot. The state's outdoor locations offered cinematographer Geoffrey Simpson good natural lighting opportunities to create different looks for scenes set in both the contemporary suburban South and the small, rural 1920s town of Whistle Stop.[62] "Generic locations," such as the convalescent home where the two lead characters meet, were also made available to the production. In addition to the creative offerings, Georgia could provide expert local production labor and facilities that were on par with those available in Los Angeles and New York. For example, in Atlanta, CineFilm, "one of the premier film labs in the south," developed in tandem with Georgia's production industry—starting as a 16 mm company catering to commercials and sports entertainment.[63] After expanding to 35 mm in 1982, CineFilm provided services to low-budget genre films and TV movies of the week, and by the 1990s, it was servicing high-profile features such as *Driving Miss Daisy* (Bruce Beresford, 1989) and *My Cousin Vinny* (1992).

In the same issue of *American Cinematographer*, Vilmos Zsigmond—best known for his location photography on films including *Deliverance, The Deer Hunter* (Michael Cimino, 1978), and *The River* (Mark Rydell, 1984)—explained that location decisions came down to budget and necessity. In his experience, directors more often preferred the control afforded by studio sets, especially for filming longer scenes. Zsigmond suggested that filmmakers reserve location shooting for times when a scene demanded a look that could only be captured on location or when location was central to the project. For example, Zsigmond explained that the ability to film the HBO film *Stalin* (Ivan Passer, 1992) in Moscow with access to the Kremlin buildings provided the impetus for making the film: "There was no way any one could have done it any other way, the results were spectacular."[64] *Stalin* was one of several projects during and after the fall of communism in eastern Europe to take advantage of the opportunities afforded by the former Eastern Bloc—newly available to international filmmakers and furnished with capable below-the-line talent who had worked for state film divisions.[65] J. D. Connor suggests in his work on production design during this period that eastern Europe appealed to Hollywood filmmakers much in the same way as the rural South had in earlier decades: "For New Hollywood filmmakers, the prospect of authentic and inexpensive locations once again proved impossible to resist."[66]

While industry-supported filmmakers explored new and expanded regional and international options for feature and television-series production, independent filmmakers were often limited to filming locally. As it was generally cheaper and easier for low-budget filmmakers—from Jim Jarmusch in New York City to David Gordon Green in Winston-Salem—to work where they lived (or near their film schools), these filmmakers helped to cultivate a new wave of regionalized American independent cinema motivated by economic limitations and creative interests. For Hal Hartley, known for his Long Island / New York City films, regional location shooting was an economic necessity because his tight production budgets limited the potential for studio rentals and travel, but the sense of place cultivated by these economic restrictions also contributed to his idiosyncratic style. Although small-budget, slice-of-life films allow for a greater degree of artistic freedom with regard to content, Hartley's working style reveals the rigorous planning needed to shoot a professional 35 mm feature on a shoestring budget. During preproduction, Hartley creates shooting plans for character positions and camera angles, akin to diagrams for professional sports plays, to ensure the maximum efficiency necessary to cover scenes quickly while working on location, whether shooting in the Cloisters Museum in Manhattan (*Amateur*, 1994) or a warehouse in Long Island (*Trust*, 1990).[67]

Abel Ferrara has similarly tied his auteurist identity to New York City, but his films demonstrate that locative authenticity need not be limited to slice-of-life, realist narratives. Ferrara's characters include mobsters, feminist killers, corrupt cops, and vampires in genre films that straddle the line between exploitation and art house. Both his style of downtown independent filmmaking and his night-marish urban vision are distinctly New York. For example, Ferrara's 1981 revenge exploitation film *Ms. 45* features a mute seamstress (Zoë Tamerlis Lund) turned vigilante after a brutal rape leads her to seduce and murder the men of Lower Manhattan. Lili Taylor plays another bloodthirsty woman ravaging New York University in Ferrara's vampire drama *The Addiction* (1995), shot in twenty days in Greenwich Village. Ferrara, whose persona evokes a street-savvy huckster, enjoys telling stories of the perils of low-budget location shooting in New York in ways that correspond with themes of urban crime and hustling that appear in his films. While recounting his war stories, so to speak, from the production of *King of New York* (1990), Ferrara described the dangers of sending his cast and crew by subway into deep Brooklyn without getting lost or mugged. Ferrara has also praised his own ingenuity in acquiring locations for free, telling the *Los Angeles Times* that he secured a room at the Plaza Hotel by promising the hotel's owner at the time, Donald Trump, that he would arrange a meet-and-greet between the film's star, Christopher Walken, and Trump's then wife, Ivana (she was a fan).[68]

Hartley and Ferrara have both maintained their reputations as independent filmmakers—in the purist sense of the term—by loosely following Roger Cor-man's blueprint for working almost entirely outside of Hollywood with financing from international coproductions and independent distribution deals. However, it was also during this time that a new wave of offbeat, independent filmmakers were beginning to garner more mainstream attention and earning commercial deals, primarily driven by film festival acquisitions. High-profile independently produced films including *Sex, Lies, and Videotape* (Steven Soderbergh, 1989) and *Do the Right Thing* (Spike Lee, 1989) earned international critical acclaim and handsome profits at the U.S. domestic box office, pointing to the economic potential of the niche art-house market. Miramax most successfully capitalized on the indie market, perfecting a model for independent film acquisition, mar-keting, and distribution for a new wave of conglomerate-owned specialty divi-sions (e.g., News Corp's Fox Searchlight, Sony Pictures Classics).[69] Although the explosion of the indie market was fueled by mergers with conglomerate Holly-wood, as Disney's 1993 purchase of Miramax underscored, the success of a hand-ful of art-house-oriented American directors helped to revive a domestic interest in character-driven studies, with an emphasis on the relationship between per-sonal identity and place. Spike Lee established his cinematic home in Brooklyn, and although Soderbergh never tied his auteurist persona to a single place, he shot *Sex, Lies, and Videotape* in his hometown of Baton Rouge. Kevin Smith pre-sented his comic-book version of New Jersey throughout the 1990s and 2000s, and Gus Van Sant developed a style informed by Portland's underground scene.

In *Walk Don't Run: The Cinema of Richard Linklater*, Rob Stone asserts, "The success on tiny budgets of Sayles' *The Return of the Secaucus Seven* (1980:

$60,000), Spike Lee's *She's Gotta Have It* (1986: $22,700), Linklater's *Slacker* (1991: $23,000), Nick Gomez's *Laws of Gravity* (1992: $32,000), Gregg Araki's *The Living End* (1992: $22,700) and Rose Troche's *Go Fish* (1994; approximately $15,000) was because each captured and communicated a realism that resulted from their innate regionalism and consequent social authenticity. They connected with empathetic audiences whose own realities had not (at least not yet) been deemed worthy of colonisation by the major studios."[70] Both Araki's *The Living End* and Rose Troche's *Go Fish* were set in major U.S. cities—Los Angeles and Chicago— but their focus on queer spaces and identities came from the insider status of their filmmakers, who presented community spaces tucked within a global metropolis. Spike Lee and Nick Gomez (and a few years later, Noah Baumbach) similarly worked in familiar territory, representing Brooklyn as a complex yet quotidian social space in contrast with the stereotypical treatment of the borough in Hollywood films. However, once *Sex, Lies, and Videotape* showed Hollywood the economic potential of indie auteurs and studio specialty divisions catered to the funding, marketing, and distribution needs of their films, the insider versus outsider status of the filmmakers who continued to make (relatively) popular and critically acclaimed niche fare began to dissolve, though the appeal of their character-driven stories and attention to local detail remained.[71] Linklater has been among the most successful of these filmmakers through his ability to strike a balance between experimentation and accessibility. His self-funded feature debut *Slacker* (1991) put Linklater, a recent University of Texas film-school dropout, and his adopted hometown of Austin on the cinematic map.

With Linklater's film-school colleague Lee Daniel behind the camera, *Slacker* meanders through local haunts as aimlessly as the characters it depicts as part of Austin's early-1990s slacker culture. He aimed for the style to be experimental but "watchable"—a comment that seemed to apply to the film's style as much as its content.[72] While the 16 mm camerawork (shot with an Arri 16SR) conveys a sense of documentary authenticity, Linklater preferred crisp photography and choreographed staging from his mostly amateur but still capable cast and crew (figure 6.4). In addition to enlisting friends to make the film, Linklater and Daniel also turned their $130-a-month house into a center for preproduction planning and postproduction syncing.[73] Through this combination of interpersonal connections and the financial freedom afforded by living and working in Austin (rather than New York or Los Angeles), Linklater and Daniel were able to complete their breakout feature. Linklater has since traded the DIY ethos for the industry support needed to sustain a career and develop a regional filmmaking scene. After Orion Pictures acquired and distributed *Slacker*, Linklater used the publicity generated by his low-budget success to secure a finance-and-distribution deal with Gramercy Pictures, a subsidiary of Universal, for *Dazed and Confused* (1993). While Linklater also shot the majority of his second film in Austin, maintaining (with Daniel) his preferred mode of "anti-slick realism," he was no longer making

Figure 6.4. An Austin, Texas, side street in Richard Linklater's *Slacker* (Orion, 1983).

a homegrown film starring friends and other locals (with the notable exception of Matthew McConaughey and some of the younger actors) but a studio-backed $7 million feature cast with New York– and Los Angeles–based actors such as Parker Posey and Joey Lauren Adams.[74] Linklater also made use of Universal Studios facilities in Los Angeles as needed.

Notably, Richard Linklater and fellow Austinite Robert Rodriguez not only helped drive cinematic interest in their chosen hometown but also contributed to the development of Austin, Texas, as a regional production hub. Linklater's production company, Detour Productions, and Rodriguez's Troublemaker Studios (largely funded by financing/distribution deals with Bob Weinstein's Dimension Films) successfully arranged their industry deals to allow them to continue to live and work in Texas. In turn, they have become integral to the development of the Austin film scene, which currently includes Linklater's Austin Film Society (AFS, established in 1985 to bring foreign and art film to the city) and Austin Studios—a twenty-acre media production complex, where Detour and AFS are housed, offering everything from youth animation courses to feature-film- and television-series-ready soundstages. The impressive infrastructure is designed to draw media and entertainment industries to Austin, while providing Austin-based filmmakers with the facilities they need to stay local. The local independent film culture, combined with the ability to draw top Hollywood talent, makes

Austin a nearly idyllic example of a regional production center—one that provides locations, efficient laborers, a cooperative government, and professional facilities to mainstream commercial features and television series in exchange for the prestige, experience, and infrastructural development that help to sustain local filmmakers. At the same time, the amount and the quality of work for local laborers in Austin or any other production outpost fluctuate considerably with production trends. It is the below-the-line workers who are most affected by aesthetic preferences, policy, and economic incentives that encourage commercial productions to seek out new places on an increasingly global scale, in search of the desired look or available facilities at the cheapest cost.

While filmmakers may drive interest in specific locations, the development of permanent infrastructure needed for a long-term production economy depends on studio backing (as the relationship between Rodriguez's Troublemaker Studios and Dimension Films demonstrates) and the cooperation of government agencies. Therefore, both the global/mainstream and the local/niche-oriented product—and in many cases the interplay between the two—have contributed to and been shaped by the dispersal of production. In *Hollyworld: Space, Power and Fantasy in the American Economy*, Aida Hozic argues that as national boundaries are broken down through globalization, the desire to construct a sense of place through architecture, the idealization of community, and storytelling is heightened.[75] The emergence of global conglomerate Hollywood thus provided the impetus for cities, states, provinces, and nations to build commissions and infrastructure to compete for their share of the global media economy, while the desire for place making and community building has simultaneously created a niche for a regionalized independent scene that is dependent on—and, thus, feeds back into—the larger system.

THE NEW GLOBAL HOLLYWOOD

Despite the rise of specialty divisions and the market for regional, independent storytelling, by the 1990s, regional U.S. production centers were losing ground to aggressively competitive international film commissions, particularly those offering direct financial incentives and impressive facilities.[76] Just four years after Joe O'Kane heralded the possibility of developing regional, independent film centers in the United States, his successor as AFCI president, Bill Lindstrom, offered a radically different vision for the organization: "Everyone is looking for American dollars and, while many countries have pursued American co-productions, they don't know how to best do it. Now they have access to all these film commissions. International is our growth area."[77] With a record number of foreign commissions represented at that year's Location Expo—including twelve Canadian provinces, Hong Kong, Thailand, Jamaica, Australia, and New Zealand—the first AFCI event of the new decade reflected Hollywood's accelerated global

interests in both production and distribution. It also made clear that national
film industries, generally conceived as a way to counter the U.S. film industry's hegemony, had grown increasing dependent on Hollywood's financial and
organizational structures.

The Canadian production centers of Vancouver, Toronto, and Montreal saw
"explosive" growth in the 1990s, together accounting for $1.26 billion in direct
expenditure in 1997, fueled by a favorable exchange rate, coproduction financing opportunities, and the introduction of the Production Services Tax Credit in
1997.[78] In 1990, Canada hosted an estimated 63 percent of Hollywood's international runaways, and by 1998, it could boast an 81 percent share (with the other 20
percent primarily split between the United Kingdom and Australia).[79] Toronto
and Vancouver (and to a lesser but still significant degree Montreal) had the
resources to invest heavily in soundstage construction beginning in the late 1980s,
making these cities the primary benefactors of the nation's efforts to inject its creative industries with additional capital from foreign production in the 1990s.[80]
Vancouver's proximity to Los Angeles and the favorable Canadian exchange rate
helped the city emerge as a popular location for filming during the television
production boom of the 1980s and 1990s. But Vancouver began to develop as
more than a "service industry for Americans" with a concerted, government-
supported campaign to attract foreign producers in 1987 that allowed the city to
double its production value over the next five years.[81] Additionally, in 1991, *Variety* reported that the single most important factor for Vancouver's success came
from money "pouring in" from Hong Kong in anticipation of the 1997 transfer of
sovereignty, illustrating just how closely production industries emerged in connection with global flows of capital.[82] With a more temperate climate and greater
landscape diversity than Toronto and Montreal, Vancouver quickly emerged as
one of Hollywood's favorite locative pinch hitters. The sharp increase in Hollywood coproductions with Canada and other international markets contributed
to a decade of uncertainty for domestic production. Florida, North Carolina,
and Texas all "suffered dramatic declines in location shooting by the end of the
1990s," and even New York's status was uncertain.[83]

Toronto's proximity to and ability to stand in for New York City had driven
the city's early production growth. Films set in Manhattan commonly shot exteriors in New York and interiors in Toronto. When several major studios boy-
cotted filmmaking in New York for seven months in 1990, following a series of
failed negotiations between IATSE Local 644 (Cinematographers) and Local 52
(Studio Mechanics) and the Alliance of Motion Picture and Television Producers (AMPTP) over overtime wages, Toronto also took a hit.[84] However, Toronto
became less dependent on New York's production industry in ensuing years due
to sustained investment in infrastructure and the introduction of the Canadian tax credits, though its ability to play New York remained vital to its success. Aurora Wallace has argued that the landscape and architecture of Toronto

changed with the city's rapid growth in the global economy, and the city began to more closely resemble a generic global city modeled on New York. This was, according to Wallace, the desired effect, as developers sought to reproduce Manhattan's trendy restaurants and boutique hotels—in part to suit the needs of production executives and international investors during their stay—which in turn allowed "Canada's NY" to more easily fulfill both interior and exterior location needs.[85] By the end of the decade, Toronto threatened to overtake New York, as the 2002 *Chicago Tribune* story "Incredible Shrinking N.Y. Film Industry" made clear. The decision to film *Rudy: The Rudy Giuliani Story* (Robert Dornhelm, 2003)—the story of the man who had just left the city's top office—in Toronto became symbolic of two major trends of the late 1990s: "the rapid decline of New York's film industry and—very much related—the rise of Canada's."[86] The blow of losing a hometown story to a more amenable or economical filming location mirrored Alabama's loss of *The Bear* nearly two decades earlier, yet the stakes of losing stories *about* New York to its competitors were much higher for thousands of New Yorkers dependent on the city's billion-dollar film industry.

The high-stakes competition between New York and Toronto in the 1990s anticipated greater challenges ahead for the growth of regional production centers and the locations industry. In 1997, Canada extended its domestic production tax rebates to foreign productions that filmed in Canada and employed local labor (the Production Services Tax Credit). Commercial productions were further incentivized to make Canada work, and both domestic and international governments were pressured into offering their own rebates and incentives in order to compete in the global production economy. By providing greater benefits through tax relief, film bureaus around the world undermined their original purpose: no longer could government-appointed commissioners champion hosting film and television production as a cheap and easy way to supplement a local economy with "found money." As Michael Curtin and Kevin Sanson explain, Canada's efforts in the 1990s were, in fact, part of a global trend in which "policymakers began to position their countries as hotspots of the 'creative economy,' reasoning that intellectual and cultural output had become distinguishing features of the world's wealthiest societies."[87] International competition also contributed to Hollywood's "race to the bottom" as governments attempted to offer producers the cheapest possible deal by weakening unions and continually bending to the industry's will at the expense of its laborers.[88]

This brings us back the questions raised by the filming of a distinctly Alabama story, *The Bear*, in Georgia. The loss of the Busey vehicle and many other Alabama-set stories to neighboring southern states appeared to be a missed opportunity for production revenue, work for local laborers, and hometown prestige; however, it is also possible that the cities, states, and nations that have, thus far, neither developed production infrastructure nor provided competitive incentives to lure the occasional feature have successfully sidestepped participation in the global race for cheap labor and tax incentives.[89] On an economic level, competition from the other southern "right-to-work" states was probably already too high for Alabama to justify continued investment. Moreover, early Alabama film commission advertisements, featuring a range of locations but little local color or specificity, suggest that production development would have done little to improve cultural capital or to produce cultural meaning in a state without geographic or iconic distinction (in comparison with cities and landscapes such as New Orleans or Monument Valley). As Aida Hozic has noted, "if we are to judge by these advertisements, successful integration into the global entertainment economy would hardy depend on the protection of history, tradition, cultural heritage or geography—all that we usually mean by 'place.'"[90] A homegrown auteur—a Linklater or a Gus Van Sant type—could theoretically do more to construct an authentically felt media presence for the state than a full-scale production center could; at the same time, without filmmaking support by the local government, young independents will continue to find inspiration elsewhere.

To date, the failures and setbacks of regional production centers—such as multiple bankruptcies filed by North Carolina studios—paired with questionable labor practices, the need for government handouts and bailouts, and the limited impact that film and television production has had on the overall economic health of cities and states (e.g., Louisiana), call into question the value and the ethics of government-supported production investment.[91] Nevertheless, governments continue to introduce controversial policies to increase regional production, looking for a place in the creative media economy, particularly as hosting a television series has become, in recent years, a form of urban branding on par with hosting a professional sports team. Driven by the explosion of digital platforms and the competition to provide the most original content, film commissions have only strengthened their position to Hollywood-based industries in the 2000s, as local governments work to tie their urban branding initiatives more closely with new media and entertainment ventures.

NOTES

1. Fay S. Joyce, "For Film, 'Bear' Defects to Georgia," *New York Times*, January 3, 1984, A16.

2. "Alabama Film Commish Touts Regional Office," *Variety*, April 11, 1984, 31. Budgets for New York, New Jersey, Massachusetts, Texas, Georgia, and Illinois ranged from $250,000 to $500,000. See Will Tusher, "49 States in a Scramble to Lure Location Work Away from California," *Variety*, October 13, 1983, 1, 15.

3. "Alabama Film Commish." Jim Harwood discusses Cole's plan for a hybrid studio and theme park in "States Mull Bonds to Lure Films," *Variety*, November 5, 1980, 54.

4. Kathy Ivens, "Hollywood Discovers Philadelphia's Charm," *Focus: Metropolitan Philadelphia's Business Newsmagazine*, May 28, 1986, 18.

5. Martin Halstuk, "The Seduction of Hollywood: States are Going All Out to Get Movie Makers to Run Away," *Los Angeles Times*, September 22, 1985, Y18.

6. "*Forrest Gump* (1994)," Internet Movie Database, accessed August 24 2018, www.imdb.com/title/tt0109830/locations.

7. Ben Goldsmith and Tom O'Regan, *The Film Studio: Film Production in the Global Economy* (Lanham, MD: Rowman and Littlefield, 2005), 9.

8. Lawrence Webb, "Remapping *The Conversation*: Urban Design and Industrial Reflexivity in Seventies San Francisco," *Post45*, June 22, 2014, http://post45.research.yale.edu/2014/06/remapping-the-conversation-urban-design-and-industrial-reflexivity-in-seventies-san-francisco/.

9. The Association of Film Commissioners (AFC) was founded in 1975 and was incorporated in 1983 with that name as an international organization. By the end of the 1980s, it had changed the name to the Association of Film Commissioners International (AFCI), which I will use going forward.

10. I am borrowing phrasing drawn from Gary Edgerton's article (which I discuss later in this chapter) "The Film Bureau Phenomenon in American and Its Relationship to Independent Filmmaking," *Journal of Film and Video* 38, no. 1 (1986): 40–48.

11. See Christian B. Long, "Burt Reynolds, Hollywood's Southern Strategy," *Post 45*, June 24, 2013, http://post45.research.yale.edu/2013/06/burt-reynolds-hollywoods-southern-strategy/. Long argues that Reynolds's string of hits set in Georgia and Florida in the 1970s tapped into and exploited the desires of the southern white working class to have its values and lifestyles recognized at the national level. However, unlike Nixon's southern strategy, which tapped into the racial resentments of the same demographic, Reynolds's characters were apolitical heroes—positive portrayals of good ole boys stripped of political complexity. Just as the Republican Party recognized the untapped political potential of the white southern demographic, Hollywood saw the economic value of making films in and about an underrepresented region with right-to-work labor policies.

12. Chris Lukinbeal, "The Rise of Regional Production Centers in North America, 1984–1997," *GeoJournal* 59, no. 4 (2004): 309.

13. Quote attributed to the film's production designer, Bo Welch, in Laurie Halpern Smith, "Look, Ma, No Hands, or Tim Burton's Latest Feat," *New York Times*, August 26, 1990, H18.

14. Julian Smith, "The Wooing of Burt Reynolds," *American Film*, July 1, 1980, 48.

15. Edgerton, "Film Bureau Phenomenon," 41.

16. "Vertical disintegration" describes the restructuring of industries, such as the motion picture business, through the outsourcing of labor that had previously been done in-house (such as production and marketing). "Flexible specialization," in this case, refers to the shift from training employees for a singular to a multiskilled approach (e.g., rather than becoming an editor's apprentice, someone attends film school to learn multiple roles), aimed toward market and technological adaptability. Michael Storper and Susan Christopherson, "Flexible Specialization and Regional Industrial Agglomerations: The Case of the U.S. Motion Picture Industry," *Annals of the Association of American Geographers* 77, no. 1 (1987): 112.

17. Edgerton, "Film Bureau Phenomenon," 41.

18. Ibid.

19. AFCI, "The History of AFCI," accessed August 7, 2018, www.afci.org/about-afci/#afci-history.

20. Ibid.

21. "Pictures: Cineposium for State Promoters of Location Shooting Features Valenti and Other Pic Savants," *Variety*, February 24, 1982, 9, 34.

22. Aljean Harmetz, "67 Locations Courting Hollywood Producers," *New York Times*, February 26, 1986, C22.

23. Halstuk, "Seduction of Hollywood," Y18.

24. Harmetz, "67 Locations," C22.

25. Ibid.

26. Ibid.

27. Warren Brown, "District Snubs Film Crew for Staying in Roslyn: District Withdrawing Film Crews Welcome," *Washington Post*, February 23, 1984, A1.

28. Edgerton, "Film Bureau Phenomenon," 42.

29. "Nevada: In a Supporting Role," ad, *Backstage*, August, 17, 1984, 14B.

30. Halstuk, "Seduction of Hollywood," Y18; see also Edgerton, "Film Bureau Phenomenon," 45.

31. Clint Goldman, "They're Shooting in the Old West," *Back Stage*, August 17, 1984, 37B.

32. Edgerton, "Film Bureau Phenomenon," 45.

33. Amy Schnapper, "Location: Studios Take to the Streets," *Los Angeles Times*, March 28, 1982, G1.

34. Halstuk, "Seduction of Hollywood," Y18.

35. Ibid.

36. As paraphrased in Lukinbeal, "Rise of Regional Production Centers," 308.

37. Ibid., 311.

38. Ibid., 314.

39. Ibid., 313.

40. "Seattle Joins the Movie Studio Race," *New York Times*, August 9, 1986, 7.

41. Tom Schatz notes that from roughly 1980 to 1989, home video went from nonexistent to overtaking movie theaters in generating the most revenue for studio conglomerates. Schatz, "The Studio System and Conglomerate Hollywood," in *The Contemporary Hollywood Film Industry*, ed. Paul McDonald and Janet Wasko (Oxford, UK: Blackwell, 2008), 21.

42. Ibid.

43. Storper and Christopherson, "Flexible Specialization," 112.

44. "Seattle Joins the Movie Studio Race," 7.

45. Edgerton, "Film Bureau Phenomenon," 45.

46. Will Tusher, "Runaway Financing New Wrinkle Facing State Film Commissioners as Location Competition Grows," *Variety*, February 22, 1984, 6, 38.

47. Edgerton, "Film Bureau Phenomenon," 45.

48. "Florida: State Officials Eye Another Good Year for Florida Productions," *Variety*, March 13, 1985, 69.

49. John Thornton Caldwell, *Production Culture: Industrial Reflexivity and Critical Practice in Film and Television* (Durham, NC: Duke University Press, 2008), 2–3.

50. Ibid., 32.

51. Goldsmith and O'Regan, *Film Studio*, 18. Saskia Sassen theorized the rise of global cities as the "nexus" of capital flows where financing, production, and distribution planning takes place. Goldsmith and O'Regan also note the applicability of Sassen's theory of global cities to Los Angeles's role as the control center of sorts for global conglomerate Hollywood. See also Saskia Sassen, *The Global City: New York, London, Tokyo* (Princeton, NJ: Princeton University Press, 2001), 36.

52. Schatz, "Studio System," 26.

53. Ibid., 28. Schatz quotes studio head Terry Semel on the significance of *Batman*'s use of "the whole machine."

54. Ibid.

55. See, for example, Mel Gussow, "Movies Leaving 'Hollywood' Behind," *New York Times*, May 27, 1970, 36.

56. Merry Elkins, "Stephen Spielberg on *Indiana Jones and the Temple of Doom*," *American Cinematographer*, July 1984, 53.

57. Ron Magid, "Batman Voodoo Mostly from Britain," *American Cinematographer*, December 1989, 58–60.

58. "Mating Film with Video for 'One from the Heart,'" *American Cinematographer*, January 1982, 92.

59. Ibid.

60. *American Cinematographer* profiled advancements in camera mobility, strobe systems, and high-speed film ideal for location shooting during this period. For example, see Robert Krey and Michael Haney, "Cam-Remote and the Future of Camera Mobility," *American Cinematographer*, August–September 1984, 104; Marji Rhea on XT 320 high-speed film

in "New Products," *American Cinematographer*, December 1992, 86–90; and "Panavision UK Takes Delivery of New Unilux Strobe Systems," *American Cinematographer*, December 1993, 34.

61. Debra Kaufman and Rick Baker, "The Arduous Art of Location Shooting," *American Cinematographer*, March 1992, 70.

62. Brooke Comer, "From the Gardens of Georgia: *Fried Green Tomatoes*," *American Cinematographer*, March 1992, 28.

63. Ibid., 30.

64. Kaufman and Baker, "Arduous Art," 70.

65. J. D. Connor, "The New Hollywood, 1980–1999," in *Art Direction and Production Design*, ed. Lucy Fischer (New Brunswick, NJ: Rutgers University Press, 2015), 127.

66. Ibid., 123.

67. Brooke Comer, "*Amateur*'s Tenebrous Images," *American Cinematographer*, August 1995, 70.

68. Patrick Goldstein, "The Prince of Darkness Director Abel Ferrara Practices a Kind of Gonzo Filmmaking, and His Violent Vision Isn't a Particularly Popular One in Hollywood," *Los Angeles Times*, 28 October 1990, T25.

69. See Alisa Perren, *Indie, Inc.: Miramax and the Transformation of Hollywood in the 1990s* (Austin: University of Texas Press, 2012).

70. Rob Stone, *Walk Don't Run: The Cinema of Richard Linklater* (New York: Wallflower, 2013), 15.

71. For more on the difficulties of defining independent cinema in this period, see Yannis Tzioumakis, *American Independent Cinema: An Introduction* (New Brunswick, NJ: Rutgers University Press, 2006).

72. Patrick Taggart, "Slacking Off in Austin: A Bold Debut for a Local Director," *Austin American Statesman*, July 27, 1990, 9.

73. Chris Pizzello, "Suburban Blight," *American Cinematographer*, March 1997, 45.

74. Ibid.

75. Aida A. Hozic, *Hollyworld: Space, Power, and Fantasy in the American Economy* (Ithaca, NY: Cornell University Press, 2001)

76. Janet Wasko, "Financing and Production: Creating the Hollywood Film Commodity," in McDonald and Wasko, *Contemporary Hollywood Film Industry*, 164.

77. Eliot Tiegel, "Location Expo Boasts Strong Non-US Contingent," *Variety*, February 21, 1990, 314.

78. Lukinbeal, "Rise of Regional Production Centers," 314.

79. Goldsmith and O'Regan, *Film Studio*, 151.

80. Ibid., 150.

81. Lester Goldsmith, "Global Report: Canada, B.C. Says Filmbiz Hits $300 Mil and Climbing," *Variety*, December 2, 1991, 85.

82. Ibid.

83. Wasko, "Financing and Production," 164.

84. Sid Adilman, "Province Pitching to Get Filmers Back," *Variety*, September 2, 1991, 49.

85. Aurora Wallace, "When the Set Becomes Permanent: The Spatial Reconfiguration of Hollywood North," in *Taking Place: Location and the Moving Image*, ed. John David Rhodes and Elena Gorfinkel (Minneapolis: University of Minnesota Press, 2011), 168.

86. Fred Kaplan, "Incredible Shrinking N.Y. Film Industry," *Chicago Tribune*, November 28, 2002, http://articles.chicagotribune.com/2002-11-28/features/0211280057_1_film-companies-film-industry-usa-network; see also Erika Kinetz, "New York Abroad: Great White Way? Try Great White North," *New York Times*, November 10, 2002, sec. 14, 6.

87. Michael Curtin and Kevin Sanson, *Precarious Creativity: Global Media, Local Labor* (Berkeley: University of California Press, 2016), 3.

88. Ibid.

89. In 2009, Alabama did pass the Entertainment Industry Incentive Act, which includes a tax rebate to encourage in-state production. As elsewhere, the incentives remain

controversial, as many people question the local economic benefit. Casey Toner, "How Much Did Alabama Film Incentives Benefit In-State Production?," AL.com, August 27, 2014, www .al.com/news/index.ssf/2014/08/how_much_did_alabama_film_ince.html.

90. Hozic, *Hollyworld*, 88.

91. See Vicki Mayer and Tanya Goldman, "Hollywood Handouts: Tax Credits in the Age of Economic Crisis," *Jump Cut*, no. 52 (2010), www.ejumpcut.org/archive/jc52.2010/ mayerTax/text.html.

CHAPTER 7

THE MODERN ENTERTAINMENT MARKETPLACE, 2000–PRESENT

Julian Stringer

It is April 2011, and cinemagoers in North America get their first glimpse of a teaser trailer announcing the imminent arrival of a movie to be released in theaters on August 5. The advertisement is visually compelling and tells an extraordinary tale. Across two dramatic minutes, it swiftly sets out its story spaces.

The plot of the promotional short, which depicts a journey that is both physical and emotional, moves in three acts from two indistinct indoor places to the world outside buildings. Here, at the outset, is a pristine high-tech research laboratory wherein homo sapiens in sharp suits and white coats experiment with a drug that allows the brain to repair itself. Now "ready to move on to the next phase," they select an ape, wheel it in, strap it down. But something goes horribly wrong. Large hairy creatures break out of a second, linked facility and bound angrily into the night; soon they are making their way down residential streets. Since, up until this point, it is impossible to know exactly where these events are taking place, the viewer starts to wonder not just about what is on the minds of those rebellious primates but about the precise topography in which those roads are located. Where on earth are we? Yet as the trailer arcs toward its violent climax, three brief shots finally reveal the relevant details. An uprising is under way on an immense structure situated between land and water; frenzied anthropoids are fighting humans on a bridge colored vivid red; and as a gorilla leaps from the metal girders to attack a helicopter buzzing overhead, the audience is at last able to comprehend the contours of the specific surroundings. This battle is happening in San Francisco. And that is the Golden Gate Bridge.

This spectacular narrative of persecuted tailless monkeys escaping their tormentors and rampaging across the most recognizable landmark in Northern California serves as prelude to the launch of *Rise of the Planet of the Apes* (Rupert Wyatt, 2011; hereafter *Rise*), a large-scale reboot of the globally successful *Planet of the Apes* movie franchise.[1] The series is already a powerful cultural presence.[2] Hollywood's famous first iteration, *Planet of the Apes* (Franklin J. Shaffner, 1968), adapted from Pierre Boulle's 1963 science fiction novel of the same name, has spawned (along with a plethora of other kinds of products) four sequel feature films (1970–73), two television series (1974–75), and, more recently, Tim Burton's blockbusting remake of the 1968 original, also titled *Planet of the Apes* (2001). As the early twenty-first century is clearly an age of rampant media recycling—demonstrated, for instance, by the highly successful contemporary resuscitations of other bygone celluloid icons such as Spider-Man (*Spider-Man*, Sam Raimi, 2002), Batman (*Batman Begins*, Christopher Nolan, 2005), and Superman (*Superman Returns*, Bryan Singer, 2006)—reviving the property at this time evidently makes good commercial sense. In line with the business rationale of the franchise reboot, *Rise*'s trailer thus speaks simultaneously to both older and younger spectators. It recalls the excitement of past glories while readying the modern variants of its genus characters—apes, chimpanzees, and orangutans—for continuing future escapades.

Why is San Francisco's Golden Gate Bridge the central and dramatic focus of the teaser trailer for this particular franchise reboot? Aside from its instant familiarity, a number of factors spring to mind. To begin with, although the Bay Area has previously been alluded to within the aforementioned series, its narrative possibilities have yet to be fully explored.[3] Then again, from the startling depiction of New York's Statue of Liberty that closes the 1968 movie to the unexpected excursion to Washington, DC, monuments that ends the 2001 one, the franchise has established a strong reputation for making innovative use of architectural icons from major U.S. conurbations.[4] At this point in time, too, the city by the bay is in cinematic vogue.[5] The years just before the release of *Rise* saw the Golden Gate Bridge serve as backdrop for cataclysmic happenings of one sort or another in *The Core* (Jon Amiel, 2003), *Hulk* (Ang Lee, 2003), *X-Men: The Last Stand* (Brett Ratner, 2006), *Terminator Salvation* (McG, 2009), *The Book of Eli* (Hughes brothers, 2010), and *Meteor Storm* (Tibor Takács, 2010)—just as, shortly after, it went on to reprise similar roles in major productions such as *Pacific Rim* (Guillermo del Toro, 2013), *Star Trek: Into Darkness* (J. J. Abrams, 2013), *Godzilla* (Gareth Edwards, 2014), *San Andreas* (Brad Peyton, 2015), and *Terminator Genisys* (Alan Taylor, 2015), not to mention *Rise*'s own celebrated sequel, *Dawn of the Planet of the Apes* (Matt Reeves, 2014; hereafter *Dawn*). So while, in 2011, there is in itself nothing remarkable in the fact that this latest installment of species survival is set on this sprawling structure, the Golden Gate Bridge nevertheless retains its allure and freshness as a movie location.

Of no less significance to grasping the geographical logic of *Rise*'s trailer is the related question of how it presents its unique imbrication of space and narrative. Two dimensions of this topic are especially noteworthy. On the one hand, with regard to emotional expressivity as well as bodily appearance, the reboot's new breed of simians—understandably livid after their imprisonment in a heartless laboratory and then a hellish holding shelter—are astonishingly lifelike. They mourn and cry and howl and smash out of their shackles more vividly than any comparable protagonists in movie history. On the other hand, the arrangement of the physical dynamics among these fantastic beings, the humans with whom they interact, and the environments in which all these characters are situated— most strikingly the Golden Gate Bridge—is exhibited with unprecedented clarity. No aspect of the cinematography appears fake: the necessary special effects have been integrated seamlessly. Indeed, internet chatter following the teaser's appearance soon focused on the news that cutting-edge computer technologies have spirited *Rise*'s fabricated apes into real-world locations in ways never previously attempted.

As the analysis in this chapter illustrates, the core creative team behind *Rise* could only attain its unparalleled photo-realist suturing of story and setting by employing the most advanced filmmaking tools available in the historical period under discussion. To understand the significance of this singular accomplishment, then, this chapter contemplates key questions of contemporary Hollywood's choice and use of movie locations: How important are they? What is their appeal? Who is responsible for the way they look onscreen? Has their function changed over time? In the context of these varied and pressing issues, the updated *Planet of the Apes* franchise may be considered as a paradigm of the distinct production circumstances underpinning the role of movie locations in high-end audiovisual entertainment today.[6]

To be more exact, the presentation of San Francisco in *Rise* and *Dawn* illustrates how, in the twenty-first century, shooting on location cannot easily be separated from the painstaking construction of a hybridized form of "location design" or "environmental design."[7] Location or environment design is distinct from mere location shooting. Moreover, it is a phenomenon that may or may not entail filming in the real-world places actually depicted onscreen.

Because this chapter offers one of the first scholarly accounts of the entire process of digital location design in contemporary Hollywood, its case studies are explored in extended depth. The downside of this approach is obvious; it leaves little room to investigate different representational practices and other films. Yet the upside hopefully outweighs this limitation. For only on the basis of careful attention to detail is it possible to comprehend how and why the two *Planet of the Apes* movies are indicative of major trends in the cultural geography of commercial filmmaking today.

The Territory of the Digital

Placing utterly convincing apes alongside humans on the Golden Gate Bridge in *Rise* and putting them here, there, and everywhere in San Francisco in *Dawn* are benchmark achievements associated with the art and industry of digital content creation.[8] This way of doing things encompasses both similarities to and differences from past creative practices.[9]

Hollywood since 2000 diverges from the earlier decades of cinema history discussed by other contributors to this book in its habit of capturing locations routinely through virtual means. More often than not, the visual environments showcased in individual titles are spawned or otherwise enhanced by computer-generated imagery (CGI).[10] While this impulse permeates filmmaking of all tiers of scale, it is most apparent in the case of those high-cost (usually franchise) blockbusters that are among the top box-office hits of this and indeed any era: *Gladiator* (Ridley Scott, 2000), *Lord of the Rings: The Fellowship of the Ring* (Peter Jackson, 2001), *Shrek 2* (Andrew Adamson, Kelly Asbury, and Conrad Vernon, 2004), *King Kong* (Peter Jackson, 2005), *Pirates of the Caribbean: Dead Man's Chest* (Gore Verbinski, 2006), *Avatar* (James Cameron, 2009), *Alice in Wonderland* (Tim Burton, 2010), *Toy Story 3* (Lee Unkrich, 2010), *Harry Potter and the Deathly Hallows: Part 2* (David Yates, 2011), *Transformers: Dark of the Moon* (Michael Bay, 2011), *The Dark Knight Rises* (Christopher Nolan, 2012), *The Hobbit: An Unexpected Journey* (Peter Jackson, 2012), *Iron Man 3* (Shane Black, 2013), *Avengers: Age of Ultron* (Joss Whedon, 2015), *Jurassic World* (Colin Trevorrow, 2015), *Star Wars: Episode VII—The Force Awakens* (J. J. Abrams, 2015). *Rise* and *Dawn* belong firmly in this lineage, as does the third installment of the rebooted series, *War for the Planet of the Apes* (Matt Reeves, 2017; hereafter *War*).[11]

The all-but-total shift toward digital workflows over the past two decades has profoundly impacted both the presentation of physical geographies in movie narratives and the ways in which production departments work together to manufacture them.[12] Regarding graphic composition, to begin with, absolutely anything can now be brought into existence, and in exact detail. (Virtual filmmaking capabilities have developed to the point where there is now little or no difference between the quality of image initially caught and the quality subsequently transmitted during exhibition. Whether a movie has been made on location, a soundstage, or a computer console, the extent of its production and reproduction is the same.) Consider, therefore, that the first thing you notice about the group of high-performing films listed above is that they do not look like a group. Certainly, they utilize a diverse range of locales for their respective scenarios.

Some encompass the known surface of the Earth; others take in unexplored or hitherto-unimagined topographies. A number are set in the present, still more in the past or future. Yet all contain a certain representational similarity. Each offers a plausible and attractive fictional universe that displays every single visual element down to its smallest particular.

More than this, at the level of textual characteristics, presenting physical geographies in twenty-first-century narratives is an agile enterprise because "digital technologies have made film images malleable, customizable, and infinitely changeable."[13] Such images constitute properties that possess economic value as well as other useful qualities. In diverse and creative ways, they function as digital assets.

However, virtual screen entertainment's remarkable pictorial agility comes at a cost when human resources are taken into account. Simply put, conjuring high-resolution environments via digital methods is an extremely labor-intensive process. Compared with every preceding era of Hollywood history—including the years between the mid-1980s and the early 1990s, when computerized image-creation programs were first integrated into features—today's "tent-pole" productions are mind-bogglingly complex.[14] It is no longer the case that there is a first unit and then a second unit that takes care of bespoke tasks such as background scenery and stunt work. Instead, there is now also a visual effects crew that itself can be as large as the first unit. In fact, digital postproduction services are so central to the commercial appeal of contemporary blockbusters that they can comprise around one-third of total production spending.[15]

A brief study of the credits for relevant movies is enough to indicate the massive increase in the number of personnel involved (to a greater or lesser degree) in location design in the digital age as well as the corresponding proliferation of new roles.[16] In 1968, *Planet of the Apes* name checked only seven staff in this area: two art directors, two set decorators, and three people working in special photographic effects. By the time of Burton's 2001 remake, however, the picture had become much more complex: illustrators, set decorators, storyboard artists, and visual effects (VF) editors are among the additional job categories thus recognized, while half a dozen digital effects studios are also acknowledged, in particular Industrial Light & Magic (based in San Francisco). Yet none of this compares to the stupendous production pipelines unraveled in the closing roll calls for *Rise* and *Dawn*. For instance, over five hundred people are named from just one of the numerous visual effects companies that participated in these dual projects—Weta Digital (based in Wellington, New Zealand)—and they appear on the basis of strict departmental headings: animation, camera, CG, compositing, environment, layout, rotoscope, shots, and so on.[17] Toiling elsewhere alongside this impressive cohort, meanwhile, are hundreds more practitioners grouped under equally curious baptismal designations: colorists, 3-D engineers, previsualization coordinators, SFX techs, virtual camera operators. Even so, and as the official making-of book of the 2011 and 2014 megahits indicates, the primary task of these untold thousands is to support diligently the vital collaborations happening elsewhere. It is their job to implement the imaginative visions of a core creative team comprising concept designer, director of photography, production designer, senior VF supervisor, and VF supervisor.[18]

Before proceeding any further, then, it is worth posing a fundamental question of any recent large-scale Hollywood spectacular: why does it need to utilize real-world locations? After all, as Aida A. Hozic observed in 2001, at the precise moment when the industry was beginning wholeheartedly to embrace CGI wizardry, "Digital effects . . . are not only blurring the line between fantasy and reality, they are also making some of the most expensive aspects of production—sets, costumes, stars, stunts, locations—unnecessary."[19] If this is true, then what is the point of going to all the fuss of scouting sites and obtaining permits? When nimble fingers can manage monitor and mouse, where is the sense in continuing to haul heavy equipment?[20] Surely, on these terms, the decision to shoot *Rise* and *Dawn* on actual city streets appears quaint, if not counterintuitive or even perverse. According to information provided by the San Francisco Film Commission, for instance, *Dawn* was granted permission to shoot at the following city locations (as well as the Golden Gate Bridge): California Street at Powell Street, Columbus Avenue at Pacific Avenue, Filbert Street between Hyde Street and Leavenworth Street, Alioto Park, City Hall, and California Street between Mason Street and Kearny Street. (*Rise* received authorization to shoot at a similar combination of sites.)[21]

In answering the question of why to film on location, it is salutary to keep in mind a textual quality that Hollywood artists have striven to attain from the silent era to the present day: believability. No matter what genre a given title may fall into, regardless of where or when it is set, the aim of technologically enabled commercial moviemaking is to transport the spectator to another world, a fabricated spatial atmosphere complete in itself. The more convincing the standards of this constructed environment, the more pleasurable the illusion. For the ultimate goal of immersing audiences in this way is to aid the efficacy of storytelling.

Integrating real-world locations into a cinematic narrative enhances its believability. This is an axiom that was not lost on many of *Rise*'s reviewers. One critic writes of its "action climax on, above and under the Golden Gate Bridge that proves perfectly satisfying."[22] Another draws attention to "the pic's climactic ape uprising, memorably staged on the Golden Gate Bridge."[23] And a third states, "If you think you've had it with special effects, wait till you see Caesar [Andy Serkis] and his ape army battling our befuddled species on the Golden Gate Bridge" (figure 7.1).[24] Then, too, *Dawn*'s production designer, James Chinlund, reports that the same aspiration motivated the staging of the sequel's thrilling final set piece. "We really tried," he says, "as much as we could, to make this film feel like a familiar place to the people of San Francisco, to make it feel like you

Figure 7.1. Caesar on the Golden Gate Bridge in *Rise of the Planet of the Apes* (20th Century Fox, 2011).

were there."[25] A well-known landmark from the downtown skyline was therefore enlisted as the model for the looming structure atop of which Caesar fights Koba (Toby Kebell). Explains that film's visual effects supervisor, Dan Lemmon, "[The tower] is based on an existing building that is in San Francisco, but re-imagining it as if it were in the middle of a renovation. So it's loosely based on the building that's currently at One Market Street, but with fairly substantial modifications."[26]

This policy of morphing genuine locations with synthetic components to forge picturesque scenes for sure-footed storytelling has guided creative talents throughout Hollywood's history.[27] To cite just one example, Jeff Kraft and Aaron Leventhal summarize the "four primary filmmaking techniques" that the director Alfred Hitchcock, working in league with a throng of collaborators including art directors and set designers, deployed to "convey the settings" of Northern California–set titles such as *Shadow of a Doubt* (1943), *Vertigo* (1958), and *The Birds* (1963):

> First, the director filmed live-action footage with the principal actors on location. . . . Second, he meticulously re-created interiors and exteriors on studio sets, exhaustively researching the subtlest details of actual locations to add authenticity. Third, Hitchcock took background footage on location, sometimes sending out a second unit led by the assistant director. He frequently used the resulting film as rear projection footage in combination with live actors on studio sound stages, known as "process shots." Finally, he often modified the images he filmed with special effects, such as matte paintings, thus adding scenery or architecture to enhance the film's setting.[28]

Today the altering of real-life locations via digital software packages, or the creation of imaginatively convincing geographies solely through CGI, is accomplished by way of a process of "rendering." This term refers to an image-synthesis procedure in which a photo-realist or non-photo-realist optical appearance is evolved from a 2-D or 3-D model by means of computer programs. In line with other treatments of this concept—for example, to describe the orchestration of sound effects to enhance the expressiveness of a film's audio track—visual rendering is concerned not so much (or only) with accurate imitation but with infusing a given scene with a particular force.[29] Walter Murch explains that rendering makes "a sound appear more 'real' than reality. . . . Walking on cornstarch, for instance, records as a better footstep in snow than snow itself."[30] Similarly, adjusting the look of a specific scene by processing individual pixels in a video-display system can intensify its credibility and attractiveness. Rendered movie locations are easy on the eye. Regardless of the actual physical appearance of a place such as San Francisco's Golden Gate Bridge, it is designed graphically to carry the heightened feelings associated with its dramatic possibilities as a story space.

Just how thoroughly the labor-intensive discipline of digital rendering can adopt and adapt actual locations is illustrated by a movie released in the same year as *Dawn*: *Big Hero 6* (Don Hall and Chris Williams, 2014). This Disney animation draws on comic-book art and live-action cinematography to shape an original hybrid environment, called San Fransokyo, out of a 3-D CGI fusion of diverse representations of San Francisco and Tokyo. (The immense red structure straddling the bay is once again included, alongside other familiar landmarks from the two cities.) Differentiating the project from a series of notable franchise hits of the period, codirector Don Hall declares, "I chose San Francisco because Los Angeles didn't feel right, and New York is the epicenter of the Marvel comics world, which I wanted to move away from. San Francisco has so many distinctive features—the Golden Gate Bridge, the hills, the painted ladies, the cable cars."[31] In blending these characteristics with the separate topographies of Japan's capital, *Big Hero 6*'s core creative team emphasize certain properties of the U.S. conurbation's exact geographical position.[32] Recounts director of cinematography (lighting) Adolph Lusinsky, "I don't know if it has to do with the winds constantly cleaning the air or if it's because a lot of light gets through the buildings, but San Francisco just has really cool lighting. We went to specific spots at specific times when events happen in the movie to try to capture it. . . . We went to the rooftop of the second-tallest building in San Francisco and photographed the skies every half hour. San Francisco's skies have a unique look because of the way the atmosphere sits really low to the water."[33] He further reports how, in pursuit of realism and believability, the crew "did a helicopter flyover at sunset in San Francisco and Tokyo. San Francisco's got a lot of old, warm, sodium lights: most of Tokyo's have a coolish, whiter hue. There's a whole color temperature difference between those cities."[34] Production designer Paul Felix, together with a small team of visual development artists, also took research trips to the cities: "You have to go to a place and feel it for yourself. Just the way spaces are arranged tells you a lot about a culture. Seeing a city firsthand gives you a breadth and richness that influences a design to be something new but also truly evoke a place's nature."[35]

Ironically, then, despite the seemingly inexhaustible supply of spellbinding illusions promoted by digital rendering—and even (or especially) in the face of "impossible" spatial mash-ups such as *Big Hero 6*'s San Fransokyo—recognizable environments remain at the heart of the appeal of contemporary cinema. Indeed, their presence is arguably more important than ever. At the very moment in Hollywood's history when, technically speaking, they are least necessary, their presentation has become egregious. To repeat, genuine locations fulfill vital aesthetic functions. And for this reason, digital location design is now a cornerstone of the manufacture of high-end audiovisual entertainment.

The ongoing centrality of tangible places to an intangible virtual filmmaking economy that does not strictly require them is only one of a series of paradoxes that characterize the choice and use of location assets in the modern entertainment marketplace. Three others may briefly be mentioned here.[36]

First, while spectacular landscapes can be generated entirely through digital means, the core business of film commissions and the interconnected culture of "incentive-mania"—or the practice of enticing productions to a given destination on the basis of competitive tax-rebate programs, help with negotiating municipal and union bureaucracy, and the like—has blossomed into a pragmatic activity of the first order.[37]

This phenomenon is linked to the development over recent decades of certain cities and regions as "media capitals"—that is to say, emerging centers of transnational cultural production (e.g., Bombay, Cairo, Hong Kong).[38] Space unfortunately precludes analysis at this time of the specific reasons why—aside from the natural topographical advantages mentioned earlier—San Francisco has arguably grown into this role. However, the factors that have led from the birth of the city's film industry to the establishment in the Bay Area of major studios and media giants such as American Zoetrope, Lucasfilm, Dolby Laboratories, and Pixar Animation Studios is a topic of interest to numerous writers.[39]

Second, the acceleration (and internationalization) of computer-oriented image-capture techniques has freed the creative imagination but raised the vexed questions of digital theft and copyright protection for electronic files that can be copied and shared quickly and easily.[40] In this respect, Portia Fontes of the San Francisco Film Commission reveals that just as a digital photograph belongs—in theory, at least—to the person who takes it, the city of San Francisco ostensibly does not exercise proprietorship over the images seized within its vicinity. So long as a shoot has been properly permitted, the recordings made by a production company are then owned by that organization, which is completely free to do whatever it likes with, say, its resulting portrayals of the Golden Gate Bridge. In her words, "We [the San Francisco Film Commission] don't control content in any way. That's something that we always mention to our productions because this is an art form and we want to protect that."[41] Having said this, of course, one fundamental purpose of a film commission is to regulate and monitor access to potential filmmaking sites in the first place.[42]

Third, although the number and variety of jobs associated with location work has risen as a result of digital science's greater flexibility, this has resulted in a deeper anxiety about the delineation and future security of distinct professional roles. How is it possible to distinguish between the contribution and importance of production designers, art designers, and digital and special effects crews as well as the increasing number of other movie personnel charged with the cinematic creation and presentation of a modern movie environment?[43] Acknowledging the force of these crisscrossing dynamics should suffice to convey the extent to which digital ways of doing things have penetrated the nature, purpose, and practice of location shooting at the point where it morphs into the pursuit of virtual location design.[44]

It is helpful to note, too, one final effect of the disruptions visited on the contemporary blockbuster by electronic workflows: production pipelines today are more dispersed and mobile than at any time in Hollywood's past. It is now much more likely that there will be a disjunction between where a movie is set and where it is filmed and between where it is set and/or filmed and where its images are rendered.[45] An individual project may draw on the unique resources of any given media capital(s) as need dictates—that is to say, on the basis of a cost-benefit weighting of the production center's particular merits relative to those offered by competing alternatives.

Turning to examine these operations in further detail, we find that in *Rise* and *Dawn*, location shooting and design took place variously in four distinct bases—namely, Vancouver and New Orleans as well as San Francisco and Weta Digital in Wellington. Once we are armed with this knowledge, the films' images of the Golden Gate Bridge and other San Francisco locations come to resemble—fittingly—mere parts of a whole. They are many-sided, useful digital assets that constitute fragments of a much-larger, complex, and fascinating jigsaw puzzle.

PIECES OF SAN FRANCISCO

Published accounts of *Rise*'s planning and assembly identify the key contributions of the U.S.-based Aaron Sims (concept designer), Andrew Lesnie (director of photography), and Claude Paré (production designer), as well as Joe Letteri (senior visual effects supervisor) and Dan Lemmon (visual effects supervisor) from Weta Digital.[46] The caliber of the group's experience is significant. Lemmon, Lesnie, and Letteri were all employed on the *Lord of the Rings* trilogy (2001–3) and *King Kong*, Lemmon and Letteri also participated in *Avatar* and *I, Robot* (Alex Proyas, 2004), Lesnie and Sims labored on *I Am Legend* (Francis Lawrence,

2007), and Paré was production designer of *Night at the Museum* (Shawn Levy, 2006) and supervising art director of *The Aviator* (Martin Scorsese, 2004) and *The Day after Tomorrow* (Roland Emmerich, 2004).[47] With a compelling mix of real-world spaces and digitally enhanced or created environments, any one of these movies offers an instructive lesson in the art and industry of virtual location design in the twenty-first century.[48]

When working together to spirit Caesar, Koba, and their fellow primates into real-world locations such as the Golden Gate Bridge, what did this creative team care most about? Regarding the film's climax, a priority was to deliver the scene in a cost-effective manner and without recourse to filming on the bridge itself, which, because of its logistical challenges, "was always going to be impossible."[49] Fontes: "The use of digital imaging has allowed productions to create a smaller footprint on the ground and impact the public less while still retrieving the same necessary shots. . . . Over twenty years ago, before the era of digital filmmaking, filming on the bridge would require major preparation with City agencies and possible closures to prevent vehicle and pedestrian access for a closed set. For example, in the 1985 James Bond film *A View to a Kill* [John Glen] stuntmen doubling for [Roger] Moore and Christopher Walken actually were being filmed on top of one of the bridge's towers. But today, the same shot can be obtained . . . after the fact using visual effects."[50]

A suitably robust production pipeline therefore had to be put in place to ensure timely delivery of the required images' constituent parts. In addition, aside from advancing the story's unique imbrication of space and narrative, the visage of apes warring on, above, and under the familiar architectural icon also needed to function—for publicity and other purposes—as a powerful spectacle in its own right. To be sure, the more convincing the standards of this composite location, the more alluring its illusion. Seeing is believing.

The job of digitally connecting actual locations with CGI renderings to form an attractive visual mosaic was complicated and painstaking. According to the available evidence, the necessary parts were joined around three more or less coterminous core junctures. Given the complexity of these procedures—and in the interests of brevity—this process will only be summarized very briefly here.[51]

Stage 1 entailed capturing authentic guide shots of the specific setting through location "plate" photography, defined as "the unaltered live-action scene to which a special effect is added."[52] A crew of twelve, forming what the movie's credits call the "Golden Gate Unit," was tasked with taking helicopter views of the watery structure with the help of an aerial-photography company. Explains director Wyatt, "We did some plate shots where we went to Golden Gate with a Canon 5D camera, and we just took stills that we then piled into the environments."[53] However, this was the extent of filming at that particular spot. Apes and other elements were subsequently inserted into the frame through CGI and other means.

Stage 2 involved reconstructing a full-scale portion of the Golden Gate Bridge on a large set built on a parking lot in Vancouver—a shooting base, selected primarily because of British Columbia's attractive tax incentive schemes, where filming conditions could be tightly controlled.[54] For Letteri, this was the toughest sequence to shoot: "We filmed on a 100-meter section of road on a backlot in Vancouver. The whole Bay Area and the entire bridge was digitally created and dropped into the road-bed, which was built to look like the five-lane highway on the Golden Gate Bridge."[55] Joe Fordham adds that Lesnie "covered the set with a big silk to control lighting.... [It] included ... traffic flanked by pedestrian walkways, backed by a 20 foot-tall greenscreen. Dan Lemmon worked with Pixel Liberation Front previz supervisor Duane Floch to determine the extent of physical and digital set builds. Second unit director Brian Smrz then worked with stunt coordinator Mike Mitchell and the ape performance team to choreograph apes overrunning a bottleneck of 80 automobiles on the bridge."[56]

Fordham outlines Weta Digital's input in this regard in more extensive detail:

> As reference for digital set extensions, Weta conducted location surveys during the San Francisco shoot, and commissioned a separate photographic study. "Chris White had friends in San Francisco who got access to the towers on top of the bridge," explained [visual effects supervisor] Erik Winquist. "They took a bunch of photos there, so we had those photos to refer to. We also had special access to the bridge around Fort Point, where we took our own photos of the underside of the bridge." Senior digital modeler John Stevenson-Galvin and lead modeler Paul Jenness then constructed a replica of the mile-and-a-half long structure.... "It was the largest hard surface asset that we've built at Weta. We managed the build by breaking the bridge down into pieces. We built one segment of the underside of the bridge, and then repeated that in a gentle arc that the bridge has over its span. The textures and shaders department then worked out procedural shading and weathering techniques, and used custom projections for closeups. The bridge asset was incredibly heavy to render in its entirety, so our digital effects supervisor Jeff Capogreco cached static spherical harmonics point clouds of the bridge in sections. Pre-calculating the lighting and occlusion data made the bridge much more efficient to render in conjunction with our image-based lighting pipeline." For the surrounding environment, Weta matte painting department head Yvonne Muinde and matte artist Daniel Bayona generated 360-degree vistas of sky and distant landscapes, which integrated with water simulations of San Francisco Bay. In most shots of the bay, the digital water was blended with a matte painting built from photo reference.[57]

In this context, Fontes confirms that visual effects personnel "often add CGI fog over establishing shots of the city. By adding in this haziness they probably do not have to add much else into certain shots (e.g., buildings in the background, cars on the road, etc.). This is best seen in the 2003 film *Hulk* where they show the superhero at the very top of the Golden Gate Bridge, but the fog blankets the rest of the city."[58] Note, too, Fordham's reference to the climactic sequence's "hazy views of the distant city," achieved when Weta Digital added "procedural shading and weathering effects" to renderings that "shrouded the bridge in fog using practical mist elements."[59] By contrast, *Dawn* depicts Koba leading apes across the Golden Gate Bridge in fog at night. Recounts Fordham, citing Winquist, "Production plates were shot without fog effects. Weta integrated atmospheric effects with city extensions of 'beautiful dense, dark, inky shadows. . . . Matt Reeves played much of this movie in shadows, and we re-created that look in our city extensions, giving nighttime scenes an orange sodium vapor cast. And if we didn't get rain or mist in plates, we added it as background ambience.' "[60]

Stage 3—which is crucial to any account of *Rise*'s unparalleled photo-realist suturing of story and setting—utilized one of the most advanced virtual filmmaking tools available in the period under discussion: motion capture, otherwise known as performance capture. This is a technology, developed for and pioneered by the *Lord of the Rings* trilogy, *The Polar Express* (Robert Zemeckis, 2004), *King Kong, Beowulf* (Robert Zemeckis, 2007), *Avatar*, and *The Adventures of Tintin* (Steven Spielberg, 2011), in which recordings of a human actor's physical skill form the basis for creating, via 2-D or 3-D computer animation, the movement of believable digital characters or objects.[61] The exact traits of "mo-cap" usage in this particular instance have been glossed as follows: "The actors playing apes wore motion-capture outfits—flannel unitards studded with tracking markers that cover the head and body—as well as helmet cameras that hover in front of the face to record expressions. Computer-graphic specialists then used software to superimpose that data onto virtual 3-D ape 'puppets' that are drawn from actual apes, and added details like hair, moisture and individual muscle simulations."[62] Referring to the Vancouver shoot on the set of the reconstructed Golden Gate Bridge, Letteri specifies, "We used more than 100 motion-caption cameras in these little birdhouses."[63]

While visual effects plate photography and built sets with digital extensions are routine implements of visual storytelling in the new millennium, it is this third juncture that distinguishes *Rise* as a benchmark achievement. For what is new in this case is the ambition to place utterly convincing apes in Northern California via a hitherto-untried combination of mo-cap and location shooting. During filming in San Francisco and Vancouver, as well as in rural British Columbia (substituting for the Bay Area's Muir Woods), Weta Digital succeeded in coupling visual effects and performance capture work outside the controlled framework of an enclosed stage (in this context also known as a "volume"). Letteri: "For the first time, we used performance capture as a fully integrated part of the live action performance. Working on *Rise* became all about the performances and the actors interacting with one another. We would take care of the rest—the actual visual effects—later."[64]

To accomplish this, staff at the Wellington company "devised a new portable performance capture rig, which could be set up in different kinds of locations. For the first time ever, notes visual effects supervisor Dan Lemmon: 'we were able to get those performances in direct sunlight.' "[65] *Rise*'s press book claims that the film "was impossible to make until the technology, invented for *Avatar* and now advanced to a new dimension, caught up to the idea behind the movie. . . . This allowed the performance capture work to be fully integrated with the live action performances—eliminating the barrier between visual effects and live action."[66] But Joe Letteri goes further: "For *Avatar*, Jim Cameron created a complete fantasy world that no one had ever experienced before. The challenge with *Rise* was a very different one, and in some ways, it was even more daunting. We applied some of the technology we developed for *Avatar* to create a real, recognizable world—modern-day San Francisco. Everything—the apes, the locations—had to feel genuine because we're exploring a story that's reality-based and not straight-ahead science fiction."[67]

Given *Rise*'s mostly glowing reviews and strong box-office performance, it appears that younger and older spectators alike were happy with the outcome of these exertions. Certainly, in *Variety*'s judgment, if "the film's stock characters and generic story components don't feel especially fresh, the technical elements are so cutting edge that the film could not have existed in such polished form before now."[68]

The story of *Dawn*'s construction constitutes in many ways a parallel journey to its celebrated precursor, albeit with crucial dissimilarities.[69] Once again, the priorities were cost-effectiveness and efficient organization of a large and dispersed international crew working across multiple media centers. Once again, mo-cap technology was used to put apes and humans here, there, and everywhere in recognizable Northern California locations, including the Golden Gate Bridge. However, audience familiarity with the earlier film's astonishingly lifelike primates also meant that a new precedent had to be established. "*Rise* was a great start," announced producer Dylan Clark. "The technology helped us tell the story in more ways than we understood when we started out. For *Dawn* we asked: what can we do better? Let's go further with the characters, let's go further with the technology."[70] So the sequel sought to nuance the presentation of its by now already well-known environment. The more convincing the standards of this revisited topography, the more potent its illusion. Believing is seeing.

As before, narrative settings were planned and assembled by a team of key contributors. The project reunited Sims, Letteri, and Lemmon, toiling this time alongside director of photography Michael Seresin (*Harry Potter and the Prisoner*

Figure 7.2. Koba in San Francisco City Hall (where the city's film commission office is located) in *Dawn of the Planet of the Apes* (20th Century Fox, 2014).

of Azkaban, Alfonso Cuarón, 2004) and production designer James Chinlund (*Avengers Assemble*, Joss Whedon, 2012).

Location plate photography enabled foundational images of San Francisco to be gathered, supplemented by a mere four days of shooting in and around the conurbation. To create "establishing views of the ruined city, wracked by ten years of decay and neglect, Weta Digital composited aerial plates of San Francisco with signs of urban decay, and revisited the digital model of the Golden Gate Bridge that it had constructed for the finale of *Rise*."[71] Also, to capture scenes of apes "in relation to recognizable Bay Area landmarks, the production conducted a two-day splinter unit shoot with a handful of ape performers"[72] (figure 7.2).

Yet as one writer observes in relation to San Francisco's perceived status as a media center, this kind of arrangement "has become the reality for an iconic city that lacks a competitive filming incentive or purpose-built studio infrastructure. *Dawn* continued the trend as a big-budget production spending just a few days in the city to get shots that established a sense of place."[73] Susannah Greason Robbins, executive director of the San Francisco Film Commission, notes that a similar approach was being taken, too, by other blockbusters of the time, such as *San Andreas* (filmed mainly in Australia), *Ant-Man* (Peyton Reed, 2015; also set in San Francisco but based in Atlanta), and *Terminator Genisys* (shot in Louisiana). On the possibility of a new California bill to support the state's production industry by expanding its filming incentive program, she adds, "It would mean that blockbusters like *Dawn of the Planet of the Apes* could remain in California and keep hundreds of local jobs, in addition to the millions of dollars that we are currently losing out on to states with stronger incentives."[74] In this respect, as well as in all the other respects outlined in this chapter, the updated *Planet of the*

Apes franchise may be considered indicative of the distinct and ever-changing production circumstances underpinning the role of high-end location design in Hollywood today.

British Columbia was retained as a production base, with four weeks of filming taking place in Canada. Recalls the project's Vancouver-based location manager, Catou Kearney, "We needed areas that looked as if there had been very little human activity in them. We also had to find locations that could support the technical requirements for the film [because] 3D and motion picture work adds an element of difficulty. Remote but not too remote!"[75]

However, *Dawn*—differently from *Rise*—also adopted New Orleans as its headquarters for a period of some months. Why? Chinlund relates, "[As] the production had no plans to shoot in San Francisco, . . . one of my first tasks was to comb the usual-suspect rebate states for a likely substitute. I stumbled upon an intersection in New Orleans that lined up well with the intersection at San Francisco's California and Market streets, which I have always loved for its wonderful perspectives and architectural complexity. The decision was quickly made to shoot New Orleans for the urban work, and Vancouver for the forest and Marin exteriors."[76] More specifically, Nick Goundry reports that New Orleans's Big Easy Studios, which offers eight soundstages and 250,000 square feet of floor space, became a chosen destination because of Louisiana's uncapped 30 percent filming incentive.[77] Weta Digital's Florian Fernandez (model supervisor) elaborates that "New Orleans was also an excellent visual resource in parts of the city that hadn't been rebuilt since Hurricane Katrina." (On top of this, staff "studied references of old buildings in Brazil and Thailand, where construction projects had run out of money and partially built structures had been left to decay, and of Pripyat, the derelict city in Ukraine, adjacent to the Chernobyl nuclear power plant disaster.")[78] And the regionally based location manager Jason Waggenspack adds "We found a dead section of highway that crossed over the interstate in New Orleans East and turned it into the Golden Gate Bridge, [and] we turned an abandoned power plant along the Mississippi River into several sets."[79]

Discussing a single shot from the scene in which an army of primates launches a vicious assault on the human colony holed up on California Street in downtown San Francisco, Lemmon illustrates how that location was blended with New Orleans to forge a wholly new story space through use of digital assets: "We took over the intersection of Rampart Street and Common Street in New Orleans for four or five months. . . . Most of the buildings in that area were abandoned. We re-dressed that small area to play different parts of San Francisco. Just a handful of shots were actually created in San Francisco, but so much digital manipulation was done to age the buildings that there was very little left of the original photography." After that, performance-captured apes were digitally added in, while other elements that actually existed, such as the military tank, had to be rendered virtually through a technique called match moving. ("We create a digital version of the camera that lines up to the physical camera. So when we add the apes, everything sticks. If you don't do it correctly, everything will slide around and they won't look like they live in the same world.") After that, the small physical set was extended with a digital version of California Street using lidar scanning: "It works like a radar," explains Lemmon, "but it's laser-based. It sweeps a laser beam in a circle and you get a cloud of three-dimensional points, and you use that to build a geometry of the location."[80] (Weta Digital's city extensions used lidar data and photographic surveys gathered after a visual effects artist traveled up and down California Street and Market Street for three days to map every contour of the architecture of fifty buildings. "The survey material was great to build from," says Fernandez. "We detailed all the hero buildings so we could light them realistically and integrate them into scenes.")[81] And after that, digital smoke and fire were added on top of the real conflagration on set to disguise the natural-gas flame bars. Lemmon states that "in service to the story," which called for a city without electricity, the details given to this background were dimmed to the point of near invisibility.[82]

Beyond all of these contemporary tricks of the trade, though, it is once again innovations in motion capture on location that signal the film's benchmark achievement. In the words of its press book, the sequel's "realism" is "enhanced by the production's ability to shoot in exterior locations. More than 85 percent of *Dawn* was shot in the forests of Vancouver and outside New Orleans. . . . Shooting a film of this scope and scale in native 3D, coupled with the complex performance capture work amidst stunning yet challenging exterior locations was exponentially more difficult than what had been achieved on *Rise*. That latter featured mostly interior sets, but *Dawn* depicts a community of 2,000 apes, living in wild surroundings, in humid, rainforest environments."[83] *Variety* reports that director Reeves "wanted to take their performance capture equipment further into the field for location shooting" and quotes Letteri: "He really wanted that feeling that we're out with the chimps. Very tribal. Very dirty. He wanted to take you out into this wet, rainy forest and so for the first time we really had to make this gear mobile."[84]

To help arrange believable physical dynamics among the numerous assembled performers, Weta Digital "had 35 people on each unit, an array of 50 or so mo-cap cameras and eight witness capture cameras that were constantly rolling on anything that involved an ape character."[85] However, these were not the only solutions the filmmakers came up with to location-related problems. According to Alexandra Wolfe, since Reeves wanted to add "an extra layer of realism by shooting on location, a feat that their special effects and 3-D camera equipment hadn't been designed to do," he ensured that, for scenes set near the apes' secluded home, "the crew lugged motion cameras and digital cameras from a studio into the woods."[86] Indeed, as Lemmon affirms, the "biggest thing on the performance capture side was that we completely overhauled all of our equipment so that we could take it not just on location but out into the elements. We could let it get rained on and take it up the side of mountains, places we wouldn't have been able to go before without it getting destroyed."[87] Weta Digital thus brought its performance capture cameras "outside and into the rainy, snowy woods of British Columbia, . . . making them wireless, hiding them in bushes and clamping them to tree branches."[88]

The actor Jason Clarke (who portrays the human character Malcolm) provides a vivid summary of what the British Columbia rain-forest shoot must have been like: "It's simply amazing—old-growth forest, 3D cameras, motion cap cameras, wires going everywhere, smoke machines, fog machines, rain and mud, a crew of hundreds and then there's 50 actors performing as apes walking around the forest. I always prefer shooting on location rather than on a soundstage. It just brings so much in terms of realism. . . . These guys are not just sitting in a volume. They've got to interact with people and the forest and the mud and everything else and the rocks and the stones and the rain."[89] And perhaps it is only fitting that the person at the helm of all this should have the final word. "We're in the woods, we're not creating the woods," says director Matt Reeves. "It was crazy hard, but what's going to be cool about the aesthetic is that you're going to feel very grounded in the real world, so just the one fantasy is that they're intelligent apes. No one has done that yet to the level that we did, so it should have a really distinctive feel and look."[90]

To the extent that the film was a box-office success and the critics were mostly happy, all these efforts appear to have been worth it. For instance, after name checking Letteri and Lemmon as the project's returning "visual-effects wizards," Kenneth Turan writes that Dawn's "vision of masses of intelligent apes swarming the screen as masters of all they survey is even more impressive than it was the last time around and reason enough to see the film all by itself."[91] Meanwhile, "Dawn is a much better . . . movie than its predecessor," adds Stephanie Zacharek. "It lives to confidently in its invented universe that you almost believe a society of apes could thrive on the outskirts of San Francisco."[92]

CONCLUSION

Some brief conclusions may be drawn from the preceding analysis. As paradigms of location design in audiovisual entertainment today, Rise and Dawn are indicative of how and why location shooting and digital content creation fuse in contemporary Hollywood. The two linked projects demonstrate that the choice and use of real-world places is of arguably greater consequence now than in previous decades. Encompassing similarities to and differences from past creative practices, they show that while a preoccupation with notions of believability and the efficacy of storytelling remain consistent, the precise function of movie landscapes nevertheless shifts over time, in line with the advent of new technologies. Certainly, despite the films' status as entries in a rebooted franchise, each advances singular ways of doing things.

The value of concentrating on the chosen case studies in such depth is that by doing so, the complexity and multidimensional nature of environmental design becomes apparent. When it comes to the production of high-cost franchise blockbusters—the biggest box-office hits of the period under discussion—antiquated distinctions between the use of sets and the practice of location shooting simply collapse. Instead, what now needs to be considered as well are the varied uses of digital assets. These are deployed alongside other modes of production and via dispersed production centers to create compelling hybrid representations. Only through close analysis of pertinent details can the full extent of these procedures be unraveled and understood.

Two specific aspects of *Rise* and *Dawn* suggest that location design will remain central to the modern entertainment marketplace. On the one hand, the ongoing growth (however precarious) of the digital postproduction and location services sectors means that production departments will need to continue to find ever more capable ways of working together to manufacture aesthetically appealing movies. On the other hand, as itemized earlier, the presentation of physical geographies in twenty-first-century narratives is likely to remain an agile enterprise because digital images are malleable, customizable, and infinitely changeable. In this reading, for example, the creative team responsible for visualizing the looming structure atop of which Caesar fights Koba in *Dawn*'s final set piece participates in a contemporary and intricate—but by no means unique—"parasitic" undertaking. ("The building was a form of parasitic architecture. . . . The ground-level structure, based on One Market Street, was a six-story art-deco building. The glass and steel skyscraper was planted on top of that, similar to the Hearst Tower in New York.")[93] Thus, too, similar to the way that, with regard to representation, "all cities are practically infinite," for filmmakers, San Francisco's Golden Gate Bridge will go on functioning as a flexible, adaptable visual asset.[94] Certainly, it is likely to continue to provide audiences with a set of instantly familiar geographical coordinates with which to navigate fresh story worlds. Referring to habitual depictions of the metallic icon's spectacular destruction, Fontes observes that recent films "involve having things like the bridge and all the skyscrapers sucked up. So people are getting tired of seeing bridges broken up. Now they want to see them sucked up!"[95]

It is 2017, and cinemagoers are getting their first glimpses of the imminent arrival of new filmmaking technologies that promise to recalibrate Hollywood on location yet again. For on the horizon dawns the age of augmented reality (AR) and virtual reality (VR). Could it be that you and I—goggle-clad mammals rising from our seats to interact with the geographies floating in front of our eyes—will soon be able to rampage for ourselves all around that magnificent red construction?

NOTES

This chapter draws on materials gathered during research trips to San Francisco and Los Angeles in July 2016. For generous help and support, I would like to thank Portia Fontes (San Francisco Film Commission), Max Maliga (Industrial Light & Magic), Rosemarie Knopka (Art Directors Guild), and staff at the Margaret Herrick Library. Thanks, too, to Nikki J. Y. Lee, Andrew Leyshon, Denise Mann, and Kevin Sanson, as well as to my colleagues Elizabeth Evans, Paul Grainge, Roberta Pearson, and Gianluca Sergi from the Institute for Screen Industries Research at the University of Nottingham.

1. For a discussion of the franchise reboot, see William Proctor, "Regeneration and Rebirth: Anatomy of the Franchise Reboot," *Scope: An Online Journal of Film and Television Studies*, no. 22 (February 2012): www.scope.nottingham.ac.uk.

2. On the *Planet of the Apes* franchise as a popular culture phenomenon, see Eric Greene, *"Planet of the Apes" as American Myth: Race and Politics in the Films and Television Series* (Jefferson, NC: McFarland, 2006); Joe Fordham and Jeff Bond, *"Planet of the Apes": The Evolution of the Legend* (London: Titan Books, 2014).

3. As Franco Moretti observes of literary works in *Atlas of the European Novel 1800–1900* (London: Verso, 1998), *"Each space determines, or at least encourages, its own kind of story. . . . What happens depends on where it happens. . . . Specific stories are the product of specific spaces. . . . Without a certain kind of space, a certain kind of story is simply impossible"* (70, 100; italics in original). A ruined San Francisco had appeared as the futuristic setting for one of the episodes in the first television series ("The Trap," 1974). Cf. Jim van Buskirk and Will Shank, *Celluloid San Francisco: The Film Lover's Guide to Bay Area Movie Locations* (Chicago: Chicago Review Press, 2006).

4. These depictions typically oscillate with the presentation of more obscure postapocalyptic landscapes, both within individual films and across the series as a whole.

5. For background information, consult Sheerly Avni, *Cinema by the Bay* (New York: George Lucas Books and Welcome Books, 2006).

6. This chapter concentrates solely on visual representation. However, the relationship between location filmmaking and the modern cinema soundtrack is a neglected yet vital topic that deserves full treatment in its own right. For a stimulating discussion of cinematic environment and sonic design, see Elizabeth Weis and Randy Thom, "The City That Never Shuts Up: Aural Intrusion in New York Apartment Films," in *City That Never Sleeps: New York and the Filmic Imagination*, ed. Murray Pomerance (New Brunswick, NJ: Rutgers University Press, 2007), 215–27.

7. Although these terms are widely used in current industry discourse, their origins and genealogies are uncertain and hence require further research.

8. The Golden Gate Bridge is displayed even more prominently in *Dawn* than it is in *Rise*. Its iconography also features extensively in both films' promotional campaigns. Full descriptions of *Rise*'s and *Dawn*'s respective plots are available on the internet. Their narrative arcs encompass downtown and suburban San Francisco as well as Muir Woods to the north of the city. In each case, the bridge serves as a symbolic threshold that joins at the same time as it separates these two land areas.

9. Hollywood in the twenty-first century is an intertwined multimedia system comprising video games and the internet as well as film and television. In order to ensure that the analysis is as detailed and rigorous as possible, though, this chapter limits its focus to the movie industry. For an account of location shooting and U.S. television drama, see Julian Stringer, "The Gathering Place: *Lost* in Oahu," in *Reading "Lost": Perspectives on a Hit Television Show*, ed. Roberta Pearson (London: I. B. Tauris, 2009), 73–93.

10. The literature on cinema and digital technologies is extensive. For studies relevant to the concerns of this chapter, see, inter alia, Shilo McClean, *Digital Storytelling: The Narrative Power of Visual Effects in Film* (Cambridge, MA: MIT Press, 2007); Stephen Prince, *Digital Visual Effects in Cinema: The Seduction of Reality* (New Brunswick, NJ: Rutgers University Press, 2012); Lisa Purse, *Digital Imaging in Popular Cinema* (Edinburgh: Edinburgh

University Press, 2013); Kristen Whissel, *Spectacular Digital Effects: CGI and Contemporary Cinema* (Durham, NC: Duke University Press, 2014); Stephen Prince, "Hollywood's Digital Back Lot, 2000–the Present," in *Art Direction and Production Design*, ed. Lucy Fischer (New Brunswick, NJ: Rutgers University Press, 2015), 139–56; and Tanine Allison, "The Modern Entertainment Marketplace, 2000–Present: Special/Visual Effects," in *Editing and Special/ Visual Effects*, ed. Charlie Keil and Kristen Whissel (New Brunswick, NJ: Rutgers University Press, 2016), 172–85.

11. *War* was unreleased at the time of writing and hence is not covered here. It is true that not all major productions of the period can be fitted into this pattern—some directors (most notoriously Christopher Nolan) continue to work on celluloid, and some films continue to be shot exclusively (or primarily) in actual locations. But as shown by the staggering financial success of the mainstream hits named in the text, the tendency holds true. Besides, when watching movies these days, one cannot always be completely certain whether this or that particular aspect has or has not been manipulated digitally. As Francis Ford Coppola puts it, "Really, in a digital medium anything is possible, depending on the concept and the budget." Coppola, *Live Cinema and Its Techniques* (New York: Liveright, 2017), 61.

12. For a lively take on the pros and cons of the industry-wide transformations wrought by digital's arrival, see the documentary *Side by Side*, dir. Christopher Kenneally (Company Films, 2012). A lack of space unfortunately precludes further analysis at this time of the concomitant changes affecting roles such as that of location manager. One member of that profession, Wesley Hagan, explains, "You definitely have to take CGI into consideration when you're selecting locations. Does this location give us the space to digitally insert the Chicago skyline into the background? In Atlanta, I've done Tikrit, Kuwait, London, and Tokyo. We've found it or created it but always with the help of CGI." Quoted in *Voices of Labor: Creativity, Craft, and Conflict in Global Hollywood*, ed. Michael Curtin and Kevin Sanson (Oakland: University of California Press, 2017), 199.

13. Allison, "Modern Entertainment Marketplace," 185.

14. Milestones: *The Last Starfighter* (Nick Castle, 1984), *Willow* (Ron Howard, 1988), *The Abyss* (James Cameron, 1989), *Terminator 2: Judgment Day* (James Cameron, 1991), *Jurassic Park* (Steven Spielberg, 1993). As a general rule of thumb, CGI innovations prior to 2000 are based more around character than geography. See Michael Allen, "Talking about a Revolution: The Blockbuster as Industrial Advertisement," in *Movie Blockbusters*, ed. Julian Stringer (London: Routledge, 2003), 101–13.

15. Michael Curtin and John Vanderhoef, "A Vanishing Piece of the Pi: The Globalization of Visual Effects Labor," *Television and New Media* 16, no. 3 (2015): 219–39.

16. For the present purposes, let us put to one side the contributions of the essential above-the-line triumvirate of writer, producer, and director.

17. For an explanation of the work of these respective departments, as well as others such as color management, lighting, and paint, see Clare Burgess, *The Art of Film Magic: 20 Years of Weta* (New York: Harper Design, 2014).

18. Sharon Gosling and Adam Newell, *The Art of the Films: "Dawn of the Planet of the Apes" and "Rise of the Planet of the Apes"* (London: Titan Books, 2014). The credits of these four films also provide evidence of a dramatic rise in the number and variety of location-management appointments. At the time of the release of *Rise* and *Dawn*, up to thirty individuals may typically be acknowledged for facilitating (in one capacity or another) location shooting on a big Hollywood production.

19. Aida A. Hozic, *Hollyworld: Space, Power, and Fantasy in the American Economy* (Ithaca, NY: Cornell University Press, 2001), 138. The year 2001 is the date of George Lucas's *Star Wars: Episode II—Attack of the Clones*, the first major Hollywood movie to be produced entirely through computer imaging (with visual effects by Industrial Light & Magic).

20. For all the reasons touched on here, the evolution of digital landscapes cannot be separated from the ongoing story of the parallel development of contemporary animation: see Suzanne Buchan, ed., *Pervasive Animation* (New York: Routledge, 2013); and Chris Pallant, ed., *Animated Landscapes: History, Form and Function* (London: Bloomsbury, 2015).

As John Lasseter, cofounder of the pioneering Pixar Animation Studios (established in San Francisco in 1986), observes, "There is not a single object in the world that can't be animated." Quoted in Avni, *Cinema by the Bay*, 146. "Filmed entirely on location," jokes the closing title for Lasseter's playful early Pixar CGI short *Knick Knack* (1989).

21. Portia Fontes, film coordinator, San Francisco Film Commission, email correspondence, July 13, 2016. Amateur footage of filming taking place at some of these spots is available on YouTube.

22. Todd McCarthy, "*Rise of the Planet of the Apes*," *Hollywood Reporter*, August 5, 2011, 9. All newspaper materials concerning *Rise* and *Dawn* cited in this chapter were sourced at the Margaret Herrick Library, Los Angeles, CA. Page references are provided where available.

23. Peter Debruge, "*Rise of the Planet of the Apes*," *Variety*, August 4, 2011, 30.

24. Joe Morgenstern, "'Apes': Something to Thump Chests About," *Wall Street Journal*, August 5, 2011, D3.

25. Quoted in Gosling and Newell, *Art of the Films*, 166.

26. Ibid. One commentator notes that the challenges of this important scene were such that "the production had to move to a completely virtual space at James Cameron's Lightstorm studios in Manhattan Beach." Kevin Noonan, "'Apes' Takes Motion Capture to New Heights," *Variety*, February 12, 2015. Noonan quotes director Matt Reeves: "There would be no safe way for us to shoot that sequence, and it wouldn't be practical to go up and shoot in an unfinished skyscraper. Basically, it's a stage that's a big fluorescent box, and you create things that represent the set, but the set isn't there." Chinlund describes another inspiration for the culminating tower sequence: "I was poking around the Web during my initial research [and] stumbled upon the image of a skyscraper fire in Russia. It appeared like a giant torch standing tall over the city." James Chinlund, "*Dawn of the Planet of the Apes*: Uncertainty Is the New Normal," *Perspectives: The Journal of the Art Directors Guild*, November–December 2014, 22.

27. None of this is novel, as "manipulation of the photograph is as old as photography itself." Dawn Ades, *Photomontage* (New York: Pantheon Books, 1976), 7. Cf. Mark Cotta Vaz and Craig Barron, *The Invisible Art: The Legends of Movie Matte Painting* (San Francisco: Chronicle Books, 2002); Richard M. Isackes and Karen L. Maness, *The Art of the Hollywood Backdrop* (New York: Regan Arts, 2016).

28. Jeff Kraft and Aaron Leventhal, *Footsteps in the Fog: Alfred Hitchcock's San Francisco* (Solana Beach, CA: Santa Monica Press, 2002), 17.

29. Michel Chion on "rendered sound": "We must distinguish between the notions of *rendering* and *reproduction*. The film spectator recognizes sounds to be truthful, effective, and fitting not so much if they reproduce what would be heard in the same situation in reality, but if they render (convey, express) the feelings associated with the situation." Chion, *Audio-Vision: Sound on Screen*, ed. and trans. Claudia Gorbman (1990; repr., New York: Columbia University Press, 1994), 109; italics in original.

30. Walter Murch, foreword to Chion, *Audio-Vision*, xix. Coppola: "All art cheats. As Flaherty said, 'Sometimes you have to lie. One often has to distort a thing to catch its true spirit.'" Coppola, *Live Cinema*, 50.

31. Quoted in Jessica Julius, *The Art of Disney: "Big Hero 6"* (San Francisco: Chronicle Books, 2014), 16. Adds Scott Watanabe, art director (environments), "San Francisco has a unique heritage and lots of natural beauty. It's surrounded by the ocean, the fog, the hillsides. . . . There's an idyllic quaintness to it we tried to hold onto." Ibid., 28.

32. Echoing Watanabe (see note 31), the novelist Frank Norris's words of over one hundred years ago evidently resonate for contemporary filmmakers: "'Things can happen' in San Francisco. . . . Perhaps no great city of the world is so isolated as we are. . . . There is no great city to the north of us. . . . To the west is the waste of the Pacific, to the east the waste of the deserts. Here we are set down as a pin point in a vast circle of solitude. Isolation produces individuality, originality." Norris, "An Opening for Novelists: Great Opportunities for Fiction Writers in San Francisco," in *McTeague: A Story of San Francisco: Authoritative Text, Contexts, Criticism*, ed. Donald Pizer (1897; repr., New York: Norton, 1997), 247, 248.

33. Quoted in Julius, *Art of Disney*, 16, 29.

34. Quoted ibid., 151.

35. Quoted ibid., 16.

36. Once again, each of these crucial topics deserves extended analysis in its own right.

37. For indicative scholarly accounts of these matters, see Paul Swann, "From Workshop to Backlot: The Greater Philadelphia Film Office," in *Cinema and the City: Film and Urban Societies in a Global Context*, ed. Mark Shiel and Tony Fitzmaurice (Oxford, UK: Blackwell, 2001), 88–98; Ben Goldsmith, Susan Ward, and Tom O'Regan, *Local Hollywood: Global Film Production and the Gold Coast* (Queensland: University of Queensland Press, 2010); and Marco Cucco, "Blockbuster Outsourcing: Is There Really No Place like Home?," *Film Studies* 13, no. 1 (2015): 73–93. Readers wishing to keep up-to-date with such issues are recommended to consult trade-press sources such as *Deadline Hollywood*, the *Hollywood Reporter*, and *Variety*.

38. Michael Curtin, "Media Capital: Towards the Study of Spatial Flows," *International Journal of Cultural Studies* 6, no. 2 (2003): 202–28.

39. On the historical origins of filmmaking in San Francisco, see Geoffrey Bell, *The Golden Gate and the Silver Screen* (Rutherford, NJ: Farleigh Dickinson University Press, 1984). For later developments, consult Avni, *Cinema by the Bay*; Gianluca Sergi, *The Dolby Era: Film Sound in Contemporary Hollywood* (Manchester: Manchester University Press, 2004); Lawrence Webb, "Remapping *The Conversation*: Urban Design and Industrial Reflexivity in Seventies San Francisco," *Post45*, June 22, 2014, http://post45.research.yale.edu/2014/06/remapping-the-conversation-urban-design-and-industrial-reflexivity-in-seventies-san-francisco/; and Joshua Gleich, *Hollywood in San Francisco: Location Shooting and the Aesthetics of Urban Decline* (Austin: University of Texas Press, 2018). Ed Catmull (with Amy Wallace), *Creativity, Inc.: Overcoming the Unseen Forces That Stand in the Way of True Inspiration* (London: Bantam, 2014), written by Pixar's cofounder and president, provides excellent insights into the links among Silicon Valley, the contemporary animation industry, and Hollywood filmmaking more generally.

40. See, inter alia, Toby Miller, Nitin Govil, John McMurria, Ting Wang, and Richard Maxwell, *Global Hollywood: 2* (London: British Film Institute, 2004).

41. Portia Fontes, interview by author, San Francisco, July 11, 2016.

42. For an account of unauthorized moviemaking via "stolen locations" in a culturally and historically specific time and place, see Julian Stringer, "Location Filmmaking and the Hong Kong Crime Film: Anatomy of a Scene," in *Hong Kong Neo-Noir*, ed. Esther C. M. Yau and Tony Williams (Edinburgh: Edinburgh University Press, 2017), 159–77.

43. For a broad-based discussion of current employment conditions, see Michael Curtin and Kevin Sanson, eds., *Precarious Creativity: Global Media, Local Labor* (Oakland: University of California Press, 2016).

44. Future research may concentrate on yet more aspects of this topic as well as filmmaking of other tiers of scale. For instance, Fontes reports that the digital has "transformed filming within San Francisco in many ways": "On a corporate and business level, there has been a steady increase of filming in our city due to affordability of professional grade filming digital cameras. We have tech companies filming corporate videos in the city daily, not only with production companies but on their own using affordable professional equipment like Red Cameras or Black Magic Cameras. In addition, entrepreneurs and web producers are creating web content to be streamed on outlets like YouTube or their own websites. As the main advocate for filming in the city and permit processing for any filming on city property, our office has become much busier due to this effect." Fontes, email correspondence, July 8, 2016.

45. See Hye Jean Chung, "Global Visual Effects Pipelines: An Interview with Hannes Ricklefs," *Media Fields Journal* 2 (2011), www.mediafieldsjournal.org/issue-2/; Chung, "Media Heterotopia and Transnational Filmmaking: Mapping Real and Virtual Worlds," *Cinema Journal* 51, no. 4 (2012): 87–109; and Christopher Lucas, "The Modern Entertainment Marketplace, 2000–Present," in *Cinematography*, ed. Patrick Keating (New Brunswick, NJ: Rutgers University Press, 2014), 132–57.

46. Gosling and Newell, *Art of the Films*; Joe Fordham, "Render unto Caesar," *Cinefex* 128 (January 2012): 40–63.

47. Letteri is a four-time Oscar winner who was also nominated in the Best Visual Effects category of the Academy Awards for *Rise* and *Dawn*.

48. Cf. Lisa Fitzpatrick, *The Art of "Avatar": James Cameron's Epic Adventure* (New York: Abrams Books, 2009); Weta Workshop, *The World of Kong: A Natural History of Skull Island* (London: Pocket Books, 2005).

49. Gosling and Newell, *Art of the Films*, 67.

50. Fontes, email correspondence, July 8, 2016.

51. More detailed descriptions are supplied by Gosling and Newell, *Art of the Films*; and Fordham, "Render unto Caesar."

52. Vaz and Barron, *Invisible Art*, 43. The authors explain that the term "probably originated when glass plates were used in photography."

53. Quoted in Gosling and Newell, *Art of the Films*, 70. Fordham elaborates that with "the exception of three digital wide views of the bridge, all scenes in the Golden Gate sequence involved plate photography." Fordham, "Render unto Caesar," 60.

54. On Vancouver's emergence as a media capital, see David Spaner, *Dreaming in the Rain: How Vancouver Became Hollywood North by Northwest* (Vancouver: Arsenal Pulp, 2003).

55. Quoted in Richard Verrier, "On Location: Eyes on the Prize," *Los Angeles Times*, November 17, 2011. The press book for *Rise* similarly claims that "Weta Digital's—and the entire production's—biggest challenge came during the filming of the film's climax. . . . The scene . . . features elaborate stunts, fire, explosions, helicopters, hundreds of cars and extras, and an atmospheric San Francisco fog—as well as the culmination of all the drama, emotion and character interactions." *Rise of the Planet of the Apes* press book, 7–8.

56. Fordham, "Render unto Caesar," 59. Previsualization ("previz"): "The rendering of film sequences in low-resolution digital animation before the production phase so that film-makers can accurately imagine each shot and plan for the practical and digital elements that will comprise it." "Glossary," in *Editing and Special/Visual Effects*, ed. Charlie Keil and Kristen Whissel (New Brunswick, NJ: Rutgers University Press, 2016), 234.

57. Fordham, "Render unto Caesar," 59.

58. Fontes, email correspondence, July 8, 2016.

59. Fordham, "Render unto Caesar," 58, 60.

60. Joe Fordham, "Ape Apocalypse," *Cinefex* 139 (October 2014): 85.

61. See Tanine Allison, "More than a Man in a Monkey Suit: Andy Serkis, Motion Capture, and Digital Realism," *Quarterly Review of Film and Video* 28, no. 4 (2011): 325–41; Ian Failes, *Masters of FX: Behind the Scenes with Geniuses of Visual and Special Effects* (London: Ilex, 2015).

62. Alexandra Wolfe, "Matt Reeves," *Wall Street Journal*, July 5–6, 2014, C11.

63. Quoted in Verrier, "On Location."

64. Quoted in *Rise* press book, 7.

65. Ibid.

66. Ibid., 1.

67. Quoted ibid., 5.

68. Debruge, "*Rise of the Planet of the Apes*," 2.

69. Full descriptions are supplied by Golding and Newell, *Art of the Films*; Fordham, "Ape Apocalypse," 66–91.

70. Quoted in Gosling and Newell, *Art of the Films*, 86.

71. Fordham, "Ape Apocalypse," 80.

72. Ibid., 79–80.

73. Nick Goundry, "*Dawn of the Planet of the Apes* Films Vancouver and Louisiana for San Francisco," *Location Guide*, July 15, 2014, www.thelocationguide.com.

74. Quoted ibid.

75. Quoted ibid. This reference to 3-D camera equipment is a reminder that *Dawn*, like *War* but unlike *Rise* (which is a 2-D production), also belongs in the lineage of major motion pictures shot and exhibited since 2000 in 3-D—a trend, initiated by *Beowulf*, that reached an initial peak with *Avatar*. Analysis of how 3-D cinematography impacts location shooting and approaches to digital rendering will unfortunately have to wait for another day.

76. Chinlund, "*Dawn of the Planet of the Apes*," 17. On New Orleans's emergence as a media capital, see Vicki Mayer, *Almost Hollywood, Nearly New Orleans: The Lure of the Local Film Economy* (Oakland: University of California Press, 2017).

77. Goundry, "*Dawn of the Planet of the Apes*."

78. Quoted in Fordham, "Ape Apocalypse," 79.

79. Quoted in Goundry, "*Dawn of the Planet of the Apes*."

80. All quotations in Patrick Kevin Day, "Bad to Worse, Digitally," *Los Angeles Times*, January 2, 2015. Failes offers the following definition of "lidar": "an acronym for Light Detection and Ranging, a system that uses a laser to measure distance from an object via reflected light, the results of which can help produce 3D spatial information about the areas measured." Failes, *Masters of FX*, 184.

81. Quoted in Fordham, "Ape Apocalypse," 80.

82. Quoted in Day, "Bad to Worse."

83. *Dawn of the Planet of the Apes* press book, 6. To help address the heightened challenges, previsualization supervisor Duane Floch "'embarked on a robust previsualization process with Matt Reeves. . . .' We found locations that fit the previs,' explained Dan Lemmon. 'We had an idea of the look and feel of the woods and what kind of palette we had to work with, based on location scouts. The previs guided shot design. We then modified shots on location." Fordham, "Ape Apocalypse," 68, 75.

84. Quoted in Karen Idelson, "Nothing in Common but Excellence," *Variety*, February 3, 2015, 69. Idelson adds that the new equipment "proved robust enough to survive the elements for long days of shooting."

85. *Dawn* press book, 7.

86. Wolfe, "Matt Reeves," C11.

87. Quoted in Noonan, "'Apes' Takes Motion Capture to New Heights."

88. Rebecca Keegan, "Such Complicated Creatures," *Los Angeles Times*, July 6, 2014. This same source quotes Letteri's observation that with *Dawn*, there is "a parallel to when film cameras started being lightweight enough that you could take them out on location and not be studio bound."

89. Quoted in *Dawn* press book, 7.

90. Quoted in Noelene Clark, "Authentic Looks Helps 'Planet of the Apes' Evolve," *Los Angeles Times*, April 27, 2014.

91. Kenneth Turan, "Captured by His Spell: Latest 'Apes' Is a Visual Triumph but Little More," *Los Angeles Times*, July 10, 2014.

92. Stephanie Zacharek, "A Society of Apes Is Living in San Francisco (Says This New Movie)," *L.A. Weekly*, July 11, 2014.

93. Weta Digital visual effects supervisor Keith Miller, quoted in Fordham, "Ape Apocalypse," 89.

94. Rebecca Solnit, *Infinite City: A San Francisco Atlas* (Berkeley: University of California Press, 2010), 9.

95. Fontes, interview, July 11, 2016.

ACKNOWLEDGMENTS

The editors would like to thank the following people: Leslie Mitchner, who expertly shepherded the book from proposal through to production—we wish her a long and happy retirement; Nicole Solano, Jasper Chang, and Vincent Nordhaus at Rutgers University Press; Andrew Katz for diligently copyediting the manuscript; the anonymous peer reviewer, whose generous and astute comments helped to sharpen up the book; and Nathan Holmes, who helped kick off the project. We would also like to extend special thanks to the libraries and archives that provided vital research materials for the book, especially the Margaret Herrick Library, Academy of Motion Picture Arts and Sciences; the USC Cinematic Arts Library and Warner Bros. Archives; UCLA Special Collections; and the British Film Institute.

NOTES ON CONTRIBUTORS

SHERI CHINEN BIESEN is a professor of film history at Rowan University. She is the author of *Blackout: World War II and the Origins of Film Noir*, *Music in the Shadows: Noir Musical Films*, and *Film Censorship: Regulating America's Screen*. Her work has been published in *Historical Journal of Film, Radio and Television*, *Film and History*, *Literature/Film Quarterly*, *Quarterly Review of Film and Video*, *Film Noir: The Directors*, and *The Gangster Film Reader*. She has contributed to the BBC documentary *The Rules of Film Noir* and the TCM Warner Bros. Gangster Collection, served as secretary of the Literature/Film Association, and edited *The Velvet Light Trap*.

JOSHUA GLEICH is an assistant professor in the School of Theatre, Film and Television at the University of Arizona. He is the author of *Hollywood in San Francisco: Location Shooting and the Aesthetics of Urban Decline*. His work has also appeared in *Cinema Journal*, *New Review of Film and Television Studies*, and *The Velvet Light Trap*.

NOELLE GRIFFIS is an assistant professor of communication and media arts at Marymount Manhattan College. Her work has appeared in *Black Camera* and the edited collection *Screening Race in Nontheatrical Film*. She is the reviews editor for *Mediapolis: A Journal of Cities & Culture*.

JENNIFER PETERSON is an associate professor and chair of the Department of Communication at Woodbury University in Los Angeles. She is the author of *Education in the School of Dreams: Travelogues and Early Nonfiction Film*. Her articles have been published in *Cinema Journal*, *Camera Obscura*, *The Moving Image*, the *Getty Research Journal*, and numerous edited collections. She is working on a new book tentatively titled "Cinema's Wilderness Past: The Dramaturgy of Nature on Screen before the 1960s."

DANIEL STEINHART is an assistant professor of cinema studies at the University of Oregon. He is the author of *Runaway Hollywood: Internationalizing Postwar Production and Location Shooting*. His work has appeared in *Cinema Journal*, *NECSUS, InMedia,* and *Bright Lights Film Journal*.

JULIAN STRINGER is an associate professor in film and television studies at the University of Nottingham. His books include *Movie Blockbusters, New Korean Cinema,* and *Japanese Cinema: Texts and Contexts.* He is the director of the Institute for Screen Industries Research, the first ideas incubator and innovation generator for the film and TV industry based at a leading UK university.

LAWRENCE WEBB is a lecturer in film studies at the University of Sussex. He is the author of *The Cinema of Urban Crisis: Seventies Film and the Reinvention of the City* and the coeditor of *Global Cinematic Cities: New Landscapes of Film and Media*. His work has also appeared in *Cinema Journal, Post-45,* and *Oxford Bibliographies in Cinema and Media Studies.*

INDEX